RICE & DIRT

ACROSS AFRICA ON A VESPA

To Will and Kate.
Enjoy the read!

Alexandra Fefopoulou
Stergios Gogos

Στέργιος
Γιώργος

Shuvvy Press

SHUVVY PRESS LTD
Banbury, England

SHUVVY PRESS LTD
www.shuvvypress.com

Published by Shuvvy Press Ltd in August 2018
Copyright © Alexandra Fefopoulou and Stergios Gogos

Alexandra Fefopoulou and Stergios Gogos assert the moral right
to be identified as the authors of this work

A catalogue record for this book is available from
the British Library

ISBN 978-0-9564-305-7-1

Translated from the original Greek by Katerina Soumani
Edited by Paddy Tyson
Proof-read by Jo MacDonald and Paddy Tyson
Typeset by Jo MacDonald at JMDesign
Cover images by Stergios Gogos
Typeset in Adobe Garamond Pro 11pt
Printed on FSC paper by Zenith Media Group, Wales

ACKNOWLEDGMENTS

In order for this journey, and this book, to happen, many people supported us in their own ways and we are very grateful to them. Without their generous commitment and the trust they placed in us, nothing would have been the same. They are way too many to mention here individually. We can only say that you know who you are and we feel lucky that we ever met you.

We are indebted to all the people we met along the way and who opened their homes and their hearts to us, without even knowing us. We thank them for their kindness and for whatever it was they offered us: a conversation, a mattress, a plate of rice.

To Effie, a simple "thank you" would not be nearly enough. If we hadn't met her on our way – each one of us separately – our lives would have been completely different; and she knows very well what we mean.

We thank Marcos, who makes us take him for long walks and reminds us to live in the present.

Finally, with infinite gratefulness, we deeply thank our families. They have always supported us and continue to do so, even beyond their own powers.

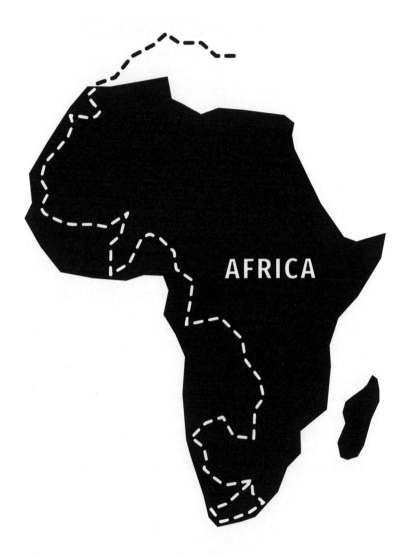

AFRICA

CONTENTS

For Thanos, Liam, Steven and Francis.
Without them, I wouldn't have such great fun.
Stergios

For Marcos, who never left my side.
Alexandra

PREFACE

In order to write this book, I drew on his personal journals, videos and photos as well as interviews I had with Stergios. For the texts about our journeys together, I also referred to my own recollections. The narrative follows the hero and unfolds through his gaze and experiences, as much as possible, which is why the chapters vary in length. The names of those who played a crucial part in the story remain unchanged. I have only omitted or changed the names of some people to protect their anonymity. There are no fictional characters or events. I have omitted certain people and events only when the omission would leave the essence of the story intact.

Alexandra Fefopoulou

DECISIONS

NEW YEAR'S DAY IN JOHANNESBURG

Dawn had broken. 2015 had been ushered in only a few hours before. The visitors were gone and I was clearing the dishes off the festive table. Effie had her own ideas. She insisted that you can't enjoy a meal unless you leave a complete and utter mess behind, until the following day at least. I didn't put up much of an objection. I just covered the melomakarona[1] with a piece of aluminum foil and collapsed on the armchair looking at the metal baobab that adorned her living room. It was full of colourful light bulbs, which we'd forgotten to turn on – again.

The dampness of the night was coming in through the open window, cooling my face. The place was dark, with the lit "Merry Christmas" sign still twinkling out in the terrace and successively tinting the walls of the room red, blue and green. Elie had long gone to bed and Effie followed him. I could flip the sofa open and lie down but instead I held still and closed my eyes without falling asleep. It seems like every time I decide to flick off the thoughts switch they want to get back at me, overflowing every nook of my mind and drifting me into a tangled ball of reflections that resemble the twisted bunch of wires from a Vespa. All crammed together, they start from the gauge on the handlebar and reach – God knows how – all of its parts, conveying every order the driver gives.

[1] The melomakarona are a kind of round-shaped, spiced soft cookies, typically soaked in honey syrup, scented with orange zest and juice and sprinkled with ground walnuts. They are traditionally served during the Christmas holiday season in Greece.

I'd already been on the road for fifteen months and lately I'd been feeling a bit confused about all the things that had happened in my life and had brought me here. Only a few days earlier I was at the southernmost tip of Africa in dirty clothes, on a dusty scooter and with Alexandra. At some point, my mind went back to Thessaloniki, to Chalkidiki, to my job and all those things that made me so sick that I had to leave them behind. I thought I might go back, in time to see them fall to pieces; join the guys from the Union again and try to help at least one colleague find justice amidst the chaos of labour rights violation; be there to plant new trees in the Skouries forest. I would go back just for all that. My mother's words echoed in my mind: "Go, go live the life we couldn't live" she said, and I could see a grin underneath my father's thick mustache. The next minute, my thoughts drifted away to all those things that I was yet to see.

"Man! You must go to Latin America!" a friend once wrote to me.

As it turned out I wasn't eaten alive, robbed or killed in Africa. All the things I was told before I left now made me laugh. Of course, I could have tried a bit harder to prove them right, by going up northeast until I reached Egypt, but then Latin America got in the way and things got complicated. Alexandra was waiting for me to make up my mind. Did she actually mean it when she said that she'd come along wherever I went? Would she really leave her life in Athens behind? I took a couple of sips of my wine, stood up and went straight to bed. Sleep was probably the only thing that could put an end to my thinking spree.

The following morning, it all seemed crystal clear. Strong iced coffee and the search for a freight company that would take charge of transporting the bike from here to Latin America. Dozens of phone calls were made with the hope that both of us would be able to leave South Africa by the end of the week, which was when my visa expired. No way of sorting it out. Most agencies were closed for the holidays and the two or three that were open informed me that I was missing some document or other.

I guess the border officer at the Namibia checkpoint did screw me up after all, I thought. I was surprised at his insistence that no document was required for my vehicle to exit the country, but I had no choice. I had already booked my own flight to Buenos Aires.

"That's it, Effie, the whole plan is off! I'll just dump the bike here and go back to Greece!"

No sooner had I finished my sentence than Effie showed up from the kitchen, her hands dripping with water. She'd taken to washing the dishes, since there was no clean plate in sight for her to place her avocado. After all those years in Africa, she felt something was troubling her.

"What am I doing here?" she asked herself aloud every time the conversation gave her the chance.

"I've made myself comfortable in the relative safety that my white skin provides me, while I sit here watching the African drama unfold from a distance." Her tenure at the university was not enough to keep her there, either. She would go back to Greece, back to her classes. Back to the agitated high-school and the kids who she hoped would wish to make a difference in their lives. We were reading the news. All indications pointed to an imminent change of government and with it, a faint flicker of hope was fading in. Or maybe that's what we needed to see.

"You think we should go back?" she asked.

GOT THE CHEESE PIES?

I overslept! When the alarm went off for the tenth time, I was sure I was late. I jumped out of bed and before putting my glasses on, stumbled on a suitcase. I turned back and looked at it angrily, as if it was its fault it was lying exactly where I left it, and only then it dawned on me.

"You're not going to work today, you idiot! You're leaving!" I said to myself. My mother and father were in the kitchen, packing up food for me, under my brother's sleepy eye.

"What time is it, aces?" I asked and when they replied, I took another look at my cell-phone and rushed to the balcony.

Oh no. Those guys have been waiting for hours and I've stood them up! I thought to myself. Or did my mother say it?

"Don't worry, I offered them some of my homemade mini

cheese pies to go along with their coffee." This time it was her.

I went into the bathroom and spent at least two minutes looking at my mug in the mirror. My beard had started to grow back, coarse and determined. My hair was hopeless. It remained faithful to the age-old family male tradition of baldness after the tender years of adolescence. It took me two minutes of careful self-observation to make an important decision: while being on the road, I wouldn't cut, trim or shave a single hair. Over the past almost ten years at work, I've always been impeccable, clean-shaven, formal and always smiling. What the hell for? My well-polished looks never stopped my employers from playing their nasty games on me. Sometimes they'd have the manager, a poor little man who aspired to achieving something by kissing his superiors' asses, scare me off. Other times, the same guy would insult me for no reason in front of customers. They thought they'd break me. Shortly before giving up, they tried pretending to be my friends to get me to sign a contract that would ruin me. In the end, they ran out of choices and were forced to lay me off. A while later, they shut the restaurant down; the entire staff was given the boot, with no compensation.

I slapped my face a couple of times, still swollen from sleeping, to snap out of it, then dashed out of the bathroom and got dressed.

All set. The Vespa was waiting, already loaded the night before. I hadn't left too many pending issues for the last minute. After all, I hadn't had the time. It was only a few days ago that I'd got back to Thessaloniki. The last few months I'd parked both the Vespa and my life in the tourist colossus of Santorini. I was away for the "high season", serving tables. I worked on top of an Aegean rock which had the misfortune to be half-torn down by the volcano that lodged in its entrails, and years later, to become one of the most popular tourist destinations in Greece. Sixteen-hour shifts on a daily basis. No days off. Even to ask about days off would sound like a joke. However, all the things I'd gone through during that time seemed to have faded away in the past, tangled up with all the things that had led me to the present day, the day of my departure. The only enjoyable moment back in Santorini was when I got back from work and sat on the balcony, to relax a bit before going to bed. That was when I realised that nothing could affect me anymore. It was in those moments that I came to realise that that was it, the countdown had begun. I would leave.

I took a couple of good sips of coffee, stole a mini cheese pie from the ones that my mother was trying to stuff into little plastic bags, and opened the door of the apartment. Always at work or in the kitchen, always trying to look after everyone, my mother. I shut the door behind me. Who knows when I would open it again? Who would I find inside when I did? When would I be back? I'm no poet so I quit the melodrama and hoisted the last backpack on my shoulders.

"Got the cheese pies?" my mother's voice sounded from the kitchen. I laughed.

Downstairs, three or four friends were waiting for me, insisting that they had to bid me farewell. I didn't want any goodbye parties and bombastic discourses. I was in no position to promise anything and preferred not to hear any promises from anyone, either. Over the last years, following the outbreak of the financial crisis in Greece, I got to know, against my will, those sides of the people around me that I'd been better off without knowing, quite frankly. Despair brings bare reality to the surface. All that varnish that once dazzled you peels off, revealing the decay hidden underneath. Back when I bought my bike the mechanic told me "Always look underneath the coat of paint."

Next thing I knew, the Vespa was posing in the yard squeaky clean and polished, and loaded with everything I thought useful for my trip. And so was the traveller! New outfit, helmet and cameras. Only my specs were kind of tattered, giving me a striped outlook on the world – literally.

Time went by and there was nothing more left to say. We were all standing together, an awkward bunch around the bike, staring at it. Now and then, someone would break the silence:

"Off-road tyres, right?"

"How are you going to charge the batteries?"

"Did you get the cheese pies?"

The time had come. I turned to my family: "Hey, aces, gather up". We hugged each other. It was the second time round that my mother had to say goodbye and all efforts not to cry were in vain. The first time was when, aged nineteen, I set off to try my luck on an oil tanker. I was a student at the Merchant Marine Academy and quite curious to see what life on a ship looked like. And I did. It only took me a month of puking twice across the Atlantic, all the way from Marseille to Southampton before I called them from the port: "Aces, please get a fine sea bream and the charcoal going – I'll be home tomorrow."

It had been seven years since then and a lot had passed. I quit the Academy and enrolled in a mechanics school, just to learn how to fix the bike I'd bought. I worked like a dog at the seafront cafés and bars just to save some money for my summertime trips. Then, the crisis came along and everything changed.

My brother held me tight. "Chill, man, you'll squeeze the breath out of me!" I told him and slipped free of his unexpected outburst of affection. I said goodbye to the guys, who had bothered to come here all the way from the indescribable west side of Thessaloniki, my hometown, to send me off. I had no one else to say goodbye to. A few months earlier, I had broken up with my girlfriend. How could I ever be with a person whose dreams were so different to my own? What's the point in giving each other a hard time over something that we both knew had no future?

Last but not least, my father. The whole time the rest of us were hugging and chatting, he pretended to be observing the bike and the luggage on it and making sure everything was alright. That's what he always used to do. He would stand aside, quiet, waiting for the right trigger to set him off. We'd have countless conversations about the world, about the existence of God and the ideal barbecue techniques. Everything I've read – History or Sociology – I owe it to him. If he hadn't, in his own special way, tucked a couple of books into my hands, I'd have been stuck with motorcycle magazines for ever. Not that I was much of a reader, anyway. Barely the basics, just to make better sense of what was going on around me. To understand why my folks had to shut the workshop down and had trouble even feeding us when we were little; to get my head around the arguments and the tension, when they nearly lost their house because of debts; to finally realise the reason why my mother was so obsessed with me getting a stable job, with no risks.

He opened his arms and hugged me. They no longer seemed as big as they used to.

"Oh, dad" was the only thing I said.

"Don't come back here", he whispered to me. I got onto the Vespa, which started right up at the first crank.

"It looks like an overloaded mule, the poor thing!" a voice sounded from the crowd and suddenly, it hit me: I had finally found the most appropriate name for my scooter. A name traditionally used for mules and donkeys in Greece!

"Come on, Kitsos, off we go!" I yelled and the two of us rolled down the slope in front of my family house.

KITSOS; WATCH OUT OR YOU MIGHT DROWN!

Luckily, it was Sunday and Dendropotamou Avenue was practically empty – which is unusual, to say the least. If it weren't for the chaotic traffic in Thessaloniki, maybe I'd never have been forced to buy a scooter. And I probably wouldn't even be here today, with all my belongings packed, heading off as far as possible. A Citroën Saxo passed me by, fully equipped with the typical sound system, tinted windows and a nickel exhaust pipe – *a fart can*, in gearhead parlance. Two young men in their twenties gave me a curious look through the half-open window and immediately stepped on it and got passed me, producing slight yet perceptible vibrations on the roadway. "Good ol' west side... gotta love it!" I said to myself.

Young dudes with small bikes and 'ricers' with twenty-year old chassis; they somehow earned my sympathy. Besides, I grew up in the same working-class neighbourhoods and the sight was pretty familiar. As soon as I reached thirteen I couldn't wait to sit in the driver's seat of our family car, a '91 Toledo, which to this day takes my family to the countryside for the summer holidays and my brother to work. I can't recall when it was the first time I ever attempted a *tête-à-queue*, which almost ended up with a busted curb...

Now, bolt upright on Kitsos, I was rolling my way out of the city in search of the Egnatia Highway. That's one of the cool things about Vespas: the erect riding posture. You don't really ride a Vespa, you just sit on its saddle and the low handlebar almost forces you to keep your back straight. I left behind the long-distance bus station, easily recognisable by its two great vaults, and I entered the highway. What a great day! Since the beginning of the week, the TV weather forecast had merrily announced that the October 28th bank holiday excursionists would have the weather on their side. There were about 300km left to Igoumenitsa. That same night, I'd be on the ferry to Ancona.

While on the road, I tried not to think too much. My top priority was to check whether all those sophisticated gadgets I was strapped up with would be comfortable, or whether I should let some of them go. Thanos would definitely crack up when he'd see me armored like *Robocop*.

I was crossing the bridge over the Gallikos river and my mind was already traversing the rivers of Africa, when I remembered reading somewhere that the river in question was once called the 'donkey-drowner'. *If this is the "donkey-drowner", then what will the Congo river look like?* the mere thought of the comparison made me laugh.

"Kitsos, watch out or you might drown!" I said out loud and realised right away that I had started to address the two-wheeled metal assembly that up until a few hours ago was just "the Vespa". Up next was the Axios river, while for the name of the third one, I used the road sign: *Loudias*, it read and I was in no position to question it. After all, my only hope of learning geography on this trip would be through observation.

The route along the Egnatia was familiar, almost boring. It was only interrupted by the successive, compulsory stops at the toll stations. Somewhere outside Grevena I stopped to refuel and called Thanos. At the other end of the line was a deep voice with the distinct accent that left no room to doubt his origin.

"Hey, man! Did you manage to get out of Larissa?" I asked in a jesting tone. We were to meet at the port, or some place before that. I put my helmet back on and continued.

While going past the highway exit, I realised that it had been years since I'd last visited my father's hometown. Kalloni is barely

20km from Grevena, and yet I never got to take a turn in that direction during my adult life. "I'll swing by when I get back", I thought to myself, unmindful of how vague that promise was.

BEERS AND VESPAS

It had been a little over a year since that day in August 2012. Back then, I was riding my scooter just like now – though it had no name then – and was losing myself in endless thoughts while on my way to Pelion. When was it exactly that I became a true "vespista"? Back in 2006, when I bought it second-hand, convinced by my friends who insisted that "Vespas are classy", the only thing I needed was two-wheels to get me to work every day. Bicycling on a hot summer's day produces rivers of sweat gushing out of every single pore of my body and, admittedly, the sight of a waiter dripping with sweat is rather unnerving, so I needed an engine.

At the first breakdown, I found myself at a service garage in Thessaloniki, packed with anything a Vespa might ever need. There, Kostas took on lecturing me and I began to understand how I should treat my curvy bike. A broken wrist, a brutally abused knee and quite a few scratches were not able to stop me from continuing to test my endurance along with that of its ten-inch wheels.

As time went by, I got to meet more and more people from the "vespisti" community and, without realising it, I eventually became one. Meetings, parties, short trips which soon got longer. From Greece to Italy, and from there to Austria – my first trip abroad! If anyone had asked me as a little boy what I would like to do in my life, I'd never have picked travelling. But there I was. For just a few days or more than that, I'd grab the chance to go away. I went as far as Portugal, to the westernmost end. But when I came back from Nordkapp – the Northern Cape – I was feeling uneasy.

The experience of getting there was unique, but something was troubling me. I had travelled 11,000km to the edge of Europe and back to Thessaloniki in twenty-four days. And what did I get to see? It looked like a speed race. Then again, that's what my whole life looked like, so why should my vacations be any different? My leave was ending and I had to go back. I always had to go back.

Predictions had it that the Greek Vespa Meeting that year would be at full attendance. Old and new friends – and maybe some enemies, too, but who cares? – would come together for three days filling the sky above Pelion with exhaust fumes. There'd be music, beer, sea and rides. The only clouds I would tolerate above my head while being there would be the ones produced by the exhaust pipes of our bikes' two-stroke engines. I was wrong. No matter how hard I tried not to, I was carrying with me all the troubles from the last few months, all the way from Thessaloniki. Although beer was plentiful and the meeting was the ideal place for me to take my mind off things, too much had piled up. To many of my friends, the word crisis, which ever since 2009 had begun to have a dramatic impact on my life, was nothing but a word that was becoming increasingly fashionable in conversation.

"Come on, give us a discount on the bill. We're in the middle of a crisis here!" I once heard.

I, on the other hand, would spend my days dashing back and forth from the Union, trying to save workers from the massive layoffs, to my mother's hometown in Chalkidiki, joining many others in a protest. I was incapable of accepting the imminent catastrophe. The one that would be brought upon our land by the unrestrained mining activity at Skouries. Day after day, I felt more pressure pushing down on me, but at the same time I felt that I was actually doing something, instead of just remaining at the mercy of circumstances. Would I get arrested? Would I get fired? I knew I was the next in line. What I didn't know was when.

As the night fell in Pellion I found myself drinking beers with some friends. Among them, a guy that I'd never met before in person; Thanos from Larissa. I can't recall what was said or how many beers it took for the decision to be made, but we would quit everything and travel around the world on our Vespas.

FROM THE IONIAN TO THE ADRIATIC

A few kilometres past Ioannina, I saw them. Thanos and a few friends of his, who had set off to accompany him to the port of Igoumenitsa, were moving ahead of me on the highway.

"Are we actually leaving?" he asked me laughing when I reached his side.

"Why? You didn't think we would?" I replied, reiterating my confidence in my decision.

Ever since that August day at Pelion, when half-drunk we first talked about it, my life had entered a different pace. No matter what I did, my mind was on the trip. When my parents saw me read they teased me saying that they didn't recall me as that bookish. Deep inside of them they hoped that, if I read enough about my venture, I would be dissuaded. However, it was precisely that certainty of many people around me that I wouldn't make it, that galvanised my will. Once more, all odds were against me. I was broke, disorganised and soon-to-be unemployed, in a country where the future looked dire. And, on top of it all, my vehicle was anything but suitable for African roads. That was all I needed; those arguments were enough to convince me to leave.

Later that evening, we were at the port waiting to get onboard the ship. Everything around me was familiar: the people, the landscape. Familiar from other times when I had done the exact same itinerary. But this time I was heading for a totally different destination. In the ship's lounge area, sleeping bags and tubs with home-made food in hand – every self-respecting Greek mother has the duty to provide everyone around her with food tubs – we were looking for a spot to make ourselves comfortable enough to sleep, but to no avail. The company's policy was strict: no lying down, unless it was in the cabins.

"Here's our chance to practice" I told Thanos. "After all, I don't think we'll be sleeping in king-size beds in Africa".

Africa! Our decision to start our journey around the world from the *Black Continent* seemed so weird. There, children starve and grown-ups live a tormented life until they die. There, life is worthless. There, people wear fancy-coloured clothes and dance all the time. There, there's only war and civil conflict. There, you get devoured by lions. There, everything is black and colourful at the same time. How is it possible to have such a vague picture of what happens there?

In the country where I happened to be born and spent the first twenty-six years of my life, I used to hear a lot about the "savages". TV news sighed in relief and preached that "this is not Zimbabwe" every time they wished to reassure the stressed-out audience about the state of the national economy. The denial of all association with anything non-European numbed our consciousness and put all our fears to rest on our common identity with the West. Nigeria, in the collective paranoia of my fellow countrymen, is a country whose population do nothing but sell CDs at the cafés all over Europe. Biafra's children are the intimidating warning to Greek toddlers who won't finish their dinner. In Ethiopia, starvation is on the daily menu and all Somalis are pirates. I persistently refused to take such simplifications seriously.

From the moment we embarked, our conversations revolved exclusively around our upcoming venture. We were laughing at ourselves. Neither Thanos nor myself had ever tried to identify with the cliché of the fearless rider – one that upon thorough and precise preparation, and armed with noble bravery, sets out for the adventure of a lifetime. Besides, as hackneyed as it may sound, isn't life an adventure in itself?

Living in a Greek provincial town, Thanos had had his own share of adversities, just like I had. This is who we were, romantic pretenses aside. I reminded him of the day I went over to his place to plan the itinerary that we'd take. We ended up with a line drawn on the map, halfway between the absurd and the impossible, and eventually, we got tired of trying to predict all possible outcomes.

"Let's just go wherever the road takes us!" This was the conclusion of that night's meeting and shortly after I found myself buying rounds of *tsipouro*[2] while Thanos plucked his bouzouki.

Although the whole organisation of the route and the schedule was practically non-existent, the preparation required in order to avoid really troublesome obstacles was painstakingly executed. Over the previous year, our arms – among other parts of our bodies – had ended up looking like strainers from all the necessary vaccine shots. We had sourced our carnets – the customs documents for

---

[2] *Tsipouro is a strong distilled alcoholic drink, made from the residues of wine production. It is popular throughout Greece, and particularly in the northern regions of Thessaly, Epirus and Macedonia.*

our bikes. We'd been racking our brains to come up with all the things that we had to carry with us. There was no travel forum left unread, in my attempt to find as much useful information as possible. High prices, corruption, illnesses and all kinds of threats lurked in Africa. And yet every time my eyes stumbled across discouraging stories I made a point of ignoring them. Every time I perceived the slightest hint of arrogance and pompous heroism in someone's words, I just stopped reading. I was sick of hearing that you had to be 'somebody' in order to make it. I wanted to see what I could do; me, the 'nobody'.

Without noticing it, we crossed from the Ionian over to the Adriatic Sea, and the following evening we were in Ancona, Italy. From there, we had to get to Livorno to take the next ship. That was the one I worried about. We would spend three days on its decks, until disembarking at Tangier.

At the sound of the Moroccan port's name, my mind wandered off in dreamy excitement: *Tangier*. How beautiful that word sounded! "Alright, as soon as we find ourselves amidst the chaos of the customs office trying to make sense of the French and Arabic jibberjabber, you're in for a bumpy landing!" I said to myself and got it together.

We spent a whole week in Italy, travelling idly to the west. The days went by quickly, with careless strolls, meeting people and talking about our trip. Before we knew it, we had arrived in Livorno and our ten-inch wheels rolled on European soil for the last time, until they were on the heavy metal ramp that led onboard the ship. The next time they'd touch the ground, it would be African.

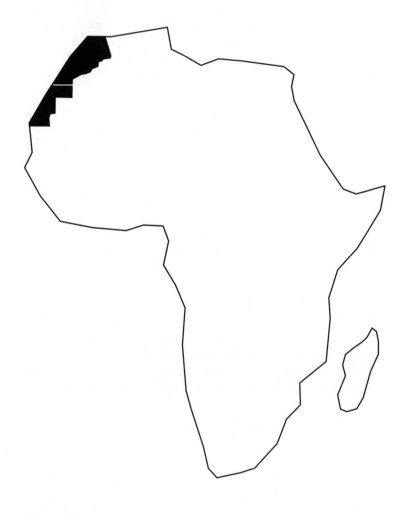

MOROCCO AND WESTERN SAHARA

MUSIC AND NOISE

The deafening buzz that came from the engine room in the ship's innards was diffused in the form of metallic squeaks, before being transmuted into fumes coming out of the smokestacks. There was commotion on the upper deck. People came up and down the stairs but everyone seemed cheerful. Our stirred curiosity soon led us to the top of the salty and slippery iron staircase. Before we even set foot on the landing the first notes got to our ears. In the back, sheltered from the strong wind, were the musicians. Around them, a Moroccan crowd had gathered, sitting on plastic chairs and watching them perform. It was the first time I'd ever listened to Moroccan music – and performed live at that!

We approached the jury-rigged stage. The singer was standing in his suit, microphone in hand. Rangy-figured, with a thin moustache that looked as though it had been glued over his upper lip, he was smiling and singing. His patent leather shoes tapped the floor rhythmically. I looked around for instruments, but the only thing I saw was a synthesiser able to produce the sounds of an entire orchestra single-handedly. The operator of this technological marvel, capable of reproducing all 80s classics straight from a can, looked drowsy. But that was nothing compared to the bar tender, who was completely worn out. I wondered how many times he had listened to the same repertoire over and over again.

The scene unfolding before us was strangely familiar. It reminded me of traditional summer fairs of the '90s in Chalkidiki. When we were kids, my brother and I would jump with excitement every time we attended such feasts. We'd rush to the fore, right in front of the stage, and stare at the band. We'd count the empty beer cans lying under the tables. We'd cover our ears when the festive gunshots cracked the air. This music had fired so many childhood memories! I asked myself could it be that we're not that different from the Moroccans after all?

We stood behind the last row of chairs and started to observe. We burst into laughter at Thanos' attempt to imitate the unintelligible word that the singer kept uttering and that roused the audience to enthusiasm. The rhythm motif and the sound volume had brought some of the attendants to an ecstatic state, and they were moving their hunched heads and shoulders in circles. Others were clapping their hands, with their palms completely parallel to one another, in ritual-like precision. "There's only men around here" Thanos noticed. Indeed as I looked around, there were no women to be seen. Were they travelling along with them? Were they anywhere around here? Or perhaps they were patiently waiting for them back home, whether that was in Morocco or some place in Europe. We could only see a few little girls dancing playfully right in front of the singer.

When we got back inside, we finally saw where all the women were: Together, gathered in small groups in the lounge area, chatting, looking after the children and preparing meals. Most of them were wearing the traditional kaftan and had their hair hidden under a scarf. While I was on the deck, I only saw one or two fez hats on the heads of the male audience, and not one *djellaba* – the typical Moroccan loose-fitting robe. Almost everyone was wearing blue jeans, jackets, and baseball caps.

So the women *out* and the men *in*; that was the deal. Did they really want the role that had been assigned to them – both men and women – or was it just a burden from the past? How had I not noticed this segregation earlier? In my eyes, the unusual remained invisible. From that moment on, I decided to be more observant. What's the point in travelling, if you don't keep your eyes wide open?

The hubbub going on in every room, instead of getting to me, seemed to have the opposite effect. The grown-ups snoring on the floor, the toddlers running up and down, the mothers waiting for them to get out of line, so that they could yell at them – everyone helped me relax. We fell asleep effortlessly, crammed in a corner in the air seat area, wrapped up in our sleeping bags. The voices of the young and the old gradually merged with the monotonous buzz of the engines. They sounded almost like a lullaby to our ears, right before we closed our eyes and started dreaming of the following day.

WATER

The time came when we would finally disembark at the port of Tangier. We wouldn't arrive until noon, but, no matter how soundly I had slept the previous night, my impatience woke me. The days had gone by faster than I could have imagined, but that morning, time seemed to be stuck. I watched the rest of the passengers arrange their luggage, take a peek through the windows now and then, get orderly outside to the deck, shading their eyes with their stretched palms in an attempt to scan the horizon for dry land. Clearly, I wasn't the only one who looked forward to arriving.

I got out to catch a glimpse of the sea. We had now reached Gibraltar and were approaching the Moroccan coastline. I leaned against the railing and finally saw the longed-for coast getting closer. I looked at the water, deep blue. We were at the exact point where the Mediterranean meets the Atlantic. The waves came and went, ceaselessly whipping the iron hull. Suddenly, a thought crossed my mind and gave me goose-bumps: I was following the exact opposite course to that taken by thousands of Africans, who, packed into decrepit fishing boats, leave everything behind in a quest for a better life in Europe. How many men, women and children – some of them unborn – have been lost in these waters? How many of the desperate, persecuted by poverty and war, finally got to set foot on the *Old Continent*? How many of those actually found the Promised Land they had dreamt of? When I thought about it, I felt deeply distressed. I no longer wanted to look at that sea.

I hastened back to the lounge room, looking for Thanos. He was now up and packing his stuff. I approached the table. My co-traveller had made breakfast and greeted me with a smile. I started a frivolous chat to take my mind off the rotten boats. The boats that either drown or save all those souls that struggle for a better life.

"I washed the tomatoes with clean water!" he said. I understood what he meant and burst into laughter. On our first day onboard, we went to the bathroom to wash the vegetables for our dinner. Much to our amazement, we became witnesses of yet another Muslim custom, of major importance in the daily life of the devout. Each of the three sinks was accordingly occupied by three men who were taking a ritual foot bath. They lifted their right foot first and rubbed it thoroughly, then repeated the exact same procedure with their left foot; this was all to prepare their bodies and souls for prayer. A good Muslim has to pray five times, no less, a day. That's quite a lot of praying. The next time we visited the bathroom and attended the same scene, it was much less awkward. Be that as it may, before putting our vegetables into the sink, we added a squirt of soap, just to be on the safe side.

In a little while, we would leave the water behind. We would set foot on dry land again. Luckily, the announcements from the ship's loudspeakers interrupted my thoughts.

"We got everything?" I asked Thanos. He nodded. Soon, we'd have to go downstairs to the cargo hold and get ready to disembark.

RIF, KIF AND THE BLUE CITY

The exhaust fumes made me sick. I couldn't wait for the door to finally open so that we could get off. While we were waiting, I noticed how overloaded the cars of the Moroccans around me were. All of them at least fifteen years old, with huge bundles strapped up on their roof racks, covered with canvasses. The children's little heads could barely be seen through the windows, crammed among boxes and suitcases.

"You think they're carrying all that stuff for their households?" I asked Thanos. He didn't hear me. His eyes were fixed on the massive mechanism of the ramp door, which was about to start up any minute now. When finally the first ray of sun slipped in through the tiny opening created as the ramp was hinging down, the drivers started to step on the gas impatiently. And so did we, no doubt. Honks, hollers and revs... We were at the port!

We went through the customs procedure almost on autopilot, and I still hadn't realised where we were. I waited patiently in line, while Thanos opted for the "oriental" way. He got past the campers and the rest of the large vehicles and, when he made sure that no one had complained, nodded at me. Keeping my eyes lowered to avoid possible reprimanding looks, I moved on. However, no one seemed to be bothered. Maybe the size of our vehicles inspired the crowd's lenience.

It didn't take us too long to get out of the port, which was far from the city. We had decided not to stay long in Tangier. Why should we stop there? Why should we move along? I found it hard to adjust my mind to the pace of a trip without schedule. Thanos was a lot more laid back. Maybe the hectic rhythm of my life over the last few years had done away with my ability to relax. Work, school, second work, gym, sleep until the following morning and then all over again. I had to reboot.

"But, our plan is to do it in three years" I was now thinking out loud. Thanos heard me and understood what was troubling me right away.

"Who says we can't spend more time on the road?". His question caught me completely off guard. By travelling slowly and with no time constraints, not only would I have plenty of time to appreciate the things around me, but also each day would cost us a lot less. I couldn't disregard either of the two.

In the end, we left Tangier without actually seeing it. The city that, ever since ancient times has been a crossroads of civilisations, would remain a mystery to us. The western port of the Mediterranean, northern entrance into Africa; a place of artists and spies. I once read in a guidebook that it was also called the *White City*.

"We'll be better off in the *blue* one!" I told Thanos, and, by "blue" I meant Chefchaouen. I was completely carried away by my enthusiasm and the desire to finally ride the first kilometres on African ground and I just couldn't wait to set off.

Being used to avoiding highways and toll posts, I chose a route through the provincial road network to Chefchaouen. We soon found ourselves making desperate zig-zags, in order to avoid the bumps and potholes. The road was so bumpy, that we couldn't actually tell whether there had once been a layer of asphalt on it or whether it had always been unpaved to begin with. But, even when we did get back on the paved section of the road, our joy was short-lived. As we struggled to escape the trucks and the cars, passing beside us at an irrationally high speed, I began to wonder whether the nasty potholes were safer after all. While remaining focused on riding, I gradually started to loosen up and observe the scenery around me.

We were already in the Rif Mountains, a range that is milder and lower than the famous Atlas Mountains, that separate the Sahara from the Atlantic coast. The valleys we came across were either grazing lands or cultivated fields and, throughout the entire route, we went through villages. At each one of them, children were waving, yelling and, at times, following us on their bicycles. Just like I used to do when I was a little boy, every time I saw tourists in their campers pass by the central road in my mother's village, where I'd spend the summers up to my adulthood. The sight of foreign travellers in strange vehicles seemed so intriguing to me that, if I got lucky enough and they stopped at the central square, I went right up to them and stood staring. Now I was the foreigner on the strange vehicle. But what remained unchanged over the years, was my disposition to observe. It wasn't just the little ones that were staring, I was staring back at them, too!

It was November and there was a cool breeze blowing. The clouds above us were rushing to hide the sun, but it always managed to outwit them, finding holes to shine through. We passed through one village after the other. The houses looked poor, built with concrete and clay blocks, and a shaded porch at the front to provide shelter on hot summer days. At every central square, women were selling their merchandise. Fruits and vegetables for the most part. Contrary to the ship's passengers, here, many men were wearing djellabas and fez hats. Donkeys were pulling carts on the roads and I, mesmerised, was looking around as if trying to "videotape" all those new images with my eyes.

I didn't even realise when we reached Chefchaouen. It was still early evening and the daylight intensified the blue colour of its buildings. When I looked at the colour of the *medina* – the old city – in pictures I was convinced that it was simply digitally tampered with. I knew I was wrong the minute it was in front of me. I'd never seen a more luminous blue!

When the central road led us to the centre of the city however, my fascination passed on to a more mundane subject. We had been moving for quite a long time and my stomach had started to complain. Its rumble was so loud, that it was impossible for me to ignore it. The irresistible smell of seared meat that came out of the small restaurants along the street in the form of a dense, aromatic cloud, forced us to stop.

"Good stuff!" Thanos shouted in excitement at the first bite of roasted meat. Even the finely chopped salad we had seemed to taste better than any other salad we had ever eaten before.

Exhausted but well-fed, we set up our tents at the camping site of the area, as the sun was going down. We were right outside the city and watched its lights turn on one by one as it got darker. Shortly before the sunset, we heard the sound of the loudspeakers, placed on every minaret in town, inviting the devout to pray. The stentorious, lyrical voice of the muezzin and the drawn-out melody of his call, almost hypnotised me and I stood quiet to listen. *"Allahou akbar"* – God is great, he proclaimed and I couldn't help but wonder which one he referred to. In all cultures there is a god, and, more often than not, he is great. What if there was no god, would we all be better people? In a while, prayer time was over and so was the sunlight. On the following day, we would visit Chefchaouen to walk around its alleys and its *souks* – its famous markets.

I had barely entered the tent, when I heard a whistling coming from the other side of the fence, which separated the camping area from the road. Convinced that it wasn't addressed to me, I turned and got back inside. But there it was again. Intrigued, I went over there to check. It was a young man, around thirty, who whispered to me: *"Kif"*. I gave him a baffled look, letting him know that I didn't have the faintest idea of what he meant. The look in his eyes was pretty straightforward. I was obviously the most clueless tourist he had ever met. Conspiringly, he gave it another shot, this time whispering a word that I would hopefully understand.

"Hashish".

"Why didn't you say so earlier? No-thank-you", I answered with my heavy Greek accent. Over the next few days, I asked around. The area was famous for its marijuana plantations, which attracted thousands of tourists every year. I never wondered again about the whistling.

WAS I GOING THAT FAST?

We've had enough of staying still. Under the pretext that we needed to adapt to the pace of life on the road, we had spent three days in Chefchaouen, passing the time mostly trying new food and beverages and wandering around the alleys of the blue medina. Before dawn on the day of our departure, my mind was already way ahead of me, on its way to Rabat. It wasn't that I didn't like Chefchaouen or that I looked forward to seeing the Moroccan capital. What kept me restless was my curiosity. If here, so close to the Mediterranean coast, everything was so different and impressive, then what was up next?

Usually, big cities tend to be the point of convergence of all noteworthy cultural elements, which make a place special and in many cases guidebooks leave aside the humble bits of the daily routine. That's why I sometimes felt that they bored me. Ever since my first trips through Europe, I would visit museums and monuments, without being sure that I wanted to. Then I would go back home and dig into my memories from each trip, but I would only remember the friends, the people, the road traffic and all those trivial moments of the daily routine in the places which I had visited.

Maybe not all of us are made to look up, towards the pieces of a glorious past of which we are taught to be proud. Perhaps if we look beside us, we'll discover the inconspicuous details that speak to our soul in another language. Then again, maybe I'm just an ignorant looking for a good excuse to have tea next to a Berber, while I watch him smoke his shisha idly at the coffee shop of any given village.

No tea for us, just coffee, and we were back on the road, on our way to Rabat. This time, we made sure that the route indicated by the GPS would lead us to our destination avoiding the bumpy secondary roads. Although I secretly hoped for a mistake to happen that would lead us astray all the way up to some rocky mountains, the highway was obviously the most prudent choice.

The scenery of the Rif mountain range was breathtaking. The road, defined by the map as the main highway, was almost deserted and this allowed me to observe everything around undisturbed. Consecutive smooth mountain ranges extended as far as the eye could see and the woodlands succeeded one another. Cedars, pines and oak trees took turns in dominating the landscape and, the harder the wind blew against my face, the more alive I felt. The level asphalt and the wide turns of the road made the ride even more enjoyable and the clear sunshine made me want this moment to last forever.

When we started to descend the mountains, conifers gave way to lower vegetation. Now and then, a majestic palm tree popped up adding an exotic touch to the scenery. Meadows and acres of light green cultivated fields made the ideal background for the little villages that every once in a while cropped up along the way. Around the streams and rivulets, the clothes of the people that washed their kilim rugs and cooking pans looked like colourful splashes.

The rock music that sounded loud in my earphones was the perfect soundtrack to the journey. When, at some point, I looked back through the mirror, Thanos was no longer in my visual range. *Was I going THAT fast?* I wondered, feeling proud of my bike's performance. But, before I got to relish my victory in a race that never existed, my fellow traveller showed up at the bend. He had stopped to take photos, as he explained, and then I realised that it wasn't the scooter that was speeding up, it was my mind.

A few kilometres outside Rabat, I noticed that the road went through the edge of a strange forest. Seen from a distance, the trees looked as if they were standing there half-dressed and the sight was at once funny and sad. Their foliage remained intact, the ash-green leaves turning silver as the wind made them flicker, but from the mid-trunk down, a human hand had stripped the bark off. The bare-butted trees looked like victims of public castigation. I went closer to take a look. I was surrounded by cork oaks. *So this is where wine stoppers actually come from!* I thought. As satisfied as I was with my newly acquired knowledge, I was filled with bitterness over the thought of how cruel we are with nature. I remembered the forest in my mother's village. The forest that was misfortunate enough to be standing over a gold placer deposit. The forest that I had defended fiercely, along with the other residents of the area, against those who were trying to destroy it. My mind started racing back again to everything that had hurt me. I turned around and moved on.

The cheap camping site that put us up at Kenitra, looked more like a truck parking lot and so we decided to get over with our errands in the capital, which was not far from there, as soon as possible. We were prepared for our first experience with African bureaucracy and, as usual, I was hoping for everything that I had read about issuing a visa in Mauritania being a daunting task to be proved wrong.

They say that we see what we choose to see or that, subconsciously, we only attract the things we want or even fear. There is, however, yet another possibility: we sometimes take every good thing that comes our way for granted and just pass it by, obsessing over the bad things. This was the only explanation that occurred to me when, in stark contrast to everything I had read, within a few hours we were holding our Mauritanian visas. "We're off to Fez!" I shouted to Thanos and we set off, riding past donkey carts and Mercedes cars.

SCENTS AND MEMORIES

It'd been only a day since we settled at the camping site in the outskirts of Fez. It was time to take a stroll around the city. Fez, apart from being the birthplace of the fez hat, the classic emblem of the oriental culture, had yet another feature that made it famous. The heart of the city, the medina, is one of the largest urban territories which are off-limits for cars. Contrary to its modern part, in which traffic chaos was one of the worst I had ever seen, once we crossed the gate to the medina, the racket suddenly ceased and we found ourselves in a funfair of voices, colours and scents. "I don't think we'll be getting out of here any time soon!" I told Thanos with a chuckle. I actually meant that, since we'd already taken the first steps on its cobblestoned streets. In travel guidebooks, there are countless testimonies of survival in the alleys, which, according to the graphic descriptions, form a tourist-devouring maze. We moved carefully, observing every single detail and making sure to remember the route we took each time. It wasn't easy. The narrow alleys were flooded with hundreds of people. Foreigners and locals all leisurely hanging out at the tiny stores that sprang up at every seemingly tumbledown building.

Multi-coloured *babouches* – leather slippers – scarves, djellabas and tones of souvenirs hanging everywhere, filled the otherwise plain ocher walls with colour. But not everything was made for the tourist's pleasure. On every alleyroad that we chose to take, we saw small blacksmith and woodworker parlours, and lots of other workshops, where the craftsmen kept working, bent over, undisturbed by the curious stares of foreigners. At the butcher stores, the sight was probably not suitable for the pampered eyes of the Western man. Heads of camels, cow calves and lambs were hanging from hooks and, below them, the bloodstained worktops where meat got chopped. Flies were perching on the syrupy sweets and the dried dates that were skillfully piled up nearby, hiding the traders.

I tried to keep my eyes and ears open so as not to miss a single moment of this reality. Until, instinctively, I covered my nose. From the alley around the corner came an indescribable stench. In a matter of seconds, we were surrounded by a crowd of youngsters. They nearly pulled us by the hand to go see the tanneries that were close by. They were holding little bunches of spearmint in their hands and suggested we shove a couple of leaves in each nostril, so that the heavy stink wouldn't bother us. Minutes before reaching the narrow door to one of the balconies with a view to the much-photographed basins, where workers plunged into foul-smelling fluids in order to dye the leather destined for coats, shoes and so many other products, I stopped. A group of tourists passed me by and went up the stairs, but my feet remained nailed to the ground. "You go ahead if you want", I told Thanos.

The smell of leather, which I managed to distinguish from the rest of the tannery materials, unexpectedly took me back to Thessaloniki. Suddenly, I was inside my parents' leather goods workshop. I went back to my childhood. I saw my mother's tired hands. I remembered the endless hours both my parents spent away from home. Then, bankruptcy came along. Leather goods from abroad were cheaper. Who would buy a leather jacket made in Greece, when imported ones are a better deal? Unemployment, efforts, disappointment, despair. That's how I grew up. No delusions.

You're being over the top! my mind was playing tricks on me and I placed my foot on the first step. *At least they get a wage!* I thought, but stayed put. *Throw them some coins if you take a picture!* that was curiosity playing its nasty game. I turned around and walked away.

I CAN'T EAT THIS THING!

"Watch out!" I yelled in Greek without realising it and honked at Thanos, who stopped dead on his tracks. The little old man, who had been running beside the Vespa for quite a few metres, without him noticing it, grabbed his arm, panting in relief. I stopped behind and watched them talk. When he left, Thanos turned back and put me at ease. As it turned out, he was the owner of a nearby restaurant and, when he saw us moving so slowly, deemed it fitting to advertise his menu.

"If you'd run over him we'd have to eat at his restaurant!" I replied sarcastically, only to regret it when, moments later, I started to count the people that tried to sell a product or service to us. Everyone in Morocco seems to be selling something. Young men dressed in their djellabas sell *kif*, women souvenirs, little kids offer guided tours around the *souks* – the markets. There is no peace for foreigners. On many occasions, I felt as if they saw a euro sign drawn on my forehead. *Foreigner! Money!* was what they thought,

I'm afraid. *If something happened to me along the way, would anyone stop and help me with nothing in return?* I wondered. I didn't want to believe that everyone around me had lost their humanity, the one feature that urges us to run to where we're needed.

"It's the law of the jungle that rules down there!" people would say, every time I'd reveal my plan to travel to Africa, and my longing to actually go deep into the jungle to see with my very own eyes the laws by which it is governed, grew stronger.

As we were leaving the chaos of Fez behind, at some point we took a wrong turn and lost our way to the camping site. We pulled over to check the map and, out of nowhere, about ten people of all ages gathered around us. Shouts, gestures and laughs. A bit of French, a tad of Arabic and lots of body language, which always comes in handy, was all it took for us to be back on the right track within minutes. For free.

The sun was going down as we were preparing our kitchenware and I, in a stroke of inspiration, assured Thanos that I was going to make the tastiest pasta dish ever. Since a few hours ago we had turned down the old man's offer to eat at his restaurant in downtown Fez, we had to cook. I was slicing onions for the sauce while watching the rest of the travellers that had settled at the camping site. Those who didn't have campers – which revealed their intention not to travel too far away from Morocco, had specially equipped vehicles, suitable for the bumpy African roads. A few motorbikes caught my eye. Big or smaller, they seemed always carefully selected to meet the requirements of a trip like this. Only a couple of Vespas stood out from the crowd for their staggering unsuitability.

"How far are we going, man?" I asked my companion, without worrying too much about the answer.

His mouth was already stuffed with the first bite of spaghetti that I had proudly prepared.

"Holy crap! I can't eat this thing!" he answered.

GOING UP

From the olive groves in Fez, we found ourselves among the cedars and oak trees, and, from Morocco, suddenly to Central

Europe. Ifrane looked as if it was perched in the Alps. There were gardens, flowers and gable-roofed houses everywhere; and the roof tops were almost vertical to prevent the snow from building up. "Is Morocco this way?" I joked with Thanos, who went past me as we were headed for Midelt.

Luckily, the "dogs" that showed up from afar, bouncing their way across the road, restored the order in place and time. "Monkeys!", I shouted, when I saw them climb up the trees. *I'm pretty sure a dog could never do that!* I thought to myself, amused. We pulled over and, for the next hour, we took to making each and every mistake that can possibly be made during interactions with wildlife. Defying every known instruction to travellers, as well as common sense, we fed, played with, photographed and tried to touch the little critters, which seemed particularly familiar with such human behaviour. Soon, as the food ran out, so did their interest in us and they just stood there looking at us listlessly from the branches of the nearby trees. A couple of travellers a bit farther, drew their attention again, when they tried to bribe them with food, in exchange of their windshield wipers that they had stolen from them. "Barbary macaques, that's what they're called", they informed us as they moved away empty-handed.

As soon as we left the last macaque-loaded trees behind us, things started to get serious. The cedars and the rest of the conifers disappeared, giving way to a vast rocky land. *Good thing I got the fleece jackets from Kenitra!* I thought. Despite being mid-day, the wind was so cold that made my face go numb. For quite some time now, temperatures at night took a real plunge, but since we started to ascend the Middle Atlas range, it remained freezing cold even when the sun was up.

When we reached 1,500m of altitude, we finally took sight of Midelt. We were going to spend the night there, although I had repeatedly proposed to Thanos that we camp up on the mountains. The little villages, the kids that were waving at us and the shepherds in their woollen, pointy-hooded djellabas, made me want to spend the night out in the wild, away from tourist lodgings. "No way, we'll freeze to death", my co-traveller brought me down to earth. He was probably right, but in my eyes, every glade beside one of the narrow streams we came across seemed ideal.

The only thing we looked for when we got to Midelt was a place to sleep. After plenty of haggling, I managed to cut the price to half for a room in a guesthouse and, as it usually happened in such cases, I felt very proud of my achievement. But the feeling didn't last long. Shortly afterwards, the tomato sauce from a jar that we somehow managed to break, was splashed all over the walls, bed and floor of the poor room. We had a good laugh at first, but, after an unsuccessful attempt to mop everything clean, the only option we were left with was to take to the streets in search of a restaurant. "This looks like my mother's *tourlou*[1]!" I uttered in disappointment, when I tasted the vegetable cous-cous that looked so exotic, served as it was in the traditional clay pot – the *tajine*.

The sharp cold of the last few days, made it harder for us to decide to abandon the room's warm blankets. The night before we left Midelt, I took all my clothes out of the suitcase and started to observe them. Back in Thessaloniki, when I was getting ready for the trip, I'd made a point of not buying anything expensive. Friends of mine that saw the tent and the sleeping bag that I had bought at a supermarket came up with the following two scenarios: a. I was kidding them and I had no intention of going anywhere, or, b. I was a total dimwit. "What if I don't like it and I want to come back?", I used to say and I actually believed that the most honest thing to do was to buy the cheapest stuff. *After all, I can always buy anything on the road*, I figured and put everything back inside. On the following day, wrapped up in our jackets, we set out for the desert.

WHEELIES

We were really curious to see how our tiny wheels would react to the desert sand. As we moved along southward to Merzouga, the landscape increasingly resembled the image we had in our minds

---

[1] *Tourlou or Briam is a traditional Greek dish, made up of various vegetables (mostly potatoes, zucchini, onions, eggplants and peppers) mixed together with tomato, garlic, parsley and other condiments and spices, and cooked in the oven or on stove-top.*

of Sahara. The air was no longer damp and the cold was milder. The buildings of the towns and villages that we passed by were all sand-coloured, fitting harmoniously in their surroundings. Throughout many kilometres, from Errachidia to Erfoud, we rode along a palm-tree forest, and we found it impossible to believe where we were! Every now and then, I opened the throttle to reach Thanos' side and let out spontaneous cry of enthusiasm. I wasn't thinking about anything, I just couldn't. The excitement had overpowered my mind and the only thing I could do was look with my eyes wide open, until the dust forced me to blink.

The beauty of Erfoud, the city located in the middle of an oasis, held us captive long enough to have some *kefta* – traditional meatballs – contemplating its almost pink buildings. After finishing our meal, as if by pre-arrangement, we both stood up at once and got on our bikes. We couldn't wait to get to the dunes. We could see them in the background, all golden-red and beautiful; a herd of camels was passing right in front of them, close to where we were, and we just had to stop for a while. "We are in the Sahara desert!" I said, but this time I was talking to Kitsos. My good ol' scooter had made it to the Saharan sand. For the first time, we kept quiet. I guess Thanos couldn't believe how far we'd got, either.

Moments before the sun went down we set our tents in a camping site at Hassilabied, not far from Merzouga. I prepared my sleeping bag and took all the clothes I could possibly wear to keep myself protected from the freezing cold of the desert out of my suitcase. Back in Greece, I had never gone camping – at least not in my adult life. Only as a kid, when sometimes in the summer our father would take my brother and me camping on an almost deserted beach, not far from our house in Chalkidiki. I don't have many memories from that time, but maybe his insistence on us to living differently for a while, even if we were just a few kilometres away from the village, had subconsciously familiarised me with the idea.

On the following day, I was up so early, that I surprised not only Thanos but myself as well. The morning light was bathing the sand dunes and, before I'd even finished my coffee, I rode Kitsos and, as if in a trance, I headed for the place that I felt was calling me. The road, full of thick gravel and eroded by the strong winds, made the wheels bounce and the entire scooter creak. I didn't care; I'd go up, regardless. Even without headphones on, in my mind I could hear my favourite classic rock songs and I sped up. I was going up the thick, orange sand of the dunes. I was flying! And then, I got stuck. No known law of Physics would possibly allow my vehicle to move on this type of soil. The front wheel sank deep into the sand at the first upslope it came up to. I started laughing and so did the two youngsters that had been following me. The oldest one dared to mock me, popping a wheelie right there in front of me, which every ten-year-old at the village square would envy. Immediately after that, and while I was still stuck, he remembered his duty. He approached me with some beads in his hands and, with professional formality, asked me if I wanted to buy any. "You little scamp" I told him in Greek. "You're not out to play, are you?". He smiled at me and didn't insist. Soon, he went back to being a child and his eyes sparkled. "Let's go!" he shouted as he wandered off on the dune.

Sand had gotten into every fabric fold of my clothes and, when I got back to the camping site and emptied my boots, a small stack of sand was formed. "Tomorrow we're going together!" I told Thanos. He agreed, although I wasn't so sure his intentions were the same as mine.

We went down to the village with the small mud-brick houses. Only the central road was paved, while on the byroads, with every step a cloud of dust rose that dyed our boots grey. There were quite a few tourists strolling around the alleys, but still their number was not proportionate to the dozens of lodgings built to cover the visitors' needs. At every corner, we were offered guided tours to the desert, to see the life of the Sahara nomads up close. "But nomads don't stay at one place" I joked. The idea of riding a camel to a pre-arranged spot in the desert where I would stare at people as if they were living objects on display did not really appeal to me. If somewhere there are people living like this, I'd much rather stumble across them by chance.

Throughout our entire stay at Hassilabied, I did nothing else but practice my skills in sand dune climbing. To Thanos, my perseverance was probably rather wearisome, but, to me, going those full 10m before sinking into the warm, fluffy sand, was a heck of an achievement. Every time I pulled out a good stunt, with patient Kitsos as my accomplice – his nickname had been officially upgraded from "donkey" to "lion" – I though of my friend, Yorgos. Back in the days of my endless shifts in Thessaloniki, when I'd get back home so tense that I'd have trouble sleeping. Right around dawn, while I was rolling around in bed trying to get my tired feet comfortable, the phone would ring. "Hey man, are you in for some wheelies?" Yorgos' voice sounded at the other end of the line and, for the following couple of hours, until the break of day, we would whip our bikes without mercy, at the parking lot of some closed supermarket.

THE MATCHMAKING

We arrived at Ouarzazate late in the evening. Gone were the days back in the desert when I couldn't wait to get out of bed; on the day of our departure, I wasn't able to get out of the tent before noon. Abdel had given us the exact address of our meeting point and we didn't want to be late, but the strong headwind on the way there made it hard for us. We stopped outside a souvenir store close to the city centre, and, while we were trying to make sure it was the right place, a man – no older than forty – came up to us and introduced himself. He was our host. He locked the store, got on Thanos' bike and led us over to his place. That was the first time that we would stay at a local's home instead of a guesthouse. As we moved through the alleys, among mudbrick houses and yards that we couldn't really tell whether they were public or whether we were trespassing, it dawned on me that, if it weren't for the internet communities which one can turn to, we wouldn't be here now. We would probably be at some guesthouse, locked up in our room.

Abdel had offered to put us up and, shortly after meeting him, we were trying to make ourselves comfortable and feel at home as much as possible in the small house which he shared with his mother, wife and two children, as well as his wife's unmarried sister. His house, like all the rest in the neighbourhood, was made with mudbricks and had exactly as many rooms as needed for his family to be accommodated. We sat in the fuchsia-black cheap nylon velvet sofas and the women of the family disappeared, leaving us alone with him and his son. He was of Berber descent, as most residents of these parts of Morocco were, with their customs and traditions having been crucially influenced by the Arabs over the centuries. It wasn't before twenty minutes later that his wife showed up with a tea serving set. She placed it in front of us and went back inside. We spent hours talking with Abdel. We asked him about his 50-dollar salary, the king, religion, and everything else that had stirred our curiosity.

I had grown particularly fond of the tea that was offered to us everywhere. Back in Greece, I had to be burning with fever and with my tonsils blown up like a balloon to drink tea – grudgingly – but in Morocco it tasted differently. I don't know if it was the mint leaves or the plentiful amount of sugar or the hands of those who offered it to me, but you could fit the entire country of Morocco in a single glass of tea. The hospitality, the smiles, the hot desert and the frozen Atlas; the little kids pulling me by the hand, the music, the noisy bazaars. With every sip I took, I gulped down real history. Why should I read about history when I could taste it?

We were worn-out, but the soirée over at Abdel's was far from over. He explained that he was expecting visitors and that the imminent visit would determine the future of his wife's sister, of which he had taken charge. The prospective groom along with his family was on his way here and we had to behave ourselves so as not to spoil the matchmaking. Soon they arrived. The women were joyful, with their eyes lowered out of respect and humility. The men were much more relaxed, affable and smiling. The table suddenly got filled with pies, dry nuts, marmalades and lots of other goodies that were probably meant to impress the guests. We stood there watching the scene unable to understand a single word. We kept smiling, trying to ease the moments of awkwardness with some sugar-and-cinnamon-sprinkled pies.

The conversation lasted for quite a while. The aspiring groom and bride were heard the least of all. At some point, I got bored and started to make up possible scenarios for the outcome of the negotiations, which I transmitted to Thanos right beside me.

"He wants more camels!" I whispered in his ear. "Mark my words: he's out of here!".

"Shut up, will you! Or they'll sell us, too" replied Thanos with a chuckle.

I don't remember what the time was when they left. And, certainly, I had no idea what the outcome of the meeting was. We were now lying down in the living-room, where only moments ago the future of two persons was about to be decided, inextricably linked with family bonds and social conventions. Did they actually love each other? Did the option of loving each other even occur to them? Did they want to get married? Who determined their destiny in the traditional society in which they lived? Then, I thought about all those things that rule our fate across the length and breadth of this earth and became even more confused.

SNAKES AND TALES

I was in a t-shirt, scorched by the sun, lying down by a pool. I couldn't believe it! It'd been only a few hours since, while on our way to Marrakesh, my glasses were fogging up underneath the helmet from cold and humidity.

We didn't spend another day at Abdel's. The rules that we had to follow were way too complicated. While he was away, it was expressly prohibited to us to be alone with the women. Problem was, our host worked late hours and so this sort of inverted curfew that kept us outside for hours was tiresome. We therefore decided to move on. We said goodbye, after a rather uncomfortable conversation about how we felt it was excessive of him to ask for one of our cameras as a "thank-you" gift for his hospitality. In the end, he kept a pair of shoes that didn't need. We, on the other hand, apart from the cameras, took with us plenty of doubts about the motives behind his offer. I didn't want to remember Abdel as the Moroccan from a typical traveller's account, in which he tries to rip tourists off. I chose the other side of the story, according to which he's just a poor man with a ridiculously low wage, trying to make ends meet for himself and his family.

Thanos was having a cold beer and I, in the shade of the parasol, was taking advantage of the camping site's fast wifi connection. "Hey, mom! How are you guys doing?" I asked and on the other side of the connection I heard the voices of the entire family in unison. My mother was expressing her permanent worry about her child's health and well-being, while my father was trying hard to keep her wild pace of asking the same old questions in check and my brother was cracking up in the background. I'd missed them all. When I assured them that, despite the high altitude and the extreme cold at the mountain passage before going down Marrakesh, surprisingly enough I hadn't gotten pneumonia, I started to describe all the different landscapes that I had seen in a single day's span. The dark shades of the earth and the gorges with the exotic vegetation, as we were climbing up the Great Atlas were gone. At 2,000m of altitude, the rocks turned white and nothing seemed to grow on the rough slopes that stretched out as far as the eye could see. Every once in a while, we'd get inside a cloud and become soaked in its frozen, silent dampness. I don't really know why, but it's awfully quiet inside the clouds. When we finally started to descend, the landscape changed once again, making it impossible for us to get bored. "Are those olive trees?" I asked Thanos, pointing at what I believed to be an olive grove. "Kermes oaks, maybe?" he replied with a question.

A few days later, while we were wandering around the *souks* of Marrakech, we saw a sign that read *"Argan Oil"* beneath the drawing of some tree that looked like an olive tree. My mother, who apparently knew all about botanicals, herbs and their properties, elucidated the issue. "The argan tree is a tree resembling olive trees and the oil from its kernels is beneficial to our health...». "You should get some!" were her last words, before I interrupted her by saying that we were late for our walk.

I knew I was being too harsh on Marrakesh right from the start. I had read so much about tourists that started to flood its alleys, from the '60s onwards, and, biased as I was, our walk around the medina left me completely unimpressed. In the *souks*, I felt I was asphyxiating for the first time. There were not that many people around, but the traders just wouldn't give up trying to catch my attention and convince me to buy something. It was literally impossible to take ten steps without having my arm pulled by someone. Thinking about everything I had read about the famous city and its square, the Jemaa el-Fnaa, where snake charmers, storytellers, illusionists and water carriers got together every evening at this huge funfair, I soon lost all interest. I pictured the square as an unbearable pandemonium with everybody that bothered me in the mornings multiplying and getting to my nerves even more. Thanos wasn't feeling the same. Almost every afternoon, he would go there to take a look around. When he came back, he described enthusiastically his day, but, though I knew I was exaggerating, I persistently refused to go along.

Amidst the fuss and the yelling, and the Marrakesh traders goading me into buying something, my mind went back to the bars and restaurants where I used to work in Thessaloniki and Santorini. I remembered the post of the "puller-in" – the elegant, all perfumed-up young man or woman, who stands outside the restaurant and, in a mellow yet persistent way, keeps trying to lure passers by in. I wouldn't even consider getting into places like that as a customer, but, ironically, I had to work in them. Slimy comments and foolish flirting from customers, who were drooling all over female staff members while they were working. What if our salaries were humiliatingly low? We worked at the fancy seafront bars and that alone was enough to make us feel important.

Thoughts like that gloomed my days and I struggled to make them go away, but sometimes they got stuck in my head and wouldn't get off. Besides, my whole life before setting off to Africa was like that. Ever since I can remember myself, I felt like there was something wrong with the people that surrounded me. But then again, could it be that there was something wrong with me? I hoped to figure that out some day.

WAKE UP!

Every sea has its own colour. And its own sound. I was gazing at the Atlantic and thinking what a terrible mistake I would have made if I had become a sea captain. It was early December and I had completely lost track of time. From the cold to the heat, from the mountains to the sea. If I were on the bridge of a cargo ship right now out in the ocean, what would I be doing? What would I be thinking? For how long would I be still able to tell the different sea blues apart? How long before I'd end up losing my sense of orientation, after seeing nothing but the sea and the sky? How long before I'd finally realise that I was a drylander?

We were at a camping site south of Agadir. As I watched the waves splashing back and forth, a thought started to sway along in my mind: one month. I didn't know when I'd go back. I didn't know if I'd go back at all. The only thing I knew was that I had to keep going. It took only thirty days for me to realise that I'd been long gone. I was in Greece, surrounded by the sweet familiarity of the place that spawned me and yet I felt like a stranger. It is hard to be in the place you know best and be spat out, rejected, cast away.

From Tiznit to Tan-Tan, southward, the endless straight roadways began. Not a trace of vegetation. Just rocks, dust and desert. The hours seemed endless on the scooter and the humming of the engine sounded like a lullaby. For the first time ever, I felt my back hurt, as I had to ride completely still, trapped in the vastness of the perfectly straight lines that went as far as the end of the horizon. Images from the past reeled before my eyes and questions, which I thought I'd answered long ago, were floating back up. Bad mood often makes us stir up painful memories and look at things through distorting lenses. Had I jumped to a hasty judgment? Had I not given enough chances? The heat was driving me nuts...

"Wake up!" I shouted to myself angrily, but it was too late. I only had enough time to hold the handlebar as firmly as I could and drag my feet a few metres along the ground. I had swerved off the road. I put the bike on the stand, rubbed my eyes until they started to hurt and stayed there staring in befuddlement. Thanos, who had been riding right behind me, stopped without really understanding what had happened.

"Are you OK?", he asked.

"I'm fine... Looks like I had too much for supper and got drowsy", I tried to explain.

As we were entering Tan-Tan, the first thing that caught our eye was the giant white camels. Realistic-looking sculptures, but slightly oversized. Pairs of dromedaries stood motionless at the entrances to the city, facing one another, without giving a dime about the vehicles passing right below them. Was it an homage to the animals which, for thousands of years, have been living close to the desert people, offering them their services? Maybe it was just another tourist attraction, but I liked the first option better. The one that makes humans look less ungrateful to nature, which they've tried to cut and sew to their own needs since time immemorial.

The scenery in the south of Morocco was quite different than what we were accustomed to in Marrakesh. The noisy imperial cities full of palaces and alley mazes that made up the medinas and the souks had become peaceful, humble coastal towns with wide streets and peace. Here, poverty could not be hidden behind complex arabesques, architectural monuments of past centuries and bazaars. It was right in front of us, sprinkled by the Atlantic mist. The inhabitants of the south, fishermen and petty traders, restaurant and hotel owners, ran their businesses in a way that could attract tourists from Europe. However, mass tourism halted somewhere near Agadir. Few were the travellers that ventured down south.

WE ARE SAHRAWI!

"Just stop or he won't leave us alone!" I told Thanos, who was fed up waiting at the police checkpoints and was in a hurry to hand his *fiché* in and go. Once we passed Tan-Tan, police checks multiplied. At the cities entrances and exits and all the big highway junctions, where there was warning street signs, we'd find one. Police officers, meticulously formal, looked through our papers and then took the document – the *fiché* – in which we had filled out our personal information. This was obligatory standard procedure for security reasons, we read. For the past few years, Morocco is not in the friendliest terms with its neighbours. We heard a lot of negative comments about Mauritanians, as well as Algerians. A Moroccan's worst enemy, however, is a Sahrawi – the inhabitants of Western Sahara – who obstinately stick to their claim for independence.

Thanos had pushed his way to the front of the line, sick of all the controls. The police officer started to growl in an unintelligible language, pointing at the intermittent line on the asphalt, behind which he had to stand. "We need to be patient with cops or we'll be making our lives complicated with no good reason", I reiterated my firm belief. We had no other choice but to wait in line and hand in one of the numerous *fichés*, of which, luckily, I had made sure to carry multiple copies. When we got to the beach outside Laayoune, the capital of this strange country, we had already shared out quite a few.

"I was wondering... Would anyone actually notice it if I gave false information?" I told Thanos and, at the same time, an idea started to nudge into my mind. I didn't say anything though.

It was not long before we found the camping site that we were looking for, but when the guard shut and locked the door behind us, we felt like we were in a military base. A high, concrete fence surrounded some dust-ridden buildings, the former use of which we could only guess. We placed the tents right in the middle of the yard and found ourselves all alone in the charmless place, while the wind grew stronger.

As I wasn't aware of the average yearly rainfall in the area, I was in for a big surprise when I found out that, coincidentally, we had arrived in Laayoune right in time for the rainy season – which lasts no more than a few days. My tent had turned into a fish tank and, while I was trying to stop the leak with the help of a cup, it occurred to me for the first time that perhaps I would soon need a new one. I didn't know what to do. My stuff was getting more soaked by the minute, but no good DIY ideas came down on me – just drops. All of a sudden, I heard a voice. It was the guard calling us. With gestures and the rather naive conviction that, if we spoke slowly and clearly enough – albeit each one in his own language – we would manage to understand each other, we finally did: he was, in fact, offering us a spot in the indoor facilities of the camping site.

Now dry and frustrated, we were cursing our bad luck, until the kind man came back. He was holding a plate of lentils and a piece of bread in his hands, and, making as much an effort as before, he explained that he had brought us food to warm us up. It was the first time that someone offered us something without being guided by the principles of tourist marketing. Moroccans were always kind and cheerful, and offered us the tea I loved so much, but that was where all of their kindness ended. The whole scenery of Laayoune and the camping site that looked like an abandoned military base was not exactly the natural backdrop for kind, selfless gestures. And yet, there it was: a plate of lentils. As simple as that. It was then that I started to regret not being able to speak any foreign language other than English. Not that I was particularly good at it anyway. I laughed at myself every time I heard my heavy Greek accent and my colossal mistakes, but regardless I got by. If I could stutter a tiny bit of French, I would be able to get closer to the people I met in all those places I visited. Of course, back in my school days when I spent most of the time looking out the window, waiting for the bell to ring, I couldn't possibly imagine the ways in which I could take advantage of that missed knowledge in the future. Where would I find the motivation to do so? People around me were either in a rush to clinch a "fixed" job in public administration so that they could kick back and enjoy, or waited tables, postponing any worries about their future to the longer-term future. Misery dressed up in expensive clothes and perfumed with *eau de toilette* knock-offs.

"Come on, man, let's take a walk now that the rain has stopped". I told Thanos. The rain had stopped completely and the sun had taken its place back up in the sky. However, the dampness and the droplets lingering in the atmosphere made up an unearthly scenery and, as we walked along the empty beach with the gigantic lampposts, it seemed like we were walking trough a ghost town. The streets of Laayoune, apart from the central one, were all unpaved. The bitter-cold sea breeze and saltiness had caused everything to be covered in rust, and, even the ground that we stepped on felt damp and salty dry all at once. There was no tourism here. Only peace and quiet, and empty houses waiting for someone to occupy them. Housing programs from the dominant Morocco were trying to bring people back to the Atlantic coast.

People were scarce, but the ones we met were really chatty. They made a point of explaining us where we were. "We are Sahrawi!" they said swelling with pride. It would be long though until I grasped the complexity of the situation in this nearly deserted country that keeps struggling for independence.

FISH 'N' CHEAP GASOLINE

Canopies, scattered tents and camels. And of course, the desert. *There is no way a country can be THIS flat and empty!* I said repeatedly to myself, as we were crossing Western Sahara with the aim of getting to Mauritania as soon as possible. I had slept well the night before. The ocean's uproar didn't bother me, although, accustomed as I was to the melodic hum of the waves in the Aegean, this deep swoosh that dominated at night, covering up every other sound. When I heard it for the first time, I thought that it came from the engines of a nearby factory that never stopped roaring. I asked a local and he laughed: "The Atlantic", he assured me.

We were travelling between the immensities of the ocean and the desert. But this was nothing like the sand dunes at Merzouga. That side of the Sahara looked mellow and safe, compared to this one. A bit further to the east, where the territory of the ex-Spanish colonies "liberated" by the *Frente Polisario* stretches, is also where the *hamada* starts – the rocky, inhospitable area of the desert, completely stripped by deflation – not even a grain of sand left on the wind-beaten soil. All the way to the military camps in Algeria, the few inhabitants of this land move among minefields and military units. Proud nomads, disheartened by war and conflicts, they have settled almost permanently, waiting for the dominant states to decide their fate. Sahrawis are no more than six hundred thousand, but they don't lose hope.

"Hey you, leave that alone!" said Thanos angrily outside the hotel in Boujdour, while I was inside, trying to haggle over the price for a night's stay. About ten kids had gathered around us and they seemed to have no intention of leaving us or the bikes in peace. They were messing around with the cameras, the helmets and Thanos, whose patience was exhausted at some point. "Stergios, come on, let's get out of here!" he shouted and I couldn't be happier with his decision.

Ever since our first days on the road, I kept suggesting to Thanos that we set camp on our own, away from tourist facilities. But he hesitated. Maybe he was not that much into the joys and pains of free camping. The only occasion in which his refusal was definitely justified, was on the frozen mount Atlas. I, on the other hand, looked forward to any kind of experience that would come my way. I knew that, sooner or later, the time would come that we'd have to camp at some random place, but I didn't want to force the situation. When I heard him say that we'd better leave Boujdour, I seized the opportunity and reiterated my suggestion. And he accepted.

We both needed a pretext, a push to make a start. I was thinking that, until then, Thanos' opposition to free camping kind of made me feel safe, as well. But when we finally put up our tents right at the edge of a cliff, where the gentle hissing of the waves was the sole soundtrack to the night, we sure didn't regret it! That night, I felt clearly and for the first time completely exposed; to anything: nature or humans. The ocean could swell up and drown me. Someone might come and steal my bike, and then kill me. *So what?* What could I possibly do? Right before I closed my eyes, I made sure that what I heard was just Thanos searching through his stuff in his tent. *I'll get used to it*, I thought and drifted off to sleep.

The following morning found me outside my tent trying to engage in conversation with some passing-by fishermen. I was becoming more and more sociable, despite language barriers. I've always been told that I was a "communicative person", but I wasn't quite sure what that meant. From the moment I stepped foot on Africa, I had spared no effort to seek as much as information as possible. Not so much about monuments and age-old history; that was not what really interested me. What I wanted to take in were people's daily stories, perhaps a bit tedious to those who actually lived them.

By the time we had to set off for Dakhla, the only information I had managed to harvest had to do with gasoline rates, which were rather low, and the Atlantic fish, the number of which had gone down, as my interlocutors, the fishermen, explained. I don't know if that could be of any use, but it was something, nonetheless.

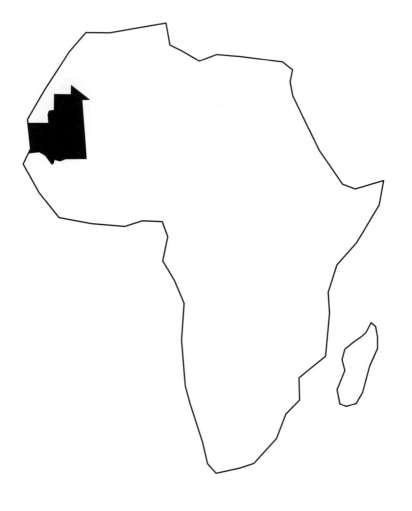

MAURITANIA

NO MAN'S LAND

From the window of our room in the guesthouse, above the last gas station before the border with Mauritania, we were watching trucks full of merchandise come and go, between the two countries. It was December and the scorching heat was but one of the new experiences that I had added to my vast collection over the past almost two months. On the previous day, we had crossed the Tropic of Cancer south of Dakhla, and it felt like we were passing through an invisible curtain that blocked the desert swelter, which would sneak up on us on the other side. The temperature suddenly jumped to 35°C, although the lack of humidity made it tolerable.

"Man, I'm so sorry about the fuss, it's just that my tent looks like a fish-tank again!" I apologised to my fellow traveller, who had grown fond of the campsite in Dakhla. Thanos understood. We didn't want to give each other a hard time. Every year, countless European campervans gathered at the same spot in Dakhla and made up an 'organised free' campsite right beside the ocean. The place next to the lagoon that is created by the sea winds and the tide is well known – we were told – to kite-surf lovers. Our two nights there were supposed to give us the chance to meet other travellers, chat and chill out. However, the weather had different plans. Throughout the entire night, the huge raindrops had ruined my sleep and with it my peace. On the following morning, we scrambled our stuff together and moved to this guesthouse by the border.

I was thinking about that South Korean motorcyclist who had told us about Dakhla's *"campervan village"*. We met him by chance and he was the first person I'd seen on a small bike. Ever since the campsite in Chefchaouen, I had watched the wheeled beasts that set out to travel around Africa and I was worried. Was I not sufficiently prepared? Was I too optimistic? Every time such thoughts sneaked into my mind, I didn't let them stay long. After centuries of people travelling around the world, quite a few of them had got by without all that "special equipment". What an absurd obsession we have with our self-perception of uniqueness! *Of course I will travel across Africa. Somehow, some day, I will get where I want.*

We left the room early. Almost immediately we reached the border and, before we knew it, we had left Western Sahara behind. We both looked forward to stepping into Mauritania and entered *No Man's Land*, this orphan piece of ground that belongs to no state and that, consequently, no state looks after. The distance we needed to travel was no more than 5km, but I had read so much about the dangers that lurked therein, that I had started to get nervous the day before. And my nervousness was only increased by the giant signs scattered all around us warning of minefields.

Since no one bothered about this narrow strip of dirt and stones, the road had been left to its fate and we had to pick the right path, looking for tracks from other vehicles. We were riding very carefully, among car carcasses that lay half-buried in the sand. Together with all kinds of abandoned objects, they made the scenery look haunted. The desert and the saltiness of the ocean had been ruthless to the metal surfaces which had been just left there, with no other choice but to rot. However, the sight of sheer abandonment was unexpectedly interrupted every time people showed up out of nowhere, to offer us currency exchange. Every trace of insecurity disappeared every time a car passed by, heading for the borders. And while we were making our way through the notorious area, all grim and uneasy, a thought crossed my mind: *How could we possibly step on a mine when so many people travel through here every day?*

I relaxed and now there was only one thing concerning me.

Ever since we started handing out all those little papers – the *fichés* – with our information on them, to countless police checks, I kept wondering: *Does anyone actually pay attention to them?* A smile cracked through on my face as I was solemnly submitting the last *fiché* before the border. In some random state logbook, maybe some day an officer will read that, around late 2013, Theodoros Kolokotronis was in Morocco...

BROTHER YUNAN

Stern, with the machine gun hanging from his shoulder and an insatiable appetite for bossing people around, he stumbled upon us accidentally.

"You park here!" he ordered.

"It's sand, we'll sink", we objected, to no avail, other than to hear him scream so loudly that it looked like he was struggling to spit his tonsils out.

There was no point in insisting. In first gear, we started moving a few metres on the sand. Our commander had summoned a couple of his underlings to push our Vespas all the way to the point at which, for some reason completely unknown to us, we had to park. Before we even reached the point that would please him, as was to be expected, we sank. He turned his eyes away to avoid meeting ours. He would have to admit his defeat and he was not at all willing to do that. Guns, power, and an empty head... We could not even begin to imagine how many people just like him we would meet along the way.

While Thanos was stuck in the cogwheels of bureaucracy, I was guarding the scooters with my life. It was a position that gave me the chance to observe life at the border. Most people around me were men. All of them in a state of constant alertness so as to fulfil – at a price, of course – every single need that the travellers might have, or, in any case, convince them that they had. I watched them rush towards every vehicle that approached to perform valet duties. If the first go failed, they approached the passengers and

---

[1] *Theódoros Kolokotrónis (1770-1843) was one of the most prominent figures of the War of Greek Independence (1821-1830) against the Ottoman Empire.*

offered to help them with the border procedures. If that didn't yield any results either, there was always the option of trying to sell vehicle insurance. Border people never gave up. Besides, all travellers would eventually give in to currency exchange. "So that's how *fixers* work!" I said to myself, as I saw Thanos coming towards me with a smile.

"All cool" he said reassuringly. "They're kind of jerks, but it's all cool". Now it was my turn to get into the office...

This mixture of tiredness and enthusiasm, which doesn't let you sleep no matter how hard you try, made me lie in my tent with my eyes wide open and recreate over and over again that day in my mind. We were so far off in our calculation of the time it would take us to cross the border, that when we set up our tents at the campsite in Nouadhibou, about 50km from there, we realised that we could have moved on south without stopping.

"A goat!" I yelled to Thanos, laughing, as we took the central road leading to the city entrance. The goat was sitting on the median of the only paved road in Nouadhibou, chewing on plastic bags from a pile of trash. I didn't have much time to look at it, as my way was blocked by a Mercedes, the driver of which had placed a huge piece of particle board on the car's roof, without straps or any fastening means whatsoever to hold it. At the sandy edges of the avenue, old men sitting on the ground were selling their merchandise and, in the alleys that cut across it, kids were playing football. Buildings were low, built of concrete blocks and sand-coloured clay bricks, with the blue windows of some houses being the only specks of colour in the monochrome scenery.

People here were different. The atmosphere was different. Djellaba-wearing Arabs and Berbers mingled with West Africans, making the country's demographic composition special. At the nearby street markets, the blue djellabas, white turbans and the flowery head coverings, blended with blue jeans and sweaters and, amidst them, the black and white parches of goats roaming around freely, with plastic bags hanging out of their mouths.

At the grocery store, the rather severe-looking store owner asked for almost eight euros for a loaf of bread and a few cookies and, when I expressed my objection, he replied with a word and a gesture.

"*Americano*" he said, as he dragged his finger across his throat, in an unambiguous evocation of decapitation.

"*Yunan!*" I responded and feigned taking offense. His eyes instantly glowed.

"*Brother Yunan!*" he replied with a smile, and the price immediately went down to two euros. It took no knowledge of foreign languages to understand that he didn't really care for Americans. But I was definitely glad about his philhellenic sentiments and, of course, the discount.

Despite my enthusiasm for the new country, exhaustion prevailed and I fell sound asleep on my leaking air- mattress, which I might have to replace at some point. The following day, we would fill up our gas tanks and set out for Nouakchott.

AND THE OSCAR GOES TO...

"*Samo?*", I asked the lady behind the counter of the small store for the third time, with my terrible French accent, as she was preparing the sandwiches.

"*Oui, chameau*", she affirmed once more. A truck driver, who had just stopped to refuel at the adjacent gas station, overheard our conversation and offered to help.

"*Camel!*" he translated into English and confirmed my suspicion about the meat I was eating. My exquisite meal consisted of pita bread stuffed with camel meat and mixed vegetables. I'd already spent five hours at the gas station, which unfortunately had only diesel, waiting for a stranger to arrive with 20 litres of gasoline. Thanos, about a 100km farther to the south, where we had been stranded, was waiting anxiously to hear from me.

The sun had not yet set when I saw a minivan approach. It stopped a few metres away from where I was sitting and the bowed silhouette of a man emerged. Skinny, with a faint moustache over his upper lip, he walked at a tired yet swift gait. It was impossible to figure out his age. From a distance, my guess would have been that about sixty years had weighed down his arched back. But when he came closer, I realised that he was no more than forty-five. He smiled and nodded to me to approach. *No way!* I thought. *It's just too early.*

I had travelled around 100km back to the gas station, north of the point where all of the extra fuel that we were carrying with us had run out and I was telling our story to the prying passers by. A taxi driver that was among them, promised me that, as soon as he'd arrive at Nouadhibou – further north – he would ask a friend who would set out in the afternoon to bring me the fuel that I needed. A complete stranger. I had no choice but to wait and see what would happen.

After five hours of waiting, I was finally holding a jerrycan full of gasoline and was flying with joy. The man was living proof that, sometimes, trust is the safest path to take.

Now the point at which we had run out of fuel was none other than a gas station! The owner, exactly half-way between Nouadhibou and Nouakchott, made it clear: there wasn't a drop left in his pump. He made us spend an entire night there, until the following morning, when the tanker was supposed to arrive. The truck, however, was nowhere to be seen and we soon realised that we were trapped in a bluffing game, the aim of which was for us to be forced into buying the only jerrycan allegedly left – and he intended to sell us the whole thing – at seven euros a litre! We had no money, but, to his misfortune, we had time.

So things led to Thanos setting out south, until he completely ran out of fuel a few kilometres away, and I was left alone waiting, killing time next to the empty gasoline pump. Around noon, an old man came up to me with a piece of paper in his hand. *"I'm out of gas, head up north. I'll meet you at the empty pump… Thanos."* it read. I got on the bike determined to do whatever I could. I headed back north, as Thanos had suggested, and I managed to get to the previous gas station which we had left behind – the one with only diesel. Late that night, our patience was rewarded.

Now loaded with a jerry can, I was going back to our meeting point beside the empty pump, where, according to the plan, Thanos would be waiting for me. My mind ran back to the two strangers that I'd let myself trust. *I bet he'll overcharge me!* I thought, while struggling to communicate with the eager man. *I bet he'll never show up!* I thought, while waiting for his friend to come. And yet two strangers kept their promise, without expecting anything in return. It'd been a long time since I last trusted someone. Over my last few years in Greece, I had received so many back stabbings from people I believed to be my friends, that I became convinced that there were no noble motives in this world. What a great way to be proven wrong!

Night had fallen and I sounded the horn to announce my arrival; Thanos jumped up and started running towards me. We hugged and burst into childlike laughter. We were so anxious to tell each other all about the things we had experienced while being apart, that we kept interrupting each other in an attempt to leave nothing out. He told me that, while I was away, he hitched a ride back to the gas station on a truck with a bunch of workers that offered to help him with no money in return. He told me that the old man that gave me the note had offered him some milk and a banana while he was trying to figure out a solution.

All of a sudden, our laughter halted. In the dark, we saw the lights of the gasoline pump – the one that, according to the gas station owner, was empty – turn on and the man, who until then insisted that there wasn't a drop left in it, rushed cheerfully towards us while we were still there.

"While you were away the tanker truck came by, but I forgot to tell you", he informed us and a cunning smile crossed his face. We looked at each other. His lie left us baffled; we were lost for words.

"And the Oscar goes to...!" I yelled, cracking up, to the man whose gabbiness had kept us hostages for two days. In the end, we filled our tanks paying the normal price and got back on our way to Nouakchott.

WOLOF

I couldn't see anything in the dark, other than what was caught in the headlights of Thanos' Vespa, as he led our way to Nouakchott. It could be that we were happy to finally have fuel or that we didn't want to spend a minute more at the gas station where we'd gotten stuck for hours on end, but, when we got back on our bikes, we felt great relief. We left at midnight, without knowing how far we would get. And we never did, actually. Exhausted, we set up only one of our tents at a random spot, a few metres away from the road, and we slept until dawn. At the first daylight, we peeked at the sand dunes in the background and got back on the road. We were in a hurry to get our visas for Senegal issued. Our only concern was to keep moving, to the extent that the sacred Friday prayer for the Muslims and the "secular" weekend holiday for everyone, which kept public administration offices closed, would allow us to do so.

We were calculating our time left in Mauritania and were hoping to be done with the procedures at the embassy of Senegal as soon as possible. Only a few days earlier, the customs officer, acting as if he had absolute control over the lives of the people that crossed the borders of his country, had allowed us to remain for only a week. He didn't care that our nation of origin permitted us more time, he just did it because he could.

"Let's go to the campsite and then we'll see", Thanos suggested and he soon proved to be right. There, we met Esteban. He rode a KTM bike and was planning to travel all around Africa in five months, but he was stuck in Nouakchott due to a mechanical failure. From the very first words we exchanged, it felt like we were old friends. Having spent quite a few days there, he had learned his way around and helped us to extend our stay permit in Mauritania, which was crucial, considering our slow pace.

"There's no way one million people actually live here!" I kept telling him as we were strolling around the capital's streets. It was too soon for me to realise it, but most African cities can be rather misleading when it comes to size. They usually spread across vast expanses and very few of their buildings have more than two floors. That was the case with Nouakchott. With wider or narrower streets, small two-story buildings that looked like cottages and neighbourhoods that were so different from one another, it was confusing. Everything was the colour of the sand that dusted our shoes. The only contrast came from the showy clothes of the people that walked the alleys and the intense colours of the fruit and vegetables at the open-air markets.

"Come on! You have to see the port!", suggested Esteban and we headed for the Atlantic coast. I had never seen anything like it! I stood and stared at the enormous domed, concrete shed, as people kept going in and out. The stench of rotten fish, mixed together with the smell of the sea barged into my nostrils and, along with the hubbub of voices and the donkeys' brays, made me dizzy.

We moved towards the beach. I didn't know where to turn my eyes. Before me, hundreds of wooden boats pulled up on the shore, one right next to the other. Behind was the sea. With every wave coming in, dozens of boats showed up on its crest moored offshore, swaying perilously. Men, women and children were walking or sitting on the sand and the wet concrete. Some relaxed, resting; others running up and down, balancing cases filled to the top with fish that were still alive and flapping on top of their heads.

The skyline was dusty and the hazy sun cast its pale rays all around. Only the boat keels, bright-coloured and flamboyant, seemed to emanate their own light. And the women. How much light exuded by the women that were sitting there, chopping, gutting and selling the fish! I lifted the camera. "*Non!*" a voice said and made me put it back down at once. I didn't make another attempt, just kept walking on the trodden, wet sand, intoxicated with the sight, the voices and the smells. A bit further down, the smell became heavier. Countless fish, salted and left in the sun until they dried completely would then be loaded onto big trucks and sent off inland.

I was wandering among the sea men, watching them closely. A man wearing a djellaba, a turban and plastic sandals was playing football. Some groups of women, wrapped in their multi-coloured scarves, were chatting, while separating the good fish from the useless ones. Two toddlers, no older than four years old, had set up a feast on an upside-down bucket that served as their table. From every batch of fish, those unsuited for the market are set apart to be consumed on the spot, and kids seemed to enjoy that. The rest, the good ones, are sent off to be frozen or dried. I sat and watched as the people were loading the cases on their donkey-drawn carts.

"Most of them are black!", I pointed out, naively. Esteban smiled.

"That's right, in here almost everyone's *Wolof*, originating from Senegal and Gambia", he explained. "They're the ones who do this kind of job".

Among the fish that were still flapping and the ones that were dead and dried out, and the water that rinsed off the fish guts and then flowed filthy on the market tiles, right there, I wondered how many of the brave *Wolof* would have been swallowed by the ocean. How many women would have been left behind mourning for their husbands and how many children would have become orphans? *What's their daily wage?* I wondered, but then I thought it over. "Whatever the sea pays them".

LIAM, ARE YOU COMING ALONG?

The four of us were sitting around the table uncomfortably, looking at the dishes lying before us full of our lunch. That morning we'd swung by the market in search of food. We weren't sure about the fish we bought, but the woman who sold them to us had taken the trouble to clean them and give us some tips for their preparation. It's a shame we didn't speak French. The fish looked pathetic, all scrambled to pieces, as a result of our attempt to flip them over in the pan. The fried squid were impossible to pierce with a fork. The *skordalia*[2] was so thick, that I could barely stir it.

"We did a hell of a good job, didn't we?" I said and we burst into laughter. Liam was joking, comparing our failure to the rather insipid cuisine of England, his homeland, while Katrina was trying to pick out the myriads of prickly bones in her fish.

"Let's just try to forget about the crap we're eating and focus on the plan", I said solemnly, and for a minute I felt like the head of an expedition. As was to be expected, nobody took me seriously and it was not until our dishes had been emptied and the skordalia thrown away that we started talking about our next steps.

It had been almost a week since we'd arrived in Nouakchott, and not once had we felt bored. Each day was a brand new experience. I tried to practice my haggling skills: the goal was to persistently demand a lower price for everything I bought. I'd

---

[2]*Skordalia is a traditional type of dip, the main ingredients of which are mashed potatoes and garlic.*

learned to never get to the checkout counter loaded with stuff, waiting to hear the amount I had to pay. I asked with exasperating precision about the price of each product, crunched the numbers and watched the exhausted look on the face of the attendant every time I corrected their maths. The only thing over which I didn't do the least of bargaining was the pizza.

The little joint where Esteban took us to have "the best pizza in the world" didn't seem like much. It was small, unpretentious, with the attendants dressed in white aprons sprinting around like crazy to serve the orders in time. Outside, cars were lining up. The customers didn't even get out of their vehicles. They waited right there, until they got the sweet-smelling carton. In the kitchen, was Danny DeVito in person – or maybe his double. A middle-aged Italian, who had the brilliant idea to bring Italian cuisine all the way to Mauritania. Agile, with a funny gait and the energy of a 25-year-old, he was oven-baking the pizzas. Until then, I avoided anything that I considered a luxury and put my grit to test. I'd always been prone to the enjoyment of food, so I'd made a bet with myself to see how long it would be until I'd miss a taste that, while I was still in Greece, I thought to be irreplaceable. That day, standing outside the pizzeria, I didn't leave a single crumb.

While washing the dishes in an attempt to scrub away the traces of our current lunch calamity, we were talking about the next stage of the trip. Neither Thanos nor I had thought about how we would proceed, but Esteban, a few days before he left, came up with a solution.

"You should go to Mali", he suggested. We looked at each other.

"Visas are really cheap, if you get them issued here", he added.

"Why not?", I thought, and Thanos agreed.

The economic factor played a crucial part in every decision made. I couldn't even recall what I said before I set off. Three years? Travel around the world? Who forced me to stick to such a sketchy plan? Gradually, a completely different one was drawn up in my mind, which seemed a lot more suitable. I would try to get by on as little as possible, my only goal being to spend as much time as I could on the road. Day after day, I watched the distance between my life back in Greece and my current situation grow.

Every kilometre I travelled on African soil made me feel more confident about not wanting the return day to ever come.

"Liam, are you coming along?" I turned to the English traveller. He was riding a Honda C90 and had reached Nouakchott loaded on the camper of a couple of other travellers, who had offered to help him cross the desert. He was my age and had left his home in Leeds to travel around Africa. Liam seemed more settled than me in his complete lack of scheme. He carried his own bit of madness around, as he rode in search of inspiration. A sketch pad and some charcoal were his inseparable companions. He drew, wrote and smoked.

"Let's go!" he replied.

I looked at Katrina. We were all impressed by the Slovenian cyclist whose goal was to reach Madagascar.

"Are you joining us?" I asked, unable to guess what she really wanted.

"I travel slowly", she responded. "But we can meet somewhere before the border". Not much more needed to be said about the route. Our only worry were the stories we'd heard about the "the most corrupt borders in Africa". I knew that, more often than not, such stories concealed a certain degree of exaggeration, but how could I be sure? The decision was made: we would avoid the much-frequented passage of Rosso and try our luck at the smaller crossing of Diama.

MAURITANIAN NOTES

We had left Nouakchott behind and were on the highway to the border with Senegal. What Liam lacked in riding experience, he made up for in self-confidence. Every time we approached a big pothole, he managed to dodge it with admirable dexterity – or at least so it seemed.

"I have honestly no idea of how I've managed to stay on the bike so far!" he confessed at our first stop. Near the small border passage of Diama the asphalt ended and we had to ride about 80km on gravel roads, some of which were smooth but others gritty and bumpy. That was when the falls began. Liam faced each and every one with humour, be it a slip or a swerve, and that eased our worry quite a lot.

Soon, we would reach the border, but, until then, the only thing I had on my mind was all those images that I had collected from Mauritania. Images from Nouadhibou, where goats chewed on trash on the sides of the road and clunkers – old Mercedes cars – looked like Frankenstein's creations, maintained with any spare parts available. Nouadhibou was the city in which the gigantic railway that extended across the Sahara, conveying iron ore freight, ends. It was the city from which boats set out, full of desperate emigrants hoping to get to the Canary Islands – to set foot on the longed-for European soil.

From there to Nouakchott, with the colourful boats and the brave fishermen. In the capital with the traffic chaos, we were not quite sure whether it was better to move around on foot or dare ride the bikes. And finally, meeting Esteban, Liam and Katrina, the first riders with whom we shared experiences and meaningful concerns, so many changes had taken place and even more changes were yet to come!

We decided not to cross the border that same day and spent the night at a random spot a few metres away from the N2 highway. Katrina, who had left earlier, was with us again and the four tents set up one next to the other made a small encampment. As we moved southwards, the landscape gradually changed. We had left the endless sand dunes and the barren desert behind, and now, small spiny bushes and shrivelled trees emerged from the pale, grey sand. Among them, the tents of nomads popped up, whose children didn't waste time coming over to welcome us. No sooner had we put up our tents than their smiling faces filled the space around us. A campfire and Mauritanian notes from Ibrahim's cellphone, (a teenager that wanted to initiate us to the local music tradition), kept us company on our last night in the country.

The sun was barely up next morning and, while we were having coffee, we saw a police car pull over a few metres away. A uniformed man, armed to the teeth, and a little kid got out. Since I hadn't had the best of experiences with the police so far, my face took on a wary and mistrustful expression, ready to fend for myself against any threat. While saying something in French and holding the kid by the hand, the uniformed man came closer, wielding a baguette.

"What does he want us to do? Make him a salami and cheese sandwich or what?" I whispered in sarcasm to Thanos, accustomed to all kinds of state officers that were constantly asking for stuff.

"Beats me! What if he wants to give it to us?" he added. He turned towards him and, playing with the odds, uttered a random *"Oui"*. Next thing we knew, we were holding a baguette courtesy of the Mauritanian police, and I was left wondering where all those mean and nasty Africans were, whose only aim was to rob or kill us.

"Where are all the terrorists that would cut our heads off in Mauritania?" I asked Thanos as I was holding the bread and waving goodbye to the man and his son. Quite a few Moroccans, who had seen their businesses go bankrupt following the cancellation of the Paris-Dakar rally due to the murderous attack by a small group of their neighbours on some French tourists a few years ago, painted Mauritanians in the darkest colours.

"It's like telling me not to go to Thessaloniki, just because someone decided to commit a crime there". I knew that things were a bit more complicated than that, but I would never condemn an entire people on the account of the acts of just a few.

The kids had gathered up again and were watching us load our stuff on the bikes. I went up to a skinny little guy that was looking at me with mischievous eyes and showed him the bag with the leftovers from last night. He took it with the same naughty look, willing to throw it away. Once we were good to go, we got on the bikes and I turned back to say goodbye. My trash bag was already hanging high from the branches of the tallest tree around and the little rascal was running around laughing, in his own improvised lap of honour, really proud of his throw.

"Way to go, ace!" I said to myself as I pulled away.

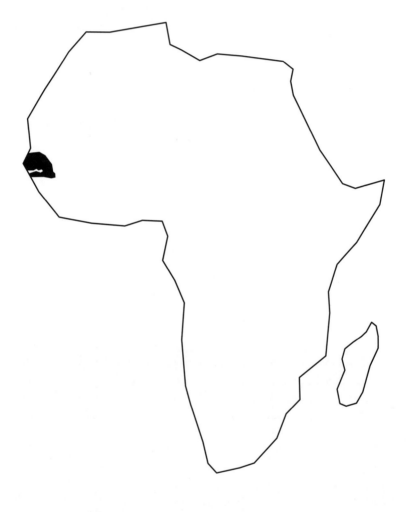

SENEGAL

SEE SENEGAL?

"Ten euros each!", said the Mauritanian officer at the customs desk. And he meant no joke, apparently.

"We paid when we entered the country", I replied, but it made no difference if that information was right or wrong. Undaunted, he went on even more aggressively.

"See Senegal over there?", he pointed far away with his finger. "You won't see it up close unless you pay!" Liam, brimming with anger, tried to give the unyielding officer a hard time, knowing that the money he was asking for would end up in his own pocket.

"Fair enough; we'll pay", he said strictly. "But we want a receipt".

The officer laughed mockingly. In a flaunting manner, he grabbed a piece of paper, tore it in three and started to write down unintelligible words and numbers with his pen. Then, in all solemnity, he took a seal and, stamping it as hard as he could on the paper, completed his mockery. My anger now made my breath come in fast, irregular pants, but I wasn't alone. The last thing I wanted to do was overreact, thus causing trouble to my co-travellers. We left.

A few metres away, the police officer that was in charge of the passports, confident that he would manage to make us pay again, asked for another five euros for the exit seal on our passports. This time I adopted a dulcet and slightly naive tone in my voice and started to recount any insane story that came into my head. My strategy of feigned western-like formality had no effect on his colleague, so I figured I might try explaining to him that, although we were white, we were also broke! I'll never know if I actually managed to convince him or if he just got fed up with my babble, but soon we were right in front of the bridge over the Senegal River.

It'd been over three hours since we initiated the procedures to cross the border and we were wondering how much more time we would have to waste. Paying seven euros per person, as the lord of the bridge demanded, was absolutely out of the question. I didn't quite realise how, but with lots of patience and the condition to skip the receipt, we made a deal of giving him seven euros for all three of us. That was it! We were finally in Senegal, ready to try out our recently acquired negotiating skills.

"Hand me your papers and ten euros each!" ordered the boot-faced Senegalese police officer.

"Yes, sir!" I replied, while Thanos was looking at me perplexed. He took all our documents, looked at them, stamped them and, before he knew it, with a swift movement I snatched them right out of his hands. He looked at me, dumbfounded.

"Wh-what about the money?" he stuttered, eventually. With a wide smile and plenty of politeness, I explained to him that I knew that this charge was not required by any authority. Suddenly, his face mellowed down.

"Brother, won't you give me a present?" I looked at him in disappointment. His clean clothes, his polished boots were totally out of tune with the imploring tone of his voice. Thanos was on the fence about whether he should feel sorry for him, or angry; he finally decided to give him a can of milk and a T-shirt, which were no longer of use anyway.

"Carbonated melon-flavoured milk from Mauritania – yikes!" he read out loud the inscription on the can before giving it to the officer. "I wouldn't give this thing to my worst enemy!" he told me, as we were getting on our bikes.

THAT'S LIFE IN AFRICA
It was getting dark and we still hadn't reached Saint-Louis. Liam's bike decided to never start again after the borders, so it had to be towed by Thanos' scooter.

"I wonder what Katrina did in the end" I said out loud, as we pulled over outside a bank, at the entrance to the city. The cyclist had changed her mind. She would cross over to Senegal through the central border station. We were curious to compare our experiences, but we didn't know when we would see her again.

Luckily, right next to the bank there was a bike garage. From the small hut, hidden behind a pile of spare parts, the mechanic showed up, covered in smudge.

"*Problème?*" was his one-word question.

"*Oui*" we answered, using up almost our entire repertoire of French words. But that was all it took for him to grab the broken-down bike and, within five minutes, bring it back to life.

"It was just the spark plug", we confirmed our diagnosis to Liam and moved on.

The campsite, which we eventually managed to locate after night fall, was heaven on earth. We didn't see the lagoon, the palm trees and the shady wooden terraces until the next morning's daylight revealed them, but, to us, heaven was our reception by the owners. A German couple had bought the land and had created the ideal haven for the dusty travellers that managed to come through the border state bureaucracy unscathed.

"Here, have a beer to cool down!" were their first words.

It was a shame we couldn't stay longer. Ahead of us, we had a true road race to Dakar, to the only place where we could get our carnets stamped, so that we could circulate freely within the country. The document we got at the border only allowed us a short stay, but Liam unwittingly had this fixed, too. A few days later, his bike broke down again and so we were stranded in Saint-Louis. Accompanied by the mechanic, we rode all the way to the police station to explain our problem. Surprisingly enough, we got a twenty-day deadline, which was more than enough time, and it also spared us the need to travel all the way to Dakar. On the way out of the police station, stay permit in hand, I turned to Liam.

"Looks like they didn't hold us any grudge from the last time we were here!" I said laughing and he smiled in complicity.

It was our first day in Saint-Louis and we were riding to the city centre. Sven and Christine from the campsite had urged us to spend time in their favourite city. Saint-Louis is situated right on the River Senegal estuary. Tongues of land that disappear into the Atlantic, lagoons, islands and a host of other geographic particularities are but a small part of its charm. The rest lies in the people and their life in the colonial buildings and the noisy markets.

The day was sunny, Christmas was near and the temperature had climbed over 30°C. With my helmet open, I let the wind carry the smell of roasting fish into my nostrils; and that of exhaust fumes, every time I got stuck right behind an old bus. Even buses were colourful. All of a sudden the whistle of a uniformed man and his fierce gestures urging us to pull over brought me back to the sad reality of the police.

"What the hell does he want?" I asked Thanos, who stopped next to me.

Always stern, just like his colleagues, he approached and asked for our papers. I reached into my pouch bag and handed them over to him. My companions didn't have theirs. Although I offered to go back to the campsite and get them, there was no way to persuade the police officer. He called a cab and ordered us to follow him. Every thought of escaping was brought to naught. We surely didn't want to become the lead characters in an African chase scene. At the police station we felt as if the entire police force of the city participated in a sad competition, where the winner was the one who would scare us the most. Neither Thanos nor I were willing to become their personal laughing stock. Frustrated, they banned us from the office and locked themselves up inside with Liam. Young fair-haired Liam, who looked baffled.

"If we keep getting ourselves into trouble with the cops on account of our own stupidity, we won't get very far" I told Thanos angrily. We didn't pay a fine; I just had to rush back to the campsite to get their papers and we got off with some reprimands and warnings.

Fortunately, it didn't take long before I went back to feeling welcome in Senegal. Only a few metres away, a group of men were hanging out next to my bike.

"What's your name?" they asked me as I approached.

"Sergio" I said, gloomily. In Africa, I became *Sergio*, since for the people there, my real name was impossible to pronounce correctly.

"What's wrong, Sergio?" they asked again.

"I'm pissed, because I just wasted my whole day in the most idiotic way." At once, they grabbed their djembe drums and threw a song together. As far as I could understand, the lyrics were words of solace for my bad luck, reminding me that I should relax because, in Africa, that's life. I went back to the campsite humming the melody of the improvised piece.

"That's life in Africa", I kept telling myself, trying to wrap my head around it.

BROTHER, I COULDN'T BE MORE CERTAIN!

Saint-Louis lies between the desert and the savanna. Right between the complete dryness of the Sahara and the land that stretches alongside the River Senegal. It's the transition from the sand dunes to the acacias and the baobabs, and from the Arab world to that of Sub-Saharan Africa. Every ride we took to the city centre made me all the more look forward to what was up next.

Days went by peacefully. Liam's bike was locked up for good in the garage and, every morning, we repeated the same drill. After coffee, we'd go to the city and watch the repair process up close. Then we'd roam around the neighbourhoods; mingle with the crowds in the street markets, watching the daily routine of the locals and, around afternoon, we'd get back to the campsite and have a splash in the lagoon. Thanos, however, had been a little distant lately.

"I bet he'll soon make the big announcement, you mark my words!" Liam told me one day. Christmas was approaching and we'd started the preparations for the big feast.

"It's the holiday season back in Greece and he probably misses his family", I replied.

"Thanos, are you sure?" I asked him.

"Brother, I couldn't be more certain" was his answer and I

couldn't argue with it. I felt sorry, but not because he was going to leave me. What made me sad was the fact that he would miss out on the chance to live the experience of Sub-Saharan Africa. I had made up such a unique picture of it in my mind that I just couldn't understand how anyone could dismiss that. But I soon accepted and even comprehended it. No matter how hard we try to walk in someone else's shoes, no matter how much we try to listen to their voice, sometimes our own voice sounds louder. With Thanos, my only travel companion up to that moment, I had a lot in common. We both wanted to travel, get away and see new places. The road – short until then – had been a great school for us both. We were ready to take the next step, but it looked like our paths would now part.

We got up from the Christmas table and, together with other travellers, we sat underneath one of the covered terraces looking at the sea and drinking cold beer. Thanos, still weak from the sickness, went to bed. He had been afflicted by fever for three or four days, but he was finally coming round.

The conversations of the people on the terrace, got to my ears like a melodic hum but I'd stopped participating. I was no longer in Saint-Louis. I'd been transported all the way back to Greece and was digging into my memory trying to remember the exact point at which I made the decision to leave. I found myself in Pelion, back on the day when, again with beers in our hands, we were plotting the big journey on the map. It would be three of us. "*Three Vespas around the world*". At once, I pictured the T-shirts I would design to support our venture. Eventually only two Vespas set out and the T-shirts became a souvenir of that first day. I ran to the Press and TV networks, which I despised, to promote our project. I remembered the reporters asking for irrelevant information, just so as to decide whether to fit us into the travel columns or the weird news section. I had changed so much since then!

A few sponsors showed up down the road. Not the magnate kind, of course. They were simple people who shared our enthusiasm and wanted to help us. However, I ended up being the biggest sponsor of myself. The journey would take place no matter what and so I started selling out all my belongings. So it was out with the bicycle, and out with my other motorbike. An Aprilia RS250 that ran like the devil. I remember trying out my speed skills on that bike and felt like flying. I'd sworn I'd never sell it. Along with it, out went all the riding the equipment. I only kept the boots that I was wearing now.

I managed to gather some money, but it was not enough. So, in the summer of 2013 I found myself serving overpriced Greek salads in Santorini. During the breaks, I'd flip the paper coaster upside down and write. I made lists of the things I would take with me, or the things that were yet to be sold. I made some rough calculations, knowing that they would be no use. But this way I managed to scrape through the day. After the 16-hour shift, I'd lie on the bed stretching my legs against the wall, to relieve my swollen feet, and I'd think of Africa. Only once, in late September, I got on the bike and went to Oia. My job term was over and I was staying on the island waiting to get paid. I thought I might go and check out just for once what the tourists were so eager to see and applaud: the sun going down. I found myself sitting with my back turned to the sunset, watching the mesmerised tourists instead. What had they found in Greece? What would I find in Africa?

"Want another beer?" Liam's voice woke me out of my slumber.

"Nah, I'll just go to bed", I said drowsily.

YOU'RE NEVER ALONE IN THE SAVANNA

I was laughing hard while watching Liam struggling to keep the fish inside the pot. I watched the poor thing twitch in agony with his mouth open wide, hoping for water to get into it instead of air. It was flapping in despair. Without realising it, I opened my mouth gasping for air. As if that would help the fish. I couldn't laugh any more. I just hope it dies soon, I wished in silence and turned my eyes away. I started thinking that we might as well have thrown it back into the river, giving it a bit more time to live, at least until the next time someone would fish it out. Or what if we'd bought it frozen, straight out of a freezer? It would still be dead, but we wouldn't have to watch it die. When it started cooking, I thought it over: As horrible as death seems to the untrained eye, I guess

I preferred it to the sterilised, massive availability of meat in the big supermarket chains. The industrialised slaughter of countless animals, many of which would probably end up in trash cans, was more atrocious than the image of a single dead fish that would be consumed within an hour.

Our retreat for the night didn't turn out to be as safe as we thought it was. Just like every afternoon ever since we'd left Saint-Louis, we took a random path and rode a few metres and, at the first clearing we came across, we set up camp. Nearby, there was a purling stream, the sound of which alone quenched my thirst. *Tomorrow I'm doing the laundry*, I thought and dipped my feet into the water.

"There's no way anyone would come here at this hour" said Liam, satisfied with the place we had found. No sooner had he finished his sentence than we heard steps. A man showed up out of nowhere, looking startled at our presence. And so were we. He came closer and the usual communication ritual commenced. With gestures and signs, he managed to explain that he was offering us one of the fish he had caught, as a token of welcome. We thanked him in any language we could speak and then the cooking operation began.

Ever since Thanos had gone his separate way, and Liam and I resumed the journey eastwards, we hadn't spent a single night in a guesthouse. Every morning, we'd calculate how many kilometres we had time to travel until sunset. We'd be in no hurry to get out of bed. We'd take either the central road, or smaller ones and we'd stop by open-air markets in villages to get our food supplies for dinner. We didn't care so much for big cities. We wanted to move among people and through random villages and collect images. The children would wave hello and shout *"Cadeau! Cadeau!"* – *Present!* – used as they were to receiving gifts from travellers. The men would come up to welcome us and shake hands with us. But the ones who seemed to have the most fun with us were definitely the women. At every market we'd stop, well-fed Senegalese women in their close-fitting, patterned dresses, ran with their baskets perfectly balanced on top of their heads and surrounded us. *"Ananas? Mangues?"* they asked, shoving the aromatic fruit right under our noses. Liam got overwhelmed. They left him no time to decide and he didn't particularly enjoy that. So then it was my turn to help out. I'd take my helmet and scarf off my head and, at once, everybody's attention shifted. My shiny bald scalp and my rough beard cracked them up! We weren't the only ones staring at the people around us in curiosity; they were staring right back in the same way.

At night we tried to relax. We picked spots that seemed to be away from the villages, put our tents up and made dinner. Despite our efforts, though, we didn't manage to spend a single night on our own in Senegal. There was always a young shepherd with cattle popping up out of nowhere. Other times, the pathways, covered in tall grass that made them seem desolate, turned out to be frequently transited by cyclists, who took a shortcut among the villages.

Then there were those nights that reminded us that the savanna was not only home to good-natured peasants. The groans and growls that resounded from within the trees around us until daybreak, were enough to keep us up. Curled up in our tents, breathing quickly but silently, we listened carefully to every single sound, hoping that, whatever the animal that produced it, it did not have an appetite for human flesh – particularly our own.

PUT THE CIG OUT AND RUN

We were only one week into 2014 and already approaching Mali. That day, we got an early start, as we wanted to go through the Niokolo-Koba National Park, in the south-east of Senegal. The savanna vegetation was getting thicker and prevented us from seeing behind the tall, yellow grass that grew right where the asphalt ended, on both sides of the road. Liam had fallen off his bike so many times, that my laughter when I stopped and waited behind him until he could get the bike back up, was starting to get to his nerves.

"Stop laughing and give me a hand, will you!" he said angrily, as he dusted off his pants.

The Senegalese, in an attempt to reduce car accidents, had studded the roads with concrete speed-bumps, which, unfortunately, were not very well-made. They looked more than irregular-shaped bulges, the same colour as the asphalt, and, to our bikes, each one of them meant an unpleasant surprise. Despite Liam's exasperation, I couldn't help myself laughing. I wasn't laughing at him though. My laughter was totally spontaneous, the result of the last few days' euphoria. I had started to realise what I really enjoyed while being on the road and I finally did just that.

Over the past week I'd set camp at random places in the wilderness, eaten fruits and food made by the locals, bathed in streams and listened to eerie sounds produced by unidentified animals that kept me up at night. The concept of time became fuzzy. How much time had it been? When was I last in Saint-Louis? When was I sitting at a table in the campsite, enjoying the festive breakfast – the only luxury that I had allowed myself? It was the best New Year's Eve I could remember. I couldn't recall ever feeling this free. Lying on the ground without worrying about getting dirty. As I was riding, I wondered what the brand new year had in store for me.

"What did we stop now for, Liam?" I mumbled from inside my helmet as my fellow traveller managed to park his bike at the side of the road without falling.

"What now?" I asked.

"Smoke!" He turned towards me and showed me the packet he held in his hand.

"There are lions here!" I said, but his addiction was greater than his fear. With the lit cigarette hanging from his lips, he talked to me about hyenas. He said he'd read that the hyena is the only animal intelligent enough to tear through a tent and attack the humans inside it.

"Ok, but right now we're not inside a tent and we're in the middle of a national park" I tried to remind him. "And why is it that all the drivers that pass by honk to us?" I added.

The answer was quick to come: A small troop of baboons cropped up from the foliage, just a few metres away from us. They stood there and stared. One of them looked really ferocious, its thick mane waving in the air, and, while the rest of them walked away, it just stayed put without taking its eyes off of us.

"Put the cig out and run!" was my only advice to Liam, who had already gotten on his bike.

NAKEDNESS

"Go fill your own bottles!" I told Liam, in a rather severe tone. We had just stopped at a gas station and tap water was abundant, but he insisted on mooching my own supplies.

Every night, before getting into the tent to go to sleep, if there wasn't any stream nearby, I'd wash myself with the water from the bottles I filled up and carried with me. The exact same water we used to put out the fire that Liam set by accident to the dry grass outside his tent. Having been brought up in a country where the concept of skill is mistaken for that of deceit, I was searching for some sort of order in my life. Liam, on the other hand, born and raised within this order that I was yearning for, had had enough of it. He didn't mind not carrying water with him; it didn't occur to him that the grass outside his tent was dry, as long as he could light a campfire. The only thing he couldn't stand was the busy outdoor markets.

"How can you possibly put up with this chaos?" he asked me. What was I to explain to him? Should I talk to him about the summer fairs in towns and villages in Greece? About the weekly street markets in the neighbourhoods where farmers competed with each other about who could advertise their merchandise the loudest?

"Stop sweating the small stuff!" I tried to ease my troubled friend. "We have borders ahead of us" I reminded him, while in my mind, I had already started to make up possible scenarios for the following day.

Another night went by peacefully and the only thing I wished for was to have many more nights like this. Lying down by the fire, we talked about our lives, our dreams and the past, until we fell asleep.

"I don't like to dream" I said and Liam found it kind of weird. I felt like dreams were, in a way, binding. The disappointment ensuing from their non-fulfilment was such that it wasn't worth the trouble. I'd rather just make short-term plans instead. In two months I'd become twenty-seven and I'd already had my share of adversities.

"Come on, let's check the route to Mali", I changed the subject.

As usual, we wanted to avoid the most transited border passages and, early in the morning, we arrived at a small village, called Moussala. There, the Senegalese police officers were so friendly and collaborative that I thought there must have been some mistake. Mali was just a few hundred metres away and I couldn't believe that we would step foot on its soil that easily.

On the bridge over the Falémé River – a natural border between the two countries – I stopped to take photos. Liam, a bit further back, was looking for his cigarettes. We had gotten over with the first check early and had plenty of time to kill until the next one. I took a few steps towards the river. The rainy season was over and the water level was low. Deep-green grass grew between each stripe of wet sand and, on top of it, laid clothes were drying out. I stood still to watch the women that were doing the laundry on the riverbank. They, too, turned to take a better look at me and then I realised that they were completely naked! I made as if to walk away, for fear that they might get angry at me for prying into such an intimate moment. However, their smiles and cheerful cries gave away anything but anger. They were greeting me, waving their arms and thus revealing their nakedness ever more clearly. I smiled and left unconcerned. They didn't mind being naked. I didn't mind them being naked either.

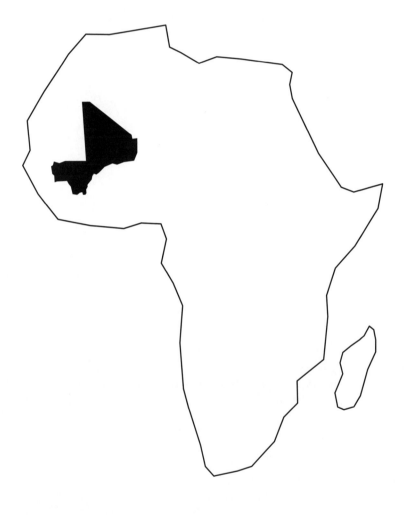

MALI

CRICKETS, NOCTURNAL BIRDS AND... A COW

"Son?" my mother's voice sounded through the headphones of the computer. "Son, where are you?" the tantalising question followed up. I was somewhere in the savanna of Mali, where I'd set camp with Liam, to spend yet another of our beloved quiet nights. I turned the computer on only to realise to my surprise that I still had some data left in the USB modem that I'd bought back in Senegal.

"Be quiet now mom, and listen!" I urged her, allowing the silence between us to bring to the fore all the sounds that would otherwise be muffled by our conversation. Crickets, nocturnal birds and animal moans in the background proving that nature never sleeps.

"It feels like I have you here by my side!" she uttered, before being interrupted by my father's hoarse laughter. No matter how impressed she was by the incredible place from where I was talking to her, her only worry was whether I was OK. I told her my news: that Thanos was gone, that now I was travelling with a crazy Englishman and his little bike and that, within a day or two, we would reach Bamako, the capital.

"We will be online the whole time!" she assured me before we hung up. *My folks will have become full-fledged hackers by the time I get back!* I thought to myself. From having absolutely no notion of computers whatsoever, they went to opening up a Facebook account just so they could follow me.

On the following morning, as always, I was the first to get up and was ready good to go. Liam was messing around having coffee and was late to pack his tent. The sound that came out of the dry grass made me turn around expecting to see a peasant on his bicycle. Yet, I found myself face-to-face with a cow that was staring at us inquisitively. We were quite used to stumbling across cattle on the off-track pathways we'd take in search of a quiet spot to set camp at. I made as if to shoo it away with an abrupt movement. It held still, undeterred. Then, a sadistic thought crossed my mind: I'd look straight into its eyes until I'd scare it off and force it to turn its eyes away. But the cow wouldn't move a hoof; it only started to snort and paw the ground menacingly.

"It's a bull!" I heard Liam say, as he locked himself up in his tent laughing.

I looked around me for cover. I had enraged a bull! I didn't have enough time to get into Liam's tent, and my stuff was already packed and loaded on the Vespa. I crawled behind it hiding myself as best as I could, without daring turn my eyes back to the animal's direction. *If you don't see it, it doesn't exist*, I said to myself laughing bitterly. This is what our whole life looks like. We ignore everything we fail to confront, by turning our back to it.

Luckily, when I finally looked back, the bull had decided that we were too stupid and unworthy of its time, and had walked away.

OLD FRIENDS, NEW FRIENDS

I was sitting in the bamboo armchair next to the entrance of the guesthouse in Bamako, enjoying the cool breeze that came in through the open doors. I was holding my metal cup, filled up with coffee. It was a gift from a Serbian friend of mine, Dejan, who always stood by me, to help me in any way he could with anything I might need. Himself a *vespista*, he enjoyed travelling and was not too shabby with kilometres. In moments like this, once I had the food and accommodation issues settled, I felt more relaxed and started to think about friends I'd left behind. Just as my life went by, so did everybody else's. I wondered which of them I'd meet again and which I'd lose along the way.

"Let's go to the city, shall we?" Steven's voice brought me back to reality.

"I'm all set", I replied and got up.

Steven was a German guy that we'd just met. He was about my age and rode a Yamaha XT125. The first thing I told him when we started talking was that, if I didn't have a Vespa, I'd like to travel around Africa on a bike exactly like his.

We took a cab to the embassies of Ghana and Burkina Faso, to get our visas. After a little bit of negotiating, the taxi fare could drop dramatically and it was a lot more convenient than taking the Sotrama – one of those green minibuses that roam the central streets, with the passengers crammed like sardines in a can and the bus driver's co-pilot hanging from the door shouting the destination. Liam, Steven and I were sitting in the back seat and, in the front, a Dutch traveller I'd first met back in Chefchaouen, in Morocco, at the beginning of my trip with Thanos. I could tell right away that I wasn't the kind of person he could take to. However, I had decided not to stress over being liked, oppressing my true self. When we met again in Bamako, he made a point of avoiding me, but there were so few of us travellers, that he had no choice but to put up with me.

If there was something I'd learned after all those years working among ill-tempered customers and rude bosses, it was to build up a wall that protected me from getting hurt. Instead, I became more and more tenacious in the face of injustice, and I only gave up when I realised that every effort was in vain.

We'd spent the previous night talking about the situation in Greece, Europe and the whole world. "You're a utopian!", my interlocutors labelled me dismissively but I took it as a compliment. I was talking about all those stereotypes that serve the purpose of keeping people divided into factions. Black versus white, Christian versus Muslim, developed versus underdeveloped and so on and so forth; words that make us keep our blinders on no matter what.

Whether we agreed or disagreed with each other, we all kept our eyes and ears wide open, reflecting on everything that was taking place around us. Except for the Dutchman. Although he had barely turned forty, he pompously asserted that he knew absolutely everything. When he interrupted me to call me back to order, stating arrogantly that the Europeans were sick of paying for the mess-ups of the Greeks, I just stopped talking. Despite the anger that I felt inside of me for my compatriots' mistakes, I just couldn't accept the narrow-mindedness of the person I had in front of me. I smiled, took a deep breath to calm my rushing heart rate and sipped on my beer. Racism sneaks into places I'd never have imagined.

SANDWICHES AND SOAP OPERAS

Our taxi drove through streets still unfamiliar to us, and we just kept watching the traffic through the rolled-down windows, without talking too much. Bamako was the first typical African capital that I'd visited and it looked like everything I'd read about cities in Sub-Saharan Africa. Everything I'd seen until then in Senegal, Mauritania and even Morocco had nothing to do with this metropolis. We crossed the Niger River over the *Martyrs Bridge* and got to the northern part, the older city quarter, in which, a few days before, I'd gotten lost with Liam, while trying to find the guesthouse where we'd be staying. Then, various armed guards chased us away, stunned, as we were about to barge into administrative buildings. Fortunately, they were quick to realise that we were just stupid tourists and gave us the right directions.

The embassies of Ghana and Burkina Faso were not far from each other, so the wisest option was to wait for the bureaucratic procedures to be over in the embassy of the first country and then go straight to the other one.

"Let's go grab some lunch!" Steven suggested. Next to some two-story concrete buildings was the "restaurant". A shack, with its three sides covered with wicker panels. The structure that supported it consisted in a few thick branches. The roof was made of some more wicker panels and threadbare canvas and, right at the front, two wooden benches for the customers to sit on. Ever since we got to Senegal, I started to loosen up on the hygiene rules I'd been observing in an attempt to avoid getting the runs and, until that moment, I'd come through unscathed. But I was still reluctant to eat whatever just happened to come my way.

The girl that prepared the "fast-food" sandwiches in the shack seemed to be fifteen years old, but she might very well be twenty-five. She made one for each of us. She stuffed the loaves with freshly made omelette and seasoned with sauces and various vegetables that came out of different plastic containers. "Ok, here we go..." I said and took the first bite.

Liam and Steven had already started to try their luck with street food before, and felt a lot more confident. Satiated and with our visas in hand we began to stroll around the streets of Bamako. We had a better sense of orientation now and so we opted for roaming the neighbourhoods and street markets.

"See? Nothing happened to you!" said Liam with the confidence of an expert. "Now have some puff-puffs as well". Without actually feeling hungry, I picked a couple of golden fried balls from a plastic bowl a little boy was holding out.

From that day on, I never questioned the street cuisine. Every day out on the streets of Bamako, was a unique culinary experience. At night, we'd walk the dark streets around our guesthouse and come across little makeshift restaurants, where women, hidden behind a counter, cooked simple meals that they sold at really low prices. We were sitting under a lamp that was blinking to the rhythm imposed to it by the power generator while enjoying a dish with rice, sauce and bits of meat, seasoned with extra hot pepper.

During the twenty days we spent in Bamako, we became regular customers of the *Senegalese lady* – as we dubbed our favourite joint –due to its owner's origin. The real name of the place, *"Petit Paradis"*, paint-written on a piece of wood, was funny and cute all at once. We used to sit together with the locals, whose main activity while they were dining, was to watch the soap operas shown on the only TV set in the area, which was hanging over the kitchen counter. We were watching them and were trying to imagine where they were and what they did during the rest of the day, until it was time to become absorbed by their favourite shows. I wondered if the pretty lead actors of those series, with their fancy cars and their luxurious mansions were their heroes.

Did they go back to their poor homes every night, at the side of city which lacked running water and electricity, hoping to get a mansion some day? Then again, they might have come to terms with the idea that that was their life and that they didn't really need much more.

Whatever their thoughts were, every evening at the "Petit Paradis" they laughed and spoke loudly, alternating comments about us with those about the soap opera that was on. And we lifted our bottles of beer and greeted them, every time our eyes met across the room.

SAY "CHEESE"

I was riding around Bamako checking out for garages, before picking the one I'd trust to get the bike's wheel tube patched. There were so many bikes there, that all central avenues had lanes reserved especially for them. They were separated from the rest of the road with a concrete curb, preventing the two-wheeled and four-wheeled vehicles from mingling with each other, and that made the traffic somewhat bearable. It was the last day before we finally reached the capital, when, while I was riding, I felt like I was moving in an unnatural way on the Vespa. *I guess I must have gotten a sun stroke and felt dizzy*, I thought, but within seconds I realised I was wrong.

"Liam, I got a flat tyre!" I shouted, to make him stop.

Whenever I talked about my scooter, I always bragged about the extra tyre that it could carry. It was the first time I'd actually get to demonstrate its usefulness. I hung the pierced tire in its place, with the intention of having it mended the first chance I'd get, and we moved on.

"There you are!" I exclaimed and turned around towards the end of the road. It was an outdoor workshop that apparently specialised in puncture repair. It had no walls, or even a sign for that matter, but the tools that were piled up on the low wooden table denoted the owner's area of expertise. It didn't take him more than ten minutes to patch the hole and about the same time for me to explain that I was looking to buy new tyres. My French hadn't become any better and his was randomly mixed up with

Bambara – the language spoken by the majority of the population in Mali. However, we managed to understand each other. The poor man seemed quite surprised at my question and explained that I could find everything I needed anywhere in Bamako. Then it dawned on me that, given the number of bikes and repair shops around, it would be reasonable to expect an abundance of spare parts, as well.

Carrying my brand new rubber, I was riding back to our lodging, when the sign of a big electronics company caught my eye. As soon as I got back, I hastily dumped the tyres next to the tent and everything else I was carrying on me and rushed back out – this time on foot – with a firm step. A while later, I was inside the electronics store.

I didn't feel the least threatened in Mali. I watched the people and took photos of them with my brand new camera. It was small, light and pearly white. The ultimate tool for a tourist! It's not that I knew nothing about cameras – I had some notions in that respect – but never until that day had it ever occurred to me to buy my own. When Thanos left and took his photographic equipment along with him, I realised how much I'd miss out if I wasn't able to immortalise some moments. Two hundred dollars wasn't that much after all, in exchange of preserving the images I saw every day. I'd smile at the passers-by and nod for their permission to take a photo. They'd consent. Toddlers with big round eyes and teenagers with the cockiness of their age would pose in front of my lens. Women with tight skirts and lustful eyes, men with their upright and lofty bearing, they'd all strike a pose.

I don't even know how many hours it took me to get back for our usual dinner-and-beers night out. I wandered around the filthy, earthen alleys and the big avenues with the traffic jams, the exhaust fumes and the enormous billboards. I crossed the *Martyrs Bridge* and took pictures of the dugouts in the Niger River. I leisurely watched the reflection of the tower that rises in the city centre, and which houses the Central Bank of West African States. I was impressed by its deep brown colour and architecture, inspired by the great mosques of Djenné and Timbuktu.

I was even more impressed, however, by the smiles of the residents of Bamako – sometimes shy and others bolder. The smiles that made me forget about my wariness towards people and finally trust their good intentions.

EXTRA-LARGE

I felt sorry that the day of our departure from Bamako had arrived, but, every time I left a place behind, the first kilometres on a road that I was yet to set a wheel on took my mind off the sorrow. There was so much more left for me to see. I got up at the first light, packed my belongings and I was already sitting at my favourite spot by the door of the guesthouse. Liam was asleep, so I started a conversation with Steven. He was thinking about heading north-east, to Mopti, to see the villages of the Dogon people, and maybe he would even reach the legendary, in European narratives, Timbuktu.

Liam and I had decided not to go that way. We said we were lazy. I must say I felt guilty for acknowledging that the idea of visiting an extremely well-known place, which was also, by all standards, worth visiting, bored me. I was worried I might miss out on some unique experiences. But then again, wasn't everything I'd been experiencing so far unique?

I got up and walked to Liam's tent. With sluggish movements, in the midday swelter, he was trying to pack his things. His face was swollen from sleeping and his eyes half-closed.

"Let's go for one last sandwich, shall we?" he suggested, hoping to buy some more time. Well, it didn't take much more for me to accept. Along with Steven, we were off to the humble yard with the delicious sandwiches, where we usually hung out at night. By the time we got there, the cook had just convinced her daughters to help her wash and prepare the vegetables. A little pile of peels had been formed at a corner of the yard and, in the stockpot, coal-black from the fire, the oil was burned. Soon, three big loaves of bread were filled with lettuce, green onions, tomatoes and fried *plantains* – cooking bananas – and were garnished with sauces and dried fruit.

"Now we're good to go!" said Liam, rubbing his stomach in satisfaction.

Sitting on our bikes, we said goodbye to Steven and the rest of the travellers and left. It was already five in the afternoon. The dry heat and the scorching sun were relentless. In my headphones sounded traditional music from Mali, which the owner of the guesthouse had passed on to my computer. *Kora* and *n'goni* and *djembe* and guitar and the awkwardly warm voices of the *jali* – the narrators that sing the history of their land – had sneaked through my ears into my heart and I felt like I was carrying the entire country with me. I remembered the markets, the motorbikes, the attempts to communicate with the store owners and their laughter. I had my new underpants on, that fitted me like a wide mini skirt, since the attendant at the little store that I'd visited a few days ago for supplies, insisted that I should definitely take the "*extra-large*".

We rode slowly, at the pace marked by the hot wind and the music notes and I was laughing by myself on the Vespa. I couldn't tell whether it was the hot sun, the baggy skivvies, or the music, but I was happy.

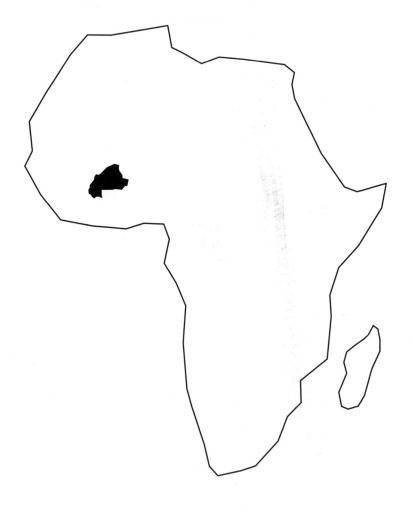

BURKINA FASO

UPRIGHT PEOPLE

We'd travelled quite a few kilometres into the new country. If there were traces of human existence, they must have been hiding pretty well behind the dense vegetation, and the utter remoteness was unsettling. At the border with Mali, the administrative procedures had taken us virtually no time and we were expecting for the green and red flag with the star in its centre and the border office of Burkina Faso to show up in front of us any minute. And yet, there was no sign of either; only the narrow, earthen road.

At last, a bit further down the road, our concern came to an end. The sight of the undulating flag indicated that the hut right next to it, with the thatched roof and the wooden chairs, was the border service station – despite its lack of walls.

"Can I take a picture of you?" I kindly asked the police officer and, after giving me a solemn look befitting his status, he refused to oblige me. His objection to me taking photos and the overall formality of the procedures made me realise that there is no need for concrete for the entry to a country to be a serious matter.

We were now officially in Burkina Faso, the "The Land of the Upright People", according to its name, which is a combination of words from different languages – those spoken by the main ethnic groups that inhabit it. All young African states that emerged after the end of colonialism had to come up with a binding element to keep them united. Thus, former Upper Volta picked righteousness to become its symbol and became Burkina Faso. However, no one is honourable or dishonourable just because a constructed reality dictates it, so I was well-prepared for even the slightest insinuation of palm-greasing. I had come up with a whole screenplay in my mind: I would remind the perjuring state officer about the honorability of his flag. I would point to the waving flag outside and make him feel guilty! However, the administrative procedures were over soon and the only conversation we had with the officers was about our venture. Then they gave us their heartfelt farewell blessings and we were ready to move on.

SANKARA

I once read about schistosomiasis, or snail fever, a really nasty disease. It is caused by a parasite that is found in freshwater in Africa... *Splash!* – Liam plunged into one of the cool, gushing streams that make up the Karfiguela Cascades. I followed his lead and found myself sitting on the slippery rocks, dipping my feet in the water, without a care in the world.

We had travelled about 100km to Banfora to visit the waterfalls. It was one of the suggestions from the travel guide I had just downloaded, along with the new navigation app since my GPS had been long dead. After discussing it with well-read Steven, who had envisioned his trip as a cultural quest, we decided to deviate a little bit from our route to see something – anything – documented in a travel guide. Waterfalls may not exactly form part of the cultural identity of an area, but we really wanted to take a bath!

Right after taking a turn south to Banfora, the landscape started to change. The earth was becoming redder, and the vegetation greener and thicker. We were entering the tropical savanna and, watching the change around me, I thought of all the geographical and climatic zones I had gone through until then. I was crossing an entire continent with two pairs of pants, five t-shirts and my bathing suit.

Among the thicket of trees a few metres away from the side of the road, a couple was standing surrounded by scattered stockpots, plastic basins and a few low wooden stools.

"Hey, Liam, lunch time!" I said and rolled over there with the scooter's engine off.

I took my helmet off and wiped my face with the bandana I was wearing on my head. I showed the brownish smear left on the light blue fabric by the red dirt and the sweat, to my companion, who was just as grimy himself, and he laughed. The man and the woman who were preparing quick meals for the workers at the nearby plantations were waiting with a warm smile. They filled up two plates with cabbage rice and sauce and, with gestures, scattered French words and nods, we tried to communicate with them. Their languid movements did not indicate laziness or indifference. Rather, this seemed to be their pace of life: heat, adverse daily conditions and tiredness from having to walk all the way there and back to the village. They couldn't rush and they didn't need to. Everything would be done eventually.

I can't remember how much time we'd spent in the cool water, but my wrinkled fingertips and my whitened nails were strong indications that it was quite a while. We had set our tents a bit further away, next to a few huts that were rented to visitors. There was absolutely no good reason for us to stay in one of those huts. They were all completely empty and the rudimentary mosquito nets in some of them were inadequate compared to any tent. Before we even had the time to heat up water for our midday coffee three toddlers showed up. Reluctant and shy at first, they got closer. Our smiles drew them out of their shells quickly and from that moment on they didn't leave until their mom's calling was heard from afar.

Throughout the entire route to the waterfalls, we kept coming across plantations. Rice, sugarcane, cotton and a whole array of cash crops that I was unable to identify. The land seemed to offer an abundance of resources and this image did not really tally with the swollen bellies of the children – a clear symptom of malnutrition. We boiled a pot of rice, put it in a bag and gave it to them. Their eyes sparkled. They dashed away into the thicket, jumping in joy, and I was left there wondering: what do the plantation workers eat? What do they feed their children? How much does it cost for the company that exploits the land to take care of the families that work for them?

In the homeland of Thomas Sankara, *Africa's Che Guevara*, as many people liked to call him, little children starve nowadays. From the struggles for self-sufficiency, which got close enough to demonstrating that Africa doesn't need anyone's "help", to now the privatisations, the multinationals and the International Monetary Fund.

On the following morning, we got ready to move on. Always accompanied by our little pals, who were now making huge efforts to communicate with us. They used every language they could speak and put on funny acts, the kind only kids are capable of to warm your heart. We sat under one of the thatch shades and, while we were sharing some oranges that we had with us, we heard voices from the back. Cheerful, youthful voices. It was a school that was on an excursion to the famous park. Within moments, the quiet clearing was buzzing with life, brought along by the teenagers that had flooded the place. We squinted at them resentfully for ruining our morning peace and got ready to leave.

Teenagers are the same everywhere. They talk loudly, laugh even more loudly and live with a passion that is so typical of their age. Their eyes are full of the cheekiness of their years. Their bodies – neither male nor female quite yet – are governed by hormones and enthusiasm. This is how I remembered teenagers back in my country. This is how Liam remembered teenagers back in his country, too. By the time the young exhibitionists had taken over the place completely, we were already far away.

GOATS AND FOOTBALL

"Should we stay in Bobo-Dioulasso?" I asked Liam, as we stopped at one of the most interesting restaurants that we'd come across ever since the day we started our trip. The look in his eyes remained cold and indifferent. I wasn't surprised at his lack of reaction. Bobo-Dioulasso is the second largest city after the capital, Ouagadougou, and, since we would inevitably have to go there, Liam preferred not to spend time in another big city. I checked the travel guide on my cell-phone. It mentioned the historical mosque, the neo-Sudanic architecture and a few more sights, but as soon as I looked up and around me, I realised that what I was seeing was much more attractive to me.

We were sitting under the tin shade of a shack. In front of us there was a wooden foosball table with its players standing perfectly still, worn out under the scorching sun, wishing no one would play with them. We'd parked next to a small bike of Chinese origin that was impossible to identify, since the owner had completely covered the original logo with a KTM sticker. My scooter, Liam's C90 and the "KTM" – at least in the local motorcycle lover's dreams – were all hanging out with a goat that was tied to the support pole of the shade, whose days were probably numbered. I was convinced that, if the goat pulled the rope with which it was tied the slightest bit, the entire shack would fall apart. A bit further down, a mysterious space was hidden behind a thatch screen; the satellite plate protruding right above it made our imagination soar!

We could enjoy the view sitting comfortably in the bus seats that were leaned against the wall, apparently reserved for distinguished visitors. However, we preferred to get up and bother the wooden foosball players. The bangs on the tattered wood and our yells soon attracted quite a few viewers. I can't remember who won the game, or who got the most cheers from our audience, but, by the time we stopped, lunch was ready.

The roasted meat was wrapped into portions. We unfolded the oven paper and its scent poured into our nostrils. I looked at the goat that was tied hardly a metre away. "Poor thing, you're up next" For the first time in my life, I saw that the amounts of meat available in the market were rational, so I didn't feel sorry for its imminent slaughter. Already since we got to the villages of Senegal, we realised that meat was becoming scarce. People in Africa wait until the animals are fully grown and, when the time comes, they use every bit of the slaughtered animal. Nothing goes to waste. I hadn't seen a single young animal be sacrificed just so that we could order a mouth melting steak.

TOMATOES

"Watch out!" my voice sounded hollow from within the closed helmet when I saw Liam riding so close to a 4×4 that he nearly scraped his knee against its door. "You dimwit! When will you finally realise that you should adapt to their ways?" I told him off severely when we stopped outside the mission guesthouse at Ouagadougou. "You have to look out for yourself here, this is not England!" I added angrily. The unruly driving behaviour in Greece helped me adapt rather easily to the, (utterly senseless to my English fellow traveller) traffic in Africa. In every city, I was terrified that he might crash. The same thing happened in Ouagadougou, which, despite looking smaller and quieter than busy Bamako, had all the typical features of an African capital.

I unloaded the luggage from the scooter carefully, so as not to squeeze the tomatoes. I'd split them into two plastic bags which I'd then wrapped carefully within the elastic luggage net and hang on top of the saddlebags so that they wouldn't get crushed. I still couldn't get my head around how, giving out a bill worth less than half a euro, I was able to buy such a big bag of tomatoes! "Tonight's special: rice with tomato sauce!" I cheerfully told Liam, who was setting his tent nearby, at the yard of the mission. We were soon ready to go out to the city with the funny name. Already since we were in Mali, place names that ended in -dougou or -bougou, made me laugh as they reminded me of caricaturesque African characters from b-side movies and series.

From the first saunter around Ouagadougou, I just loved the city. It had everything Liam and I were looking for on our idle trip. Smaller in size and with more peaceful corners than Bamako, the capital of Burkina Faso was full of markets, little stores, bazaars and street music. Green taxis and brown buildings, men and women on small motorbikes, meat skewers and beers; it was all there.

We got into a supermarket, one of the big, "Western" ones and started looking around to see if there was anything that we'd missed badly enough to buy it. "Look at the price of the cheese!" I said in astonishment to Liam, who was flirting with some fruit-flavoured yogurt desserts. "80 euros a kilo! 80 euros!" I kept repeating in total disbelief.

Burkina Faso is one of the poorest countries, and the contrast between life in the supermarket and that outside of it made my blood boil! Inside, white customers were clearly more than the black ones, but this is not necessarily proof that the capital is mainly in the hands of the former. I hadn't been long in Africa, but I had started to understand. Wealth has no colour; what it does have, in most cases, is contacts, hand-greasing and exploitation.

I felt uncomfortable at the supermarket with the overpriced cheese. It might have been the first time I'd felt uncomfortable in my own skin – literally – and the luck I got for having been born somewhere else. And yet I felt like I didn't belong to either side. Neither inside the supermarket, nor outside of it. Almost twenty-seven years alive and still clueless about where my place was.

OUAGADOUGOU – THESSALONIKI

I wasn't even done with my breakfast yet – which lately consisted of tomatoes, bread and green onions – when I heard a familiar sound of a bike engine and, with it, the distinctive honk that announced an arrival. "Steven! You came!" I shouted in Greek, knowing that he understood me, and jumped off my seat. Liam also got out of his tent and started messing with the German member of our team, who, despite having made clear that he would go to Northern Mali, he ended up looking for us in Ouagadougou only two days later.

"Come on! We'll take you sightseeing!" I suggested and, in no time, we were outside the guesthouse and headed to the neighbourhood with the little stores, where Liam and I usually strolled around. We were roaming the city streets without ever stopping talking and looking around us. There were clearly fewer paved roads than in other cities and, by the sides of the wide boulevards there were open drainage pipes that looked more like sewers. A Belgian traveller we once met along the way advised us to never drink tap water in the cities; his advice proved to be wise. We were on one of the most central streets, when, right in front of us, a woman lifted her colourful skirt and, squatting down over the edge of one of those pipes, with her back turned to the passing cars, decided to relieve herself!

"Turns out I'm right to drink only sodas" Liam congratulated himself but my answer came as a timely reminder.

"I was your designated nurse for three days after eating that cabbage rice in Banfora that gave you the runs, remember?"

"Nothing ever happens to you or your bloody Vespa!" he said, faking offense.

We passed by the supermarket with the expensive cheese and, while the two of them got inside to get their beloved yogurts, I wandered around the market that was right outside. Surrounded by women who were trying to sell me pineapples, bananas, strawberries, papayas and a bunch of other fruit I'd never seen before, I remembered the weekly street markets in Western Thessaloniki. There was a time when I worked as a potato salesman, in an attempt to complement my income. My female customers would come up to me all worked up over the bad quality of the potatoes, when in fact they just wanted to get a better price.

"The potatoes you sold me the last time turned out lemons!" they'd complain. "Cut the price a bit and we're even!" they'd finally cut to the chase.

"Save your complaints for my boss, will you?" I'd reply, denying all liability.

This was pretty much how bargaining worked in the market of Ouagadougou, a few thousand kilometres away from Thessaloniki. I might not understand a single word, but the extravagantly theatrical movements and gestures left no room to doubt about the content of their conversations. I approached a counter, ready to feign anger myself. But the young woman that was standing behind it surprised me with a broad smile. Her eyes brightened up as she revealed her pearly teeth. "Go ahead, take your pick", she said calmly, and I found it hard to believe that, amidst the chaos and racket of the market, I would ever find that kind of behaviour. This is what I must have looked like myself in the eyes of the customers of the market back in Thessaloniki, when they leaned over piles of potatoes and saw me hunched over my laptop, cramming for the trip I was about to set out on. I just smiled at them and let them take their pick.

I got back to the guesthouse with a bunch of avocados and a few pictures of the girl's sweet smile.

BABY, PLEASE DON'T GO

We sat at one of the plastic tables. The yard behind the stone fence was full of plants and paved with fine gravel. In the back, there was a rudimentary stage bathed in pink and yellow lights, on which the band were grooving hard.

"*Brakina, s'il vous plaît!*" I ordered assertively.

All three of us, Liam, Steven and I, sipping the beer straight from the bottle and tapping our feet to the rhythm, started to discuss our route options.

"It would be better to cross Nigeria together", Steven suggested and we agreed at once.

We'd read quite a few stories about traveller who got robbed, had trouble with the local police, or, for one reason or another, ended up regretting having ever set foot in the country. Some of them chose to load their vehicles on ships or planes to spare themselves the risk altogether. I agreed with his idea, confident as usual that nothing could go too wrong, but also thinking that there's no need for us to challenge our luck, either. Besides, it seemed that the new member made a good match for our team and I wanted to see how the three of us travelling together for a while would work out. On the following day, we would leave Ouagadougou and be headed for Ghana; the decision had to be celebrated with a few more beers. And so it was.

"You've really messed me up, guys!" Steven would say every time we joked about how he'd eventually give up on his cultural quest and join forces with us. But deep inside, he knew that our way of travelling was not really that different or worse than his. He understood the reasons why we shunned most popular tourist attractions and he concurred on our wish to get to know the "unremarkable" aspects of the African daily life as much as possible.

"This, too, is a cultural quest" he admitted in the end, as the show was coming to its end and we were getting ready to get back to the guesthouse.

It was shortly after noon that we finally managed to get going. I had adapted to Liam's pace, who was anything but a morning type.

We said goodbye to Steven, who had made his own schedule, and arranged to meet again several days later in Ghana. The camera was hanging from my neck and I didn't miss a chance on taking photos. Liam gave me a weary look every time I pointed my lens to him. I had rightfully earned the title of the "tourist asshole with the camera", but how else would I ever learn to take photos?

We passed by outside the little stores with paint-written product brands on the half-plastered walls. At the neighbourhood with the disc stores, there seemed to be a party going on. We went closer. A couple of store owners, in their almost completely empty stores, were cranking up an old, familiar tune. *"Baby, please don't go"*; Muddy Waters was in charge of entertaining the passers-by.

There was no need for me to put on my headphones that day. I was singing a few mixed-up lyrics that I'd retained from the song, at the top of my voice, without caring the slightest bit about my mistakes.

SNEAKING MANGOES

We had just left Léo behind, with our tanks topped up with gasoline of particularly doubtful quality. According to the official demographic data, thirty thousand people were supposed to be living here, but the gas stations were empty. We stopped at a "gas kiosk" downtown, looking at the unsettling dozens of bottles that were lined up on makeshift shelves. Right across the road, a Total Gas retail station stood deserted, with a rickety gas pump. Liam, more worried than I was, was watching the attendant count carefully, with his glasses on, the amount of liquid poured into our plastic containers.

"I'm in for another breakdown – mark my words", he said with cynical certainty, as we rode along the earthen road that led out of the city.

Burkina Faso, a country with a predominantly agricultural economy and all the flaws brought upon it by the International Monetary Fund, is full of small villages mostly populated by farmers and workers at the plantations that are exploited by various multinational companies. Livestock breeders live in the north, leaving the fertile lands of the south for cultivation. I stopped outside every mudbrick hut we came across on the way and took photos of the playful thatch roofs. Their cone shapes looked like pointy wizard hats straight out of a fairytale. They popped up on every side of the road, among trees and reeds and I couldn't decide what the best frame for my shots would be. The road, despite being a laterite track, was fairly smooth. I guess the Chinese paving machines that we had first seen in Ouagadougou did their job. There were very few vehicles passing by and, fortunately, the cloud of dust that they raised settled quickly.

At some point, a ray of intense light came through one such cloud and hit me straight in the eyes. I squinted a bit and that was all it took for me to see more clearly. It was Elias, a fellow countryman of mine, on his bike; he and his girlfriend had also been travelling around Africa. We'd been in contact for days trying to get together. He had texted me that he was somewhere in the area, but I hadn't received the exact information about his location.

We set camp close to the border with Ghana, where we spent two days talking about our trips. I parked the little Vespa right between the two XR250 and we all laughed at the huge difference in the size of our bikes. Christina, with her spontaneous laughter and her bright eyes, transmitted her urge to know everyone and everything that came her way. Elias, focused on his venture – to travel around Africa – talked more about the practical aspects of the issue. I was speaking Greek for the first time in months and I really enjoyed the fact that I could finally joke in my own language.

"So I see this bundle on wheels heading towards me" Elias recounted. "Must be a local – I say to myself". "No, wait! It's Gogos on his Vespa!", he concluded, laughing.

When the sun went down, we got into our tents. But I was feeling uneasy. I was thinking about... mangos! For over three months I'd been avoiding fruit that I hadn't tried. The last vestige of conservative thinking in my mind had to do with fruit. It was Liam who had convinced me to try one some time ago. I can't recall feeling more stupid and at the same time more complete in my life. Its juicy, bright yellow flesh, its sweetness and intense aroma drove me crazy. "I will only eat mangos from now on", I declared solemnly-and kept my promise.

Liam hardly ever bought anything that he didn't consider a first necessity. Only when he needed something, provided that I wasn't carrying it in my luggage, did it occur to him to get it. In many cases I pretended to tell him off. I told him that, if I had enough luggage space on the Vespa, then he did, too, on his own bike. In fact, I'd never refused to share anything with him. The only thing I found hard to share, were the mangos. I had only two left and I was hungry.

"Did you hear those weird noises late last night?", Christina asked me when I got out of my tent, the next morning.

"It must have been some little critter that sniffed out the leftovers", I replied.

I lied! That night it was just me trying – secretly – to wash myself clean of the juice of my last two mangos.

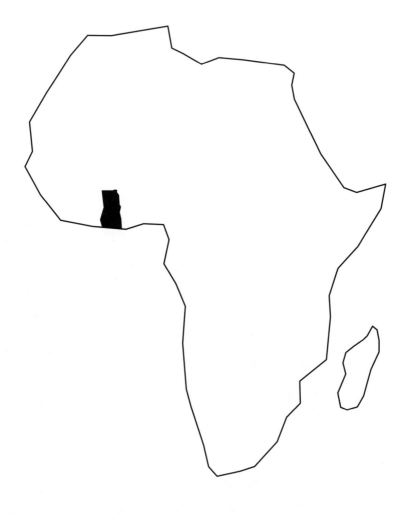

GHANA

ALL ALONE

I had stopped somewhere past a town called Wa, waiting for Liam, who had vanished from my rearview mirror at some uphill section. Since the previous day, he had been complaining that his bike didn't work too well and that the engine sounded kind of weird.

"It must be that bottled gasoline we poured in at Léo", I told him, acknowledging, however, that most of his engine's issues were due to his own exaggeration.

The first 200km in the north of Ghana were a plunge into a subtropical climate, dampness, luscious vegetation and potholes. I was curious to see the country that, over the past years, had become the leading example for the rest of West African countries. Implementation of development models with the blessings of the International Monetary Fund and big investments had transformed the former British colony into a financial paradise. I remember catching a glimpse of its position in worldwide rankings: moderate corruption, moderate dangerousness and moderate stability. For African countries, "moderate" as per global organisations, equals success. *Something similar happens with Greece!* I thought as I traced with my foot the outline of the continent that had sheltered me over the past few months on the powder-fine soil.

Liam wouldn't answer the phone. I wondered how far behind he had been left. I didn't want the distance between us to grow too much, but the paved section of the road that we had finally reached, seemed to be begging for more speed. It didn't last long, but it was enough for me to sprint ahead. We'd been in Ghana for only a day and we were both thrilled.

"You should have got the visa back in your country", the obnoxious Dutchman in Bamako had reproached us, struggling to demonstrate that we did everything wrong. "There's no way you'll get in without the *carnet*", he tried to scare Liam. Apparently, he looked forward to seeing us get back from the embassy of Ghana frustrated. An ungainly grin – a twisted smile of pretended politeness – was carved on his face, when we got back holding our visas.

"Well, now let's see if you can make it across the border" he mumbled, insisting selfishly.

At the border, the police officer invited us into his office with a smile. He was willing to help Liam sort the problem of not having a *carnet*. Twenty minutes later, we were getting out of the border station with our papers stamped and Liam holding a special permit, which allowed him to circulate on his vehicle around the country legally. Nobody wanted their palms greased and nobody gave us a hard time.

Excitable as I've always been, I wanted to log into all travel forums out there and comment in huge, capital letters: "EVERYTHING IS POSSIBLE". The more time I spent on the road, the more I realised that travelling is an experience unique to each one of us and that there is no need to follow all the advice we read to the letter. That's what I used to tell Liam, who, despite his overall kickback attitude, usually ended up more stressed than I was.

"Read less and look ahead of you more", I kept repeating every time that he looked overwhelmed.

I was trying to shake as much dust as I could off me, when the incoming text tone sounded on my phone. I was fed up waiting so I'd decided to ride back a few kilometres, in a last attempt to find Liam. I didn't go too far. I stopped again, this time at a road shoulder, which apparently served as a parking lot for the trucks of the Chinese construction company that was building the road. I didn't know what else to do, but I wasn't willing to go through the same dust ordeal all over again. Besides, I wasn't worried.

Right before being lost to sight, my fellow traveller had given me a thumbs-up from a distance.

"I got back to Wa", read the text message. "I'll stay here until I get the bike fixed; you go ahead"

I found it weird.

"Don't you want me to wait up?", I asked to make sure.

"No" came the answer. "It's been a long time since I last travelled on my own and I've missed it. See you in Accra", he said. I was alone. For the very first time since I'd started the trip, I was all alone.

KUMASI

I rode through plantations of tobacco, mango, banana and cocoa. Ghana, this rapidly developing country I was travelling across, did not seem too different from the rest. Perhaps the plantations owned by multinationals slightly outnumbered the others, but the people in the villages and towns that I came across on the way did not really seem to have better lives than the ones in other countries I'd seen.

The dense tropical vegetation was not enough to conceal the poverty of the residents of the countryside. Dirt everywhere; four or two-wheeled clunkers and tin shacks; wooden benches on the road; fruit, vegetables and women sitting in the shade selling them; kids in dirty school uniforms that laughed their hearts out at the sight of the Vespa; trucks that rushed by through the settlements, carrying crops to the great urban areas for export, leaving a thick layer of dust on everything behind them.

Not too shabby! I thought, as I made myself comfortable at the rather weird spot I'd chosen to spend the night before getting to Kumasi. The vast stretches of land that belong to the corporations are guarded, and I didn't particularly like the idea of being charged with trespassing. I'd discovered a path cutting through the corn fields and, at the first clearing I ran into, I snuck in among the tall undergrowth and set the tent.

I didn't cook that night. I tricked myself into believing that there was fire danger. Deep inside I knew, though, that it was the lack of company that made cooking seem boring. I just ate half a pineapple and hung the other half on a tree, wrapped up thoroughly in plastic bags. I lay inside the tent and my mind immediately started to process the new conditions. I was all by myself and the best I could do was to enjoy it.

I was entering Kumasi right in the heart of the land of the *Ashanti*. I was in the capital of the legendary kingdom that over past centuries played dominance games with the other ethnic groups of the area, the English colonists and the rest of the Europeans that sought land and slaves. I accidentally bumped into the city's central market at rush hour and my only chance of surviving was to turn the engine off, buy a few popsicles from the ice cream huckster and enjoy them in the shade, for as long as the endless traffic jam would last. When I had devoured the last one, I looked around me. The *tro-tros* – minibuses that move like crazy around cities in Ghana and are the main transport means for the residents – were swirling in the avenues around the market, adding to the existing havoc. I was trying to orient myself, so that I could find the guesthouse where I'd stay, but to no avail. *What the heck! I'll just ask*, I thought and got back on the bike.

The guesthouse was not far. Following the owner's instructions over the phone, I soon found myself in a strange room. There were chipboard sheets that divided the entire floor into compartments big enough to fit a bed and a bedside table right next to it. The mischievous thought of pushing the "wall" to see what happens crossed my mind. I imagined the consequences of such an action: scenes from a sitcom. I pictured the chipboard tumbling down at a single stroke, revealing intimate moments of the next-door tenant!

I couldn't even remember how long it'd been since I'd last laid on a mattress. I fell asleep.

ANTS AND PINEAPPLES

While riding, I prayed to the African gods of rain asking for their intervention, so that the big grey cloud that was hovering in the sky would drain itself dry over my head. I was coated from head to foot in a layer of the same thick red dust that covered everything around me. However, the foreign gods couldn't understand the language of my pleas. The blackness dissipated into numerous puffy little clouds which, like tufts of cotton, drifted off in the strong wind.

The peasants that gathered up when they saw me set camp at one of the road shoulders didn't come closer. When I nodded that I was planning to spend the night there, they just waved from afar and then left. I hadn't spoken to a soul for days and that had fuelled my imagination into making up fictional dialogues, adapted to the make-believe scenarios I came up with.

On the following day, I woke up early and got back on the road. After endless kilometres on an incredibly bumpy dirt road, which looked like an arduous practice session for the routes that, according to my research lay ahead of me, I reached the coast. At last, the sea! I washed the dirt off and surrendered to the bliss that one can only experience when completely submerged underwater. It's like a voluntary baptism, stripping the body of all the tiredness and filth that ends up weighing it down over time. I walked along the beach, leisurely looking at the palm trees. I kept track of my footprints on the sand to find my way back, just like when I was a kid playing on the beach. I cooked some rice, ate the mangos I had with me, and promised to myself that, for as long as I travelled on my own, I would never buy a pineapple again. It made absolutely no difference that, a few days ago, when I camped among the cornfields, I had wrapped it almost airtight in plastic bags. The ants still found their way in and when I woke up the next morning there was nothing but peels and a stalk left. How was I supposed to eat an entire pineapple by myself anyway? *Better off with company!*

I placed the towel on the floor boards and lay on my back. No walls seemed to ever have existed in the abandoned building that would be my home for the next two days. Its skeleton was only there to support the thatch roof with the wide triangular openings, and the whistling wind was getting in and out of the exposed wreckage, which, in all probability, was initially destined to be a hotel.

I wasn't afraid of being alone, I didn't mind not sharing my food with anyone; I was only thinking that I was in one of the most beautiful places I'd ever been to and felt sorry that no one else would see this beauty with me.

GOLD COAST

I was lost. I had an old habit of getting into alley mazes while looking up at the sky, as if someone would magically draw signs and arrows made of clouds to show me the right way. I looked straight ahead, at the muddy lane with the shacks and the colourful hanging clothes. A bit further, some kids were playing football, pretending to be famous football players. I nodded at a man that was walking my way and asked him how I could get to the Elmina Castle.

"Why did you come this way?" were his first words.

"To see the town", I replied.

He looked at me in bewilderment, as he earnestly thought that there was no good reason for me to be there.

"You should go to the castle. *That* is worth seeing", he advised me and gave me directions to get back on the *right* track.

The Portuguese, the Dutch and the English had all left their mark on the history of Ghana, the country that takes pride in being the first one in Africa to cast off the yoke of colonialism, in 1957. The English dubbed it the *Gold Coast* to emphasise the importance of its soil, rich in gold deposits. However, the land was even richer in soul deposits. The Elmina Castle still stands as a reminder of the millions of African people that were violently uprooted and carried all the way to every corner of the Old and the New World. Those who made it there alive were forced to work to death, having lost the right to be called humans. Europeans and Africans that belonged to the powerful kingdoms of that period bled the poorer regions of their resources for centuries, in order to build a reality the remnants of which still affect our lives to this day.

Back on the bike heavy rain was soaking my face and I felt like I was waking up. Ahead of me was the notorious castle and its "door of no return". It wasn't racism that spawned slavery. It was the other way around. It was the slave markets throughout the centuries where the evil seed of racism was planted and germinated. I hit the brakes. I didn't go to the Elmina Castle.

BLACK STAR

"You're not allowed to be here!" sounded the guard's severe voice. I was standing a block away from the US Embassy. Its walls were high and impenetrable, and the guards were armed to the teeth. I tried to explain to him that I was looking for an address nearby and wondered how it was possible for me to be only person banned from stepping on the sidewalk. Around me there were dozens of kiosks and counters and people and nothing seemed to prevent them from being there.

I guess my beard has grown too much and I look like the terrorists he sees on TV, I thought as I was walking away. Luckily, it wasn't long before I found the house. I made a phone call and, right at the main entrance, Steven showed up with a smile.

"I've been wasting my money on this fucking hostel for three days now!" I complained and followed him to the house of the diplomat who would put us up during our stay in Accra.

The first night I had arrived in the capital of Ghana, I rented a room at a hostel that I ran into by chance. On the third day, I realised that the price I had agreed on wasn't in the local currency, but in US dollars. I swallowed my tongue, packed my stuff and got the hell out of there. I shared the over-priced dorm with three Indians, a Ghanaian, a Swede and an American, all of whom were there on business. "*Development*", I thought bitterly. The images of all the endless landfills and the ragged little kids playing on top of trash mountains in the villages I had passed through were still fresh in my mind; and so were the luxurious lodges found all along the coast – mighty fortresses beyond reach, exclusive to the beneficiaries of this development.

We spent a week at the diplomat's house with the antiques, the valuable books and the opulent cellar. It was a special experience, but the persistent cough that had been troubling me made me want to go back to the dirt roads and the shacks. The air-conditioner worked around the clock to protect the old books from dampness and, whenever I told someone about the luck I had to get sick in the "civilised" environment I'd found myself in, they'd laugh and say that luxury just didn't become me.

While waiting for our visas for Togo and Benin, I wandered

around the wide avenues of Accra. Flags with the colours of Africa and the black star in the centre were waving everywhere. If the national identity of the citizens of Burkina Faso was constructed on decency and peacefulness, this one was different. The star is a symbol of black pride and even the country's name was chosen as a reminder of the belligerent nature of its inhabitants. Glorious kingdoms and wars for independence and dominance mark the past of this former British colony. I didn't know much about history, but it seemed that the cast-aside people in the villages had been sacrificed so that oil, gold, cocoa and tourism would become the new symbols of Ghana.

Rather listlessly and without the motivation I had in Bamako and Ouagadougou, though still curious to observe life around me, I went over to the city centre. I went past the Black Star Square, saw the Independence Arch, the statue of the Unknown Soldier and then got to the beach. People of all classes and ages were hanging out by the sea. Two young women in uncomfortably tight skirts and sky-high heels were trying to maintain their balance on the sand, as they swayed their slender figures. I raised the camera to take a shot of them. They smiled at me – not shyly at all.

"Which one of us do you want to marry?" they asked playfully with a suggestive look in their eyes. I burst into laughter.

"I really don't think I'd make a good husband!" I said.

I kept walking, until I heard him. *Another sermon!* I thought. I first saw the pastors who, with a microphone in their hand, take to the streets and preach about God in Kumasi. Stentorious voice, intense, dramatic movements and an expression on their face that, to my eyes, looked infuriated. They yelled, raised their hands up in the air and showed their teeth like rabid beasts. As if people will end up loving God, if someone keeps threatening them with sin and the punishment of death. Next to the angry pastor, a dozen children were playing joyfully, shamelessly sticking their tongues out at fear and death, in defiance. A lanky man on horseback passed by looking up at the horizon, confident and proud. A couple of girls were giggling while flirting with a group of young men.

And the pastor kept preaching.

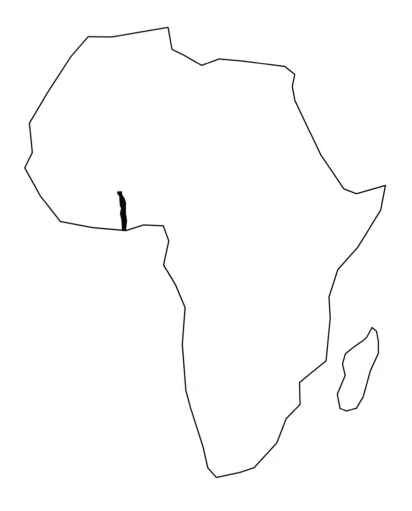

TOGO

TOGOLAND

It was around mid-March when we reached Lomé. The atmosphere was already clean of the dust brought along by the Harmattan wind, which had been blowing from the Sahara over the last few months. If it wasn't for the border checks, we wouldn't even realise that we had entered another country, since the line that was once drawn to separate the English from the French Togoland in the early 20th Century was based on an administrative allotment rather than some natural border.

We arrived around afternoon and the sun, which at that time was dipping into the sea, painted the sky orange and cast its light on the palm trees and the endless beach. We didn't take a turn to the city centre, but just kept on riding leisurely along the beach road. Overall, Togo has an extension of barely 600km from north to south and another 150 from west to east. We had no important business in its capital. We only needed to get our visas for the *Congos*, so we would spend the rest of the time there, waiting for Liam to join us from Ghana and then we'd move on.

"Time for a well-deserved break!" I told Steven as we were setting up our tents at the guesthouse, a few blocks away from the beach. He looked at me and laughed.

"A break from what?" he asked playfully.

On the following day, the heat and the hordes of mosquitoes that nested among the tropical plants of the yard woke us up at dawn. From the fixed 16°C of our host's air-conditioned mansion in Accra and the cough it had caused me (and which continued to trouble me) the temperature now soared to 30 humid and smothering degrees.

"Let's go to the beach and cool down a bit!", Steven proposed. The wind coming from the Atlantic was our only hope if we wanted the sweat to ever dry off our bodies and find the slightest relief from the mosquito bites and the sticky atmosphere. The coastline of Togo is no longer than 60km, so the only thing that we had to do was to pick a sandy beach to spend our day on. We didn't have to walk far. At any sea-side spot there was a place for us to sit.

We chose *Coco-Beach*, a little beach bar with no particular luxuries, just parasols, chaises-longues and plastic chairs. Its customers, though, were mostly foreign residents, European travellers and middle-class locals. In front of us, pale white tourists were enjoying the sun lying on colourful towels. Boys and girls who – as far as we could tell – spoke French, were relaxing on the golden sand making the place look like one of those exotic paradises from a travel agency brochure. The last time I'd seen tourists enjoying their flight-and-hotel getaway was back in Morocco. These groups were not dusty or tired, and they hadn't set foot inland. I wondered what had brought them all the way here to lie on this particular beach. Our chat with a French businessman answered our question. Togo, he said, had become popular among his country folk over the last years as the ideal destination for "exotic" and economic vacations. Besides, up until the '60s it, too, was a French colony.

After spending the entire day drinking coffee and reading on the beach, we went back to the guesthouse, where more travellers had now gathered. Among them were two motorcyclists: Charlie, from England and Francis, from France.

Francis was a weird guy. He'd lived in Africa for years. He was a teacher in Sierra Leone and was familiar with the reality of the continent he was in, with no idealisations or illusions. Without a hint of colonial superiority, he approached people in a way that left no room for misinterpretations. Sometimes he'd joke with the locals and other times, with paternal severity, he'd tick them off when they asked for a handout or tried to trick him. He was my father's age and travelled on an BMW F800GS. He wanted to travel around Africa, with no fixed itinerary or schedule. He didn't say much about his life and I didn't ask much, either. But he seemed to have been through a lot. And he drank beer – lots of it.

BLACK COFFEE

"We'll never find it!" I said disappointed. The embassy of the first Congo – the *little one* – gave us no trouble at all. We had everything settled within an hour and so we set out to find the other one, that of the *big* Congo. Early that morning, we got on our bikes and went on a mission to get the visa procedures started. It was almost noon and we still hadn't located the elusive embassy of the Republic of the Congo. "Let's go ask someone" Steven urged me.

We were lost in the dirt alleys of the city, and we could be really enjoying the ride if it weren't for our pressing eagerness to get our pending task over and done with. Lomé, despite its confusing vast coastal avenue, its palm trees, and the three or four modern, eye-catching skyscrapers that dominate its skyline, is not that different from other African capitals. Its central market is a chaotic maze of narrow streets full of small motorbikes, cabs and street vendors either carrying their merchandise on top of their heads or laying it down on makeshift counters. The drivers' honks, loud and continuous, give you a headache, and the exhaust fumes suffocate you.

The embassy was located on the floor of a building that looked like any other house in the neighbourhood. It was hidden behind a fence, while, right next to its entrance, some goats were literally hanging from a tree, chewing on its tender foliage. We went in and then out, frustrated. In order to get a visa for the Democratic Republic of the Congo, we should either be residents of Togo or go back to our countries of origin and have them issued there. We were surprised, but we soon came up with a solution. We would go to the nearest police station and file for a permanent residence permit.

We went back to the city centre and left our bikes at the parking lot close to the police station. There, a really gifted valet, capable of cramming all two-wheel vehicles together in such a way that absolutely no space was left between them, applied his skills on our bikes, making the best of every bit of space available. They were impossible to steal.

We stepped into the office. The officer in charge, always with a smile, made clear that the speed of the service offered, depended on one euro. He could either have our papers ready within an hour, provided that we paid, of course, or within a week. I remembered the Greek term coined by a journalist to describe the extra fee required to speed up some supposedly time-consuming procedures in public administration: the kickback stamp. Inside the police station, right at the heart of law enforcement, we were being asked to break the law.

We had a whole hour to kill while we waited for our papers, and we were poorer by one euro. We stood at the sidewalk in front of the police station. There, on make-do counters, women were cooking and chopping fruit, while men with carts were making coffee. I ordered a black coffee out of habit – a pitch-black one. I hadn't taken sugar or milk with my coffee ever since I left Greece. I'd grown accustomed to the dark liquid; plus, this way I was spared the burden of two extra items in my luggage. The sweet-tasting, light beige beverage that reached my lips had clearly nothing to do with what I expected. The coffee guy had decided – God knows why – to pour the entire can of evaporated milk he had available and then add a couple of generous teaspoonfuls of sugar to the mix. I laughed and kept sipping. It reminded me of my military service, more specifically the time I spent at the border. There, coffee could be nothing but strong, sweet and with plenty of milk.

SUNDAY IN LOMÉ

It was another hot day and *Coco-Beach* was dressed up to the nines to welcome the customers that swarmed to its tables every weekend. Contrary to weekdays, the wooden fence's little gate, which separated it from the rest of the beach, was closed to those who weren't willing to pay the corresponding fee to enjoy their day by the sea. People of all ages – almost exclusively white – flocked in for a place under the shade of the palm trees. We got in, reluctantly, to experience racket, music and people who talked loudly, while enjoying the show of a Togolese dancers group. The folklore spectacle, offered in exchange for some coins, had earned the tourists' attention. Through the chinks of the crooked reed fence, I could see a bunch of little heads, trying desperately to take a sneak peek inside the magical universe of the Coco-Beach. We didn't stay. Steven took the road back to the guesthouse and I headed to the side of the beach that wasn't reserved to the lucky VIPs.

All humans have some common codes of communication and one of them is entertainment. I could see no difference between the local families that were sitting on colourful pieces of cloth laid on the sand, and the customers of the *Coco-Beach*. Nor did the kids playing football outside do anything different than the ones on the other side of the fence. I sat at a refreshment stall nearby with chairs a bit more ragged than the ones at the *Coco-Beach* and tables that wobbled. I ordered a beer. The customers – almost exclusively black – didn't show any signs of surprise at my presence. The wind blowing on this side was exactly the same as the wind on the rest of the beach, the beer I drank was just as cold and the meat and fries I had just as tasty. The only difference was the quantity of garbage – there was a bit more. I looked towards the sea. *What are those people doing over there?* I wondered, surprised. Scattered around right in front of me, two or three individuals with their pants off were squatting down, hunched over the sand. Then I got it. The refreshment stall had no bathrooms...

Late in the afternoon I was on my way back to the guesthouse. I had taken dozens of pictures of Vespas that circulated on the streets of Lomé. I thought I might call Costas, my mechanic back in Thessaloniki and joke about opening a branch of his repair shop, right here in Togo. Maybe someone could use my services. In the countless repair shops around the city, loads of little scooters just lay around gutted, waiting to get fixed. I'd caught a couple of locals red-handed while taking pictures of mine. It was the first time I'd seen local vespisti. I remembered when, a few days earlier, at the border, I'd asked for permission to take a photo of a snazzy little Vespa. At once, the owner and the police officers went into panic, and made sure to warn me that taking photos is strictly prohibited all over Africa! Were they trying to scare me or did they get some law completely wrong?

"Hey, Steven! You won't believe what happened to me today!" I hollered cheerfully when I got back.

"Liam is not coming", his reply took me aback. "He got his passport stolen inside the Embassy of Benin in Accra and so he's stuck there".

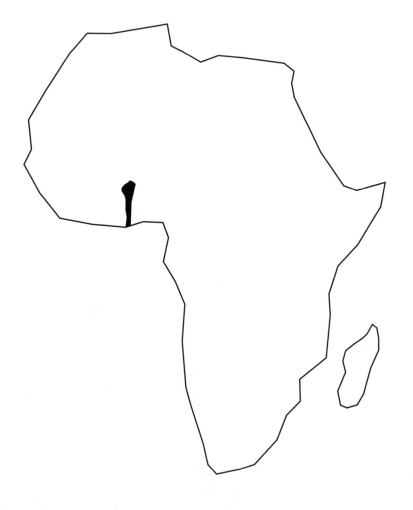

BENIN

THE FIRST DROPS

"It's a good thing I got new tyres!" I kept repeating to myself with a good dose of sarcasm, while trying to dodge the abysmal potholes of the motorway in Benin.

It looked as though there was some invisible life-balance supervisor who had seen us relax under the palm trees in Lomé and deemed that it was now time to get our share of torture. No more summer languor or cold beer for us. Right after crossing the border to Benin, we took a plunge straight into trouble.

It was the first day on the road together for Steven and me. We were trying to figure out a pace that would work for both of us. He could keep up a steady speed of about 75km/hour, but I was forced to go to the extremes. I would either travel at 40 or 90km/hr. At any speed in between, the scooter would shake so badly, that I thought every part of it was about to come unscrewed and fall off. However, when we got past Allada, the road became so bumpy and the traffic so chaotic that we were only left with one choice: run for our lives!

I found it hard to digest the scenes unfolding before my eyes. The central highway, which connects the country's north with the south and its great ports, was full of hundreds of heavy cargo trucks overloaded with merchandise. Bewildered, I was laughing nervously at the deadly driving behaviour of the oversized vehicles which, without thinking twice, were perfectly capable of squashing anything that would come their way.

As if the horrible roads and the nightmarish truck traffic weren't enough, rain came along to complete the apocalyptic setting. It was late March and the rainy season was menacingly close. However, we were hoping to have a little more time until April, which is when it begins officially. Unfortunately, our hopes were dashed by the *avant-première* of the first drops. In tropical storms, the first drops are usually the forerunner of the ensuing disaster. They plough thick into the soft ground with such impetus that their impact produces tiny water jets. And then the cataclysm strikes.

Splashing in the waterhole that had formed within seconds at the side of the road, we managed to stabilise the bikes on their stands making sure they wouldn't get lost under a sea of mud. We ran along with some locals under a shed and we all crammed together there, waiting for the storm to pass. The sound of the rainwater falling on the tin roof of the closed store that offered us shelter was deafening. We didn't know which village we were in and we didn't really care. Our temporary room-mates under the shed, a motorcyclist and three or four women, were smiling uncomfortably; being trapped with two white guys was apparently an awkward situation for them. We're all equal before the almighty nature. We looked at each other: we were soaked to the bone.

A little while later, the sun broke through the black clouds. We said goodbye and everything went back to normal.

HALF-BROTHERS

The baguette I'd been carrying with me since Togo had sponged up so much water, that I threw it away without second thoughts – a treat for toothless ants. It was the last piece. I'd felt such great joy when I finally tasted decent bread after such a long time, in Lomé. The loaves we bought in Burkina Faso and Mali would go dry and crumble at the first whiff of wind, like charred wood logs in a fire. In Ghana, bread was sweet and the thought of accompanying it with onions and tomatoes made me sick. In Togo, though, I had the best sandwiches ever!

Steven and I had agreed on a strict daily road schedule, at least until after we'd get through Nigeria. We would ride from dawn till dusk, with the fewest stops possible.

From Allada to the city of Bohicon, the route was a true nightmare. The truck traffic continued unchanged and the quality of the asphalt did not get any better. When I saw Steven getting between two huge cargo trucks in an attempt to go past them, right when one of them was pulling ahead of the other one, I opened my mouth as if to scream at the top of my lungs. But terror muffled my voice. I went past them as fast as I could and got beside him again. My popped-out eyes spoke louder than words, and he knew what I wanted to tell him. But there was no time for talking. Before I could utter a single word, the next menace was already dashing towards us. This time, it was a heavy truck, which had crossed over to the opposite lane – ours – in order to avoid a pothole. The only option we had if we were to survive was to abandon the motorway altogether and continue our journey off road.

That same afternoon, we reached Nikki, a town barely 20km away from the border with Nigeria. I found it hard to straighten my body up when I got off the scooter. My back was killing me, no matter how I tried to keep it straight while riding and my butt made its discontent pretty clear through a piercing ache in my tailbone.

"Remember that baboon back at the guesthouse in Lomé?" I asked Steven, while he was stretching up. "I bet this is what my butt looks like right now!" I added with a giggle.

That poor baboon, which, together with a monkey and an African grey parrot, lived a miserable life locked up in cages, displayed as exhibits at the guesthouse where we were staying. Seeing them behind bars, listlessly staring at the void while swaying back and forth monotonously, seemed so wrong. I don't know why I didn't say anything then, why I didn't ask. Maybe I didn't want to know the answer.

We got into a hotel that we ran into by chance. We asked the receptionist. The price was rational. We asked for a two-bed room.

"You mean two rooms", he said.

"No, we only want one" I corrected him, thinking that I might have said something wrong.

"I'm afraid that's not possible", he said politely yet assertively. Steven and I looked at each other.

"How so?" we asked confused. The clerk faltered. It was his duty to explain, but he was embarrassed.

"Wh-what is the nature of your relationship?", he asked in a low voice. Then we got it. He feared that Steven and I might be a couple. We knew nothing about the laws in Benin, but many countries have banned homosexuality over the last few years, as if it were an abomination to do away with. Yet another human right violently trampled over, well into the 21st Century.

"We're half-brothers", answered Steven, without hiding his annoyance. I don't know if the receptionist actually believed us, but apparently our answer was good enough for him and so he gave us the keys to one room with two single beds, placed sufficiently far from each other.

I SAW NOTHING OF BENIN

That night at the hotel, I couldn't sleep a wink. Across the room, Steven was also tossing around in his bed.

"Are you having nightmares about Nigeria?", I whispered. "Fuck off!" was his answer.

We wanted to avoid Lagos and this was why we'd gone to the north of Benin. We'd cross the border from there and then ride all the way to Abuja. After that, we'd head south, to Cameroon. We'd heard the news that, a few days ago, Maxim, the French cyclist we'd met on the road and who travelled together with Katrina, on and off, was assaulted in the outskirts of Lagos. They smashed a glass bottle on his head and snatched all his belongings, except for the bike. Katrina was travelling on her own by bus at the time, so as to avoid cycling until safely crossing the border of Nigeria.

On the following morning, we were all alone at the border post. It looked like the wooden stands put together at the artisan markets in Greek villages. We were waiting, without knowing for whom or until when. A passer-by saw us and offered to give the only officer a phone call.

"He's taking a bath, but he'll be here any minute", he assured us, so we prepared coffee, made ourselves comfortable and started placing bets about how long it would take the guard to finish his bath.

"Oh, man! I didn't get to see anything of Benin!" I complained as I took a look around. The only images of the country I was taking with me were its road network and everything found on it. I also saw a couple of really funny Vespas along the way. One had become a make-shift motor tricycle pulling entire trunks of palm trees. The other one, after being subjected to an elaborate customisation process by its resourceful owner, had ended up with a steering wheel on it. I didn't get close to either one while on the road, just to be on the safe side. I remembered the bumper stickers on the vehicles of the Ghanaian drivers, which, in capital letters, thanked God for protecting them on the road. In Benin, they would have been more useful. Blind faith is the only thing that can help you steer your way through this chaos!

Benin is a sparsely populated and laid-back country. I guess... We didn't get to visit the capital, or any of the big cities of the former kingdom of Dahomey, the birthplace of Voodoo, or *vodoon*, as probably the most well-known African religion was called there. I'd read about the fetish markets – where macabre items are sold – and the spreading of the voodoo over to the Caribbean through the slaves. The imagination of white people and, most of all, their inability to understand the voodoo, soon turned it into a senseless practice involving magic spells and potions, the ideal theme for horror movies. The only thing that really horrified the locals, however, was falling in the hands of the more powerful ethnic groups, which, in collaboration with the European slave traders, sold the weaker as slaves. The Slave Route passed through here, as well.

The more I learned about African history, the better I understood that, since time immemorial, exploitation was a matter of power. And that little had to do with the colour of people's skin.

"Good morning!", all of a sudden, we heard a mellow voice behind us. It had been a full hour and, finally, the border officer had arrived, freshly shaved and smelling like early morning breeze.

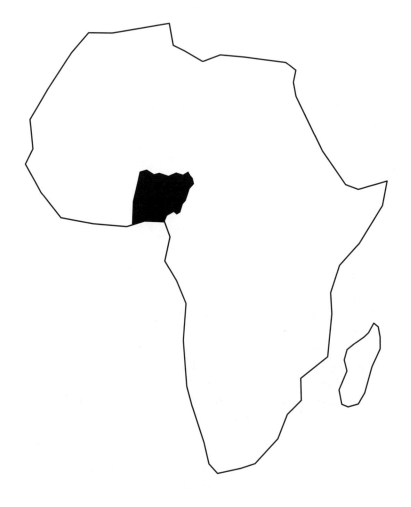

NIGERIA

27 – HELL YEAH!

"*It's my birthday*, man!" I shouted to Steven from within my helmet, right before we took a plunge into the mud. We had just entered Nigeria and copious rain was pouring down, transforming the awful dust roads into torrential streams. "*Happy birthday!*" the German's voice sounded, muffled by both the excitement and the hood he had on. We shook hands and opened the throttle, ready to face everything that would come our way.

As I rode the scooter, I thought about my birthday. I'd just turned 27, and had had the time to grow up in a family that struggled to provide for my brother and me as much as possible. I'd had the time to go to school in a working-class neighbourhood of Thessaloniki and play football in its alleys. I'd had the time to speed like a maniac on a fast bike, thinking that death couldn't run as fast as I could. I'd had the time to see people fall apart, because it turns out that death does run pretty fast. I'd had time for more: to build my teenage years on dreams that weren't really mine, to work longing for the next day off, to say "yes" to employers even knowing that I was being given the rough end of the stick; to lose friends and lovers because I could no longer understand them. I belonged to the "crisis generation" – as TV networks dubbed people my age – bound to go through frustrations, one after another. *Hell yeah!* I was 27 and I was fighting against rain and mud in Nigeria.

The water level at some points had risen so much, that we could only guess where the road ended. Around us was the savanna.

During the past few months, people in the savanna lived for the day that the first clouds would gather up, for the day that the arid ground and the parched trees would finally be watered. The day that the water would wash away the scorch of the burned fields and make the earth fertile, so that it can be sown again; that the wells and water tanks would be full again and the children's faces will be cleansed of the dust and dry snot; that the cattle and the goats would bend down over the creek and the women wouldn't have to carry so many buckets on their heads. And that day had come.

Everybody was waiting under the awnings or inside the tin-roofed shacks. Villages looked haunted. Not even an animal in sight. Only a few clunkers, parked here and there, bore witness to human presence. Steven was ahead of me and I followed, struggling not to get sucked in by the huge potholes. For the big wheels of the XT that was a piece of cake, but for my ten-inchers, it was a genuine nightmare.

"Come on, Kitsos! Come on, boy!" I was cheering my bike up. It'd been a long time since – rolling around the alleys of Thessaloniki – I'd christened the 100-kg bundle of metal that carried me. "You're a grown boy, now, 11 years old, not a good time to let me down!" I kept on talking to him, while kicking the crank to get it started after another big plunge. A faint purr that gradually built up into an intermittent roar was his answer. "*Braap!*"

We moved on. Kitsos and I, and the burden of my 27 years, and all the worldly goods I had left. The more time went by, the less I remembered my daily routine before the trip. I'd only been on the road for five months and yet the only memories I kept were from my childhood, as well as the turbulent time right before I left. That was the time of strikes, protests, and the hope that I wasn't the only one drowning in that reality.

The rain finally let up and we got to a village to spend the night. As soon as we stopped, people turned up everywhere. Some came closer, rather reluctantly, whereas the children, without thinking twice, surrounded us laughing. This was what always happened in villages. Our arrival was like a funfair for the locals, who always gathered up to take a look. At the front row were the toddlers, with their playful disposition and their inquisitive nature still untarnished by excessive thinking and inhibition. Right behind them, older children and teenagers – boys and girls – trying to hit the balance between childish innocence and the undertaking of the first adult responsibilities. Then the adults. Women were a bit more hesitant, more serious. Men were always up for a joke. I took the camera out of my luggage. All of them, grim or grinning, elbowed their way into the shot – they just had to be in the photo no matter what.

BRIBERY IS PENALISED

The minute we laid wheels on the muddy Nigerian soil – mindfully avoided by most – we witnessed immediately and unequivocally the diametrically opposite faces of the country. Each of the ten days we spent travelling across it offered us at least one unpleasant and one pleasurable experience, succeeding one another within an overwhelmingly short space of time. Their common feature was that all of them, both unpleasant and pleasurable, depended exclusively on the people that happened to cross our path.

Being no different to most African regions that had been split, dealt out and claimed by aggressive foreign forces, Nigeria was "constructed" by the English. Its borders remained the same after its independence in 1960, enclosing hundreds of ethnic groups with completely different backgrounds. People that up until then might have been on bad terms, would suddenly have to become fellow nationals under one and only identity: that of the Nigerian citizen. Presidents and dictators that walked in and out of the government buildings in Lagos and Abuja, did nothing but contribute to the instability and tense situation, and the great industry and oil economic interests, along with the ineffably corrupt administration, shredded the laws and the constitution. Even Boko Haram, the extremist organisation the infamy of which managed to reach Europe, was born in the northern part of the country and, over the past few years, has terrorised, murdered and displaced big parts of the population, who fear its attacks or reprisals.

Although the media, worldwide organisations and many travellers provide dire warnings about Nigeria, describing it in the darkest colours, I didn't want to be biased.

"Would you care for contributing to the work of the police?" asked the servile police officer in a tone of feigned politeness.

"What do you mean?" we looked at him, already suspecting what would happen next.

"Keeping the borders safe costs a lot of money" he said, emphasising the necessity of his existence.

"Look! The state does not even provide us with a fridge" he added, pointing at an empty corner in the office, where he figured they could fit one. Steven was irritated and eager to show it.

"Are you asking us to bribe you?" he asked firmly. The police officer sprang out of his chair, as if hit by an electric shock.

"Shame on you! Shame on you for not understanding!" he started yelling, while his face went red with anger. As he stood behind his desk, he was hiding the sign behind him that read, in English: "BRIBERY IS PENALISED".

"I only asked for your contribution; who said anything about bribery?" His tone was now menacing. He had such nerve that, for a minute, I felt unsure about whose punishment the sign referred to. By way of revenge, he only gave us three weeks to cross the country instead of four, which was what our visas allowed for.

A few metres away was the customs office. From the raging police officer to the kind female clerks with the metaphysical inquiries and their zest for chit-chat, which helped us forget about the unfortunate incident and go our way nonchalantly.

GOOD AND EVIL

"Dinner's on me tonight!" I told Steven. The restaurant at which we would celebrate my birthday was in a small, half-empty building, with its chipped-off walls full of cables that lead to a disproportionately large amount of switches and plugs – especially since there was no power. There was a greasy plastic curtain hanging over the window, trimmed with patterns of roses and crushed mosquitoes. Our plates were filled with rice, covered in a thick layer of spicy red sauce. We clinked our beers and drank to everything working out just fine.

A while later, at the guesthouse, I was on the bed staring at the ramshackle ceiling and thinking about our first day in Nigeria.

I wasn't so surprised by our reception by the police officers at the border. Both in Senegal and Mauritania, we'd had similar experiences. There's nothing unusual about the authorities, especially the armed ones, abusing their power. However, the clerks at the customs office were a whole different story. They wanted to know about Greece, Germany and Europe; they wanted to chat and joke. Even when we refused to add our religion in the papers we had to fill out, they didn't seem to mind – on the contrary. Steven's origin and mine, being German and Greek, explained everything: we were *philosophers*! I laughed my heart out when I heard that. This idea was so radically different from whatever I believed myself to be that I felt like that laughter was the only appropriate reaction.

"Has my beard grown too much?" I joked, thinking about the busts of the bearded ancient Greeks.

Just before falling asleep, my mind went back to the children that surrounded us back at the village where we'd stopped. Some were raggedly dressed, at best wearing a pair of mangy, wrong-sized flip-flops and a muddy T-shirt, others were completely naked and barefoot. Many of them had their bellies swollen from malnutrition. I saw poverty around me. It would be mindless of me to choose to see only their smiles; to just take pictures of them thus perpetuating the compassion and romanticism about the *Black Continent*. I'd feel so foolish to just stand there, among the beautiful, pristine landscapes and the *genuine* faces – brochures of exoticism for 'humanitarian' organisations and travel agencies – without looking beyond all that. Covert racism, the kind I feared the most, is the one that lurks behind the pity that the 'civilised' feel as part of their supposed superiority, furnished with 'love' and guilt.

"All people are good!" I once heard. How naive! The people I met were just people. Good and evil exist everywhere, and to make things more interesting, they can exist in the same person, at the same time. Everyone, regardless of the kindness they might have in them, may also carry the same amount of malice. The man that smiles at me today might have beaten his wife yesterday. The man that gives me a hard time at a police blockade might hug his children when he gets home from work. The same person that tries to cheat me with the scales may hand out food to his starving neighbour. Maybe the Christian, last month at the riots, killed a Muslim; or maybe the other way around.

STICKMEN

Steven was determined not to knuckle under when it came to border backhanders. We were on the same page on that. I'd stuck to the same tactic ever since I started the trip, but when it got me nowhere but pointless conversations and wasting time, I'd be more flexible.

"Just say you're a Christian and be done with it!" I begged him during one of the dozens of police blocks, which we had to go through before getting to Abuja.

"No, they need to understand that they have no business asking that bullshit", he insisted.

"We have no business preaching to them about atheism, either" I replied, weary of the hopeless conversation with the police officers. I didn't know if I was right or wrong, but I felt that the time I'd wasted on talking to such narrow-minded people had already been too much.

"Yes, we have been baptised Christians", we answered diplomatically, in an attempt to cast off the guilt of our defeat. Steven, raised in a Protestant environment, had soon opted for atheism. As for myself, just like the vast majority of infants in Greece, I had been baptised an Orthodox Christian, within a year of birth. I cried a lot during my baptism. And perhaps so did my folks, though on the inside, since despite both of them being atheists, they had succumbed to the commands of a conservative society.

We were only a few kilometres away from Abuja, but the blockades were taking far too long. The sun was about to set when we finally met the *stickmen* – the men with the poles – in person. We'd read about this habit of some Nigerians to set up barricades on the central roads outside cities and ask the passing drivers for money. We were curious to see if that was actually true.

From a distance, a group of people standing on both sides of the road caught my attention. I remembered the official tolls I'd come across along the indescribable roads of Ghana. When I passed through the toll booths, I didn't even bother to slow down and ask whether I had to pay. Here, however, things were different. The men with the yellow vests were holding wooden poles and planks in their hands, some of which had nails jutting out of them. Steven was ahead of me; he didn't slow down, just manoeuvred past them from the right, leaving them bewildered. They were all looking at him, so they didn't see that there was a second motorbike passing. I seized the opportunity and went through. We got lucky at the first block and even luckier at the next one, where, again following Steven, I saw in terror a stick almost grazing his helmet, missing it by just a few centimetres.

I was trying to understand what had pushed these people to set up makeshift blockades and threaten the passers-by. Perhaps they were sick of surviving on the crumbs tossed to them by the governors and the multinationals that plundered their land. Perhaps they watched their neighbours thrive while they remained unable to provide for their families. Or perhaps they simply had nothing to lose, since no one seemed to be in control of the situation. And, while around cities the practice of the *stickmen* flourished, why was it that in the villages we had never felt threatened? With all these thoughts in my head I didn't even realise that, by the time we reached Abuja, it was already dark. The arduous venture of finding accommodation in a big African city was about to begin.

BOMBS AND INEQUALITIES

The time had almost come to leave the hotel and we could still not believe our luck. On the night before, we thought luck had forsaken us, as the hotels we came across asked for amounts that were way over our budget. Just when we were about to give up and stay at one of these hotels, a Mercedes with tinted windows showed up out of nowhere and blocked our way. From the rolled-down window, the driver – who I couldn't see from where I was standing – said something to Steven and my fellow traveller nodded me to follow them. I got furious at him, but there was no other option at that moment. As we were riding behind the dark

Mercedes, I kept yelling at Steven, accusing him of breaking the rule we had set when we started riding in Nigeria: "Every decision will be discussed beforehand", we'd promised one another. And yet, there we were, following a stranger in the middle of the night.

To cut a long story short, we soon found ourselves at the bikers' club of the well-off of Abuja and from there, to a more than decent hotel, all paid for. The mysterious driver turned out to be an hospitable Nigerian, a speed lover and an expensive motorbike enthusiast. We spent quite some time at the bikers' club with the pool tables and the expensive liquour; everything on them. The massive economic inequalities between the citizens of Nigeria, from the villages and the children with the swollen bellies, to Abuja and the heirs of rich families, was no novelty for an African country. I'd become used to seeing them around me, but it was the first time I'd actually experienced the two parallel realities to such an extreme, from one moment to another.

On the following day, we loaded the bikes and headed to the house of the couple that were going to put us up while we stayed at the capital. The night before, they'd accepted our online request for accommodation. The girl worked at some NGO and her partner was an IT engineer. We went along with them to the places they usually hung out and took a look around Abuja. Both of them had long avoided specific neighbourhoods of the city for fear of possible assaults. Assaults by whom? It was unclear. To whom? As usual, the heedless passers-by.

It was Sunday noon when we visited the fish market, the famous *Abacha Barracks*. As always, the four of us in the car, we stopped at a spacious, guarded parking lot.

"You should leave your cameras and cellphones here", they urged us. "They're not allowed in the market".

We moved towards the place where that splendid scent of grilled fish emanated. In a big round kiosk, a dozen women were standing. They were cooking the huge blood-red fish that lied before them. Each one of them was standing behind her grill on the counter and prepared, upon order, sating portions of grilled fish, with fries and salad. The customers took their plate and sat on benches near the kiosk. We each took our own and sat down to eat. I'd had enough time to snatch a picture with my phone, disobeying the couple's urge to leave it in the car.

"So why is it forbidden to take photos?" They explained it was New Year's Eve, back in 2011, when a bomb exploded in the area, killing and injuring citizens that were celebrating the arrival of the New Year. Ever since then, although it'd been three years, security measures had remained rigid. Who had placed the bomb? All evidence pointed to Boko Haram, which, although already in existence since early 2000, had begun to make its nasty presence known again from 2010. Muslims against Christians, in a war with thousands of casualties. Killed or displaced, refugees, desperate people sacrificed under a sacred pretext. I wondered if religions weren't there to be used as an excuse for war and the pursuit of power. What else would humans come up with to exterminate everyone around them? I bet they would find some other pretence…

FEAR

After a week in Abuja, without much strolling around its streets and neighbourhoods, we got ready to leave. We'd heard a lot about assaults and robberies and we were kind of wary. "Why push our luck?" Steven wondered and I agreed. Our visas for Cameroon were ready, but our ego slightly wounded by the embassy clerk who, as we realised afterwards, had swindled us. We'd paid 15 euros extra, which apparently ended up in her big pocket.

We had about 600km left to the border with Cameroon and, to amuse ourselves, we placed bets on how many blocks – official or otherwise – we'd stumble upon along the way. Our laughter was soon cut short as we reached the first barricade of the *stickmen*. We were forced to stop. They had laid wooden planks with nails on the ground, which made it almost impossible to escape. Before we knew it, we were surrounded by a mob of peasants that yelled unintelligible words and wielded clubs. We were dazed. Things were taking a bad turn. "Police, Police!" I started shouting, hoping that someone would hear me. Suddenly, a man walked up from the enraged crowd that seemed somehow calmer. He asked for our passports. Without letting go of them, we held them up so he could see them. He turned to the crowd saying something we couldn't understand and, at once, they made way for us to pass through. We never knew what really happened that day. They didn't ask for money. The only possible explanation was fear. It was impossible for them to imagine that someone would ever pass through their village meaning no harm.

The rest of the blocks along the way to Gboko were just annoying, since the continuous checks kept delaying us. Once more we'd reached our destination after sunset. Gboko, a town of five hundred thousand inhabitants and insufficient infrastructure, was pitch-dark. I was exhausted. The last few kilometres had been a speed race with bad lighting and even worse roadway. I blindly followed Steven's red tail light and hoped I wouldn't fall again into one of the huge potholes. We got inside the first hotel we stumbled upon.

"No vacancy!" the receptionist was quick to hold us back. He was lying. The hotel seemed almost empty. We explained that it was impossible to keep riding in the night, but he remained intransigent. We stepped out to the yard. There, a crowd had started to gather and stood staring. They didn't talk to us. They seemed reticent and distant. A woman in her thirties walked up from the observing crowd and approached us.

"Come back into the hotel, I'll help you get a room", she said. She had a long conversation with the receptionist, who eventually accepted grudgingly to put us up, under the condition that we would leave first thing in the morning. We didn't understand. The stranger introduced herself and explained that, in her hometown, people were afraid. She assured us that she tried to make them understand that they had no reason to mistrust us.

We went up to the room. We'd just taken a bath and were ready to go to bed when around fifteen fully armed policemen banged on our door. At once, we found ourselves surrounded and started showing every document we had with us. Behind them, outside the room, was the woman who had self-appointed herself our personal consultant.

"Follow them, it's for your own safety", she urged us. We had no choice. We started loading our luggage on the police 4×4, under the vigilant eye of the local crowd, which remained gathered outside the hotel.

"That's it! We're being kidnapped" I said and kicked back in my seat. There was nothing else I could do. I had to accept things as they were. So did Steven. We were sitting there quietly, as the car bounced along the bumpy dirt roads of Gboko. We were dragged from one police station to another. They checked our documents and put us back into the 4×4, which sped around the streets of the town. A few hours later, Steven, the stranger who wouldn't leave our side and I, were back at the entrance of the hotel where we had started. The woman was right. The crowd began to disperse. Their worries were eased after the police assured them that we were not terrorists.

"Did they actually think we were terrorists?" I asked her.

"In my hometown, people are afraid" she replied.

GO AWAY!

Displaced populations are due to Boko Haram in the north, and environmental immigrants in the south have been driven out by oil scandals and *Shell* – at the Niger Delta. Ethnic group conflicts and economic interests abound. The most densely populated African country was in distress and I was trying to figure out why. All the countries I had travelled across on my little Vespa to that day had a dark story to tell; a story that goes on to this day and no one knows for how long it will continue. However, the way in which I found out about the doomed side of Africa was disarmingly plain in Nigeria.

We were riding through the region that once was the Republic of Biafra, the territory that dared to split off from the rest of the country in 1967. The horrendous war and the complete blockade of Biafra lasted for three years. It took harrowing pictures of children trudging towards their death for the public eye to see a problem that, until then, everybody seemed to ignore. The expression *"Biafra kid"* remains to this day a metaphor for squalor and extreme emaciation. A million people died back then, mainly of starvation. A number too big for the human mind to process. How can our mind possibly imagine one million people being lined up and killed? No matter how hard it tries, it can only think about the number, not the souls.

I couldn't enjoy the beautiful trip across the savanna. I couldn't enjoy the tropical forest that gradually started to emerge as we rode south, to the edges of the Cross River National Park. Nigeria got me confused. Good and evil, constantly interchanging before me left me quiet and troubled, more than ever. The melody of "*Zombie*", Fela Kuti's song came to mind, whose lyrics lambasted the depravity of his homeland's uniformed officials.

A few kilometres before leaving Nigeria and crossing the border to Cameroon, we stopped at a police blockade, expecting the annoying check, as usual. However, something felt different this time. One of the men, unfortunately the highest in rank, started screaming to us in such rage to get off our bikes, that he gave me the giggles.

"Calm down, please, I'm getting off", I said cheerfully. The only thing we heard was the sharp sound of him unlocking his machine gun.

"He's drunk!" whispered Steven. "He stinks of alcohol! Do whatever he says".

I got serious. Even at that point, I refused to believe that he would actually shoot me. The police officer kept on yelling. He bent over and scooped dirt from the ground with his hands. He brought it all the way to his chest and, with his fists clenched tightly, he pounded his chest.

"I'll shoot you!" he kept saying. His bloodshot eyes were popping out. I suggested he checked our documents, our luggage – whatever. The rest of the squad, a few kids that seemed more dumbfounded than ourselves, were looking at him without knowing what to do. One of them plucked up courage. He approached him reluctantly and told him something. He stood there thinking. I couldn't tell whether he was actually thinking or whether it was his drunken haze that kept him from moving. He got into the car and sat in the driver's seat, leaving the door open. The machine gun was propped up beside him. The man that had calmed him down turned our way. "Go away!" he said.

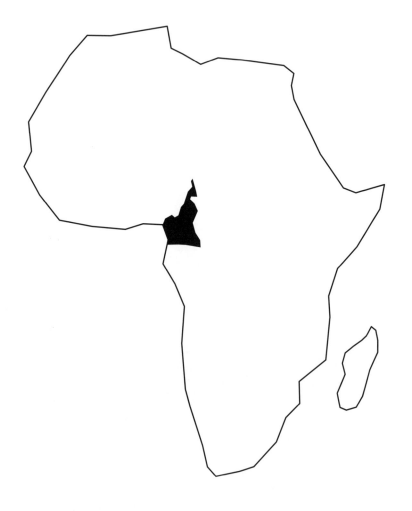

CAMEROON

BREAKDOWN

It was with mixed emotions that we crossed the bridge that connects the two countries and passed over to Cameroon. There was not a single moment in Nigeria that was adrenaline-free. The surprises that lurked around every corner of the road made our passage through the country unforgettable. I'd chosen to keep the pleasant memories, but I was still struggling to understand what had caused all the mishaps. After all, nothing dramatic had happened. The kidnapping was not really a kidnapping, the shooting was not really a shooting, and eventually, we avoided getting lynched by the enraged mob.

"You'll sure have lots of stories to tell about Nigeria!", I told Steven as we said goodbye.

"Right, it would have been so boring without you", he teased me as he revved up.

He would head north. Before getting to Yaoundé he wanted to check out some other regions that he planned on visiting with his family, which would soon come over to pay him a visit. I, on the other hand, thought I might just stay on the central highway, which would lead me straight to the capital.

I kept riding accompanied by a relentless downpour. I had no doubt I would get soaked to the bone in Cameroon. The climate here is tropical and the rainy seasons in the centre and the south, endless. The deluge washed the red dirt off the giant trees and left their bright green leaves all shiny and polished. Even my boots looked brand new, although my feet were soaking in the filthy puddles formed inside them. I thought about Liam. He was still stuck in Accra, trying to sort out the lost passport issue. We'd get in touch once in a while, hoping that somehow he'd manage to catch up with us – in vain. In the end, we left the date of our reunion open; be it in the Congo or further south.

As I was reaching Bamenda, I decided to look for accommodation, where I could take my soaked clothes off and dry them out. It was more than certain that the next minute I'd get wet again, yet the idea of spending a quiet night in a room was becoming more and more appealing to me. As I entered the city, a nice little restaurant caught my eye. I was craving a cup of hot coffee. Without thinking it twice, I got off the bike and walked in. There, on my left, at the only occupied table, was Steven!

"You can't stay away from, me can you?", his voice sounded, drowned in chuckles. He, too, had stopped because of the rain.

The hotel where we stayed was one of the tallest buildings in Bamenda. From the balcony, among the hung-out underpants and the yellow T-shirts that were still dripping, we watched the lightning that tore the night sky in two. Months before setting off, I'd ordered about a hundred yellow T-shirts with the "*Worldvespa*" logo on them – of my own device. I handed them out among friends and acquaintances, who bought them to support our venture. I took the remaining five along with me. Liam and Steven disliked them. Their bright colour, they said, drew too much attention. I liked them precisely for that same reason.

We were sitting in our plastic chairs lazily and the smell of moist earth blended with exhaust fumes reached our nostrils. Below us was the hubbub caused by the chaotic traffic in the capital of north-western Cameroon.

"Do you understand their English?", I asked Steven.

"Of course not!", he replied, serious.

Just like in Nigeria, we had trouble communicating with the locals here, as well. The language they use in their daily interactions is a mixture of English words and local languages, which left us befuddled every time we heard it.

On the following morning, we took advantage of the short break that the rain had taken and left each other, for good this time, headed in different directions. From the English-speaking region of Cameroon, I was heading to the French-speaking part, which is the largest. Throughout the route to Yaoundé, the landscape was beautiful. There was barely any traffic. The paved road – though curvy – allowed me to look around carelessly. Little mountains one after another were carpeted in lush green vegetation. Sweeping corners made riding really pleasurable and successive slopes, which, as I climbed them, allowed me to take in the view of the jungle that spread out before me. Every now and then, I stopped to take a picture of a lake, a house with laundry hanging in the yard, like colourful splashes on the green backdrop, herds of cattle with their herders leading them to the fertile grazing lands.

I was so close to the capital that, as night started to fall, I thought looking for a place to camp wasn't worth the trouble. Steven had found a guesthouse on the internet that belonged to some Benedictine monastery and we arranged to meet there, when he'd come to Yaoundé. I was riding the perimeter of the mountain at the foot of which the city is situated, searching. The GPS was a bit confused due to the successive turns of the ring road and, as if this wasn't enough, the engine started to make weird noises. After having spent hours on end every day on the scooter, I was perfectly capable of detecting the slightest jarring sound in its engine, and the intermittent stalling I perceived, really started to worry me.

Within the pitch-dark night, I made out the entrance of a hotel. I stopped, but the five stars that accompanied the hotel's name on the sign made it abundantly clear that there was no way I could spend the night there. I asked the guard of the parking lot for directions to the monastery. He willingly gave me all the information I needed. I got back on the scooter and tried to start up. But, for the first time during the trip, the engine wouldn't start.

"Man, you got a breakdown!" I said to myself and stood concerned beside the machine.

CAPPUCCINO

The receptionist that was on shift that night at the luxurious hotel looked at the white man with the dust-stiffened beard and the awkward hair fuzzing out at the sides of his head – leaving the rest of the scalp exposed to grease and smudge – with a frozen smile of surprise. Without losing his cool and always preserving a professional attitude, he eventually took up the courage to utter "good evening", as if there was nothing weird about me. I put up an act and told him that I was interested in spending the night there, but, before picking a room, I needed to use the restroom.

As soon as I got into the bathroom and saw myself in the mirror, I realised the reason of the receptionist's bewilderment. I looked much worse than I thought. I was hopelessly grimy, full of smudge and axle grease, and terribly sweaty after all the strenuous effort to make the scooter start. My yellow T-shirt was now black and disgusting. I burst into laughter. If I'd walked into a similar hotel anywhere in Europe looking like this, I would have been kicked out immediately. Here, however, I was the *white* man. I thought I might take advantage of this sad realisation a bit further and took a seat by the pool.

I ordered a cappuccino, turned the laptop on and started messaging my mechanic, describing the scooter's symptoms one by one. Costas was always on guard, ready to answer any question I might come up with, even at a distance. I sipped on my coffee slowly. Every long sip from the bright white porcelain cup reminded me of the simple things of a daily routine that I had long forgotten. My mind got muddled. I was tired, it was late, and I had no idea how the hell I'd fix my bike. The monastery guesthouse was only 300m away, but, in order to get there, I had to climb up an almost 90-degree slope, carrying my heavy luggage along. My other option was a kingsize bedded room with freshly washed sheets, a soft mattress, power, tap water and a clean bathroom, for which I'd have to pay 150 euros. I took my calculator out and started crunching the numbers. The money I'd spend on a single night at the hotel would allow me to get by for about ten days, maybe more. Ten days of freedom! This is what my days on the road seemed to me: "days of freedom". And my only goal was to gather up as many as possible.

A conversation with my folks and Costas' comforting reply, which was quick to arrive, soon cheered me up. I paid for my cappuccino, walked out of the posh cafeteria feeling the eyes of all the white lodgers fixed on me and left the hotel.

RELIGIOUS BUSINESS

I'd been up early, and, sitting at the terrace of the guesthouse, I was waiting next to Steven's tent. He'd arrived the previous evening and was pretty tired, so I thought I'd let him sleep a bit longer. The Benedictine monastery that put us up perched on mount Fébé, overlooking Yaoundé, and the view from there was extraordinary.

I was thinking about the repair of the scooter, which I kept postponing, when I heard the chilling screams of a woman. They came from a room nearby, which, from what I understood, served as the auxiliary event hall of the monastery. I jumped up. The woman kept screaming and, as I got closer, I could discern male voices. I pressed my face against the window glass and looked inside. I unintentionally became witness to an exorcism! A priest, a couple of monks and two more women, who seemed to be relatives of the screaming woman, participated in the ritual. The priest was reading extracts from some Bible, the monks were forcibly holding down the woman, who was reacting violently, while the relatives were watching the scene and crossing themselves now and then.

I heard Steven's steps behind me and turned around to him. "Let's get out of here, I can't stand this bullshit!", I told him. He agreed without second thought.

"Perhaps it's better this way", I added as we walked away. I thought maybe after all this brutality is preferable to the woman being lynched at some neighbourhood of the city, on accusation of witchcraft.

Most missions and monasteries we came across on our way were little more than yet another form of colonialism. They "saved" the locals from sin, built schools and medical centres, which, however, always came at a price. Conversion, exploitation and money. Lots of it. From the moment I set foot in the Benedictine monastery, all sweaty and exhausted, I realised that its policy and modus operandi was no different than any other business. Even its webpage made sure to highlight the accommodation facilities and the hosting of events. I had to go through onerous negotiations with the monk that received me over a spot in the yard to set my tent. During the days I spent alone waiting for Steven to arrive, I watched well-dressed locals in huge SUVs and expensive accessories gather up to attend the Holy Week masses. I was at some place of worship for the rich and I found it hard to wrap my mind around.

Apart from the locals, throughout our stay, we saw quite a few groups of European students flock in. Our guess was that they participated in some volunteer labour program, but neither Steven nor myself were really interested in knowing the details. As if in a parallel universe, we were completely invisible to the crowds that walked in and out of the monastery. We were impressed at how nobody would ever come near us. Even the monks only remembered our existence on "paydays", when they came to collect the rent.

MOTHERS

"Slow down, man!" I yelled to Steven from the passenger's seat. He cast a sarcastic look through the rearview mirror. He couldn't imagine that I was actually scared when I wasn't the one steering. Back in my teenage years, my brother and I would snatch the car or bike from some older friend and go get our kicks by performing all sorts of foolish stunts. A few crashes and falls had made me more prudent as I got older. It was the last time I'd go downtown with Steven. On the following day, he and his family – who had arrived in Yaoundé just a few days earlier – would set out on an excursion north.

Tall buildings, lots of concrete, brown and ash green walls and surroundings made up a unique scenery that I'd never seen in another capital before. The vehicles that roamed its streets took me back to the '90s. Maybe it was just the neighbourhoods we visited, but Yaoundé did not look that chaotic at all. There were market stalls and pretty merchants and cars everywhere and yet somehow everything seemed quiet.

"Let's grab a coffee, shall we?", I proposed to Steven. He eagerly accepted, under the condition that we hide in the mezzanine of a café. "To get some peace and quiet", he said. I wanted to sit outside, right by the traffic and the passers-by, but he was baffled by my apparent imperviousness to the racket produced by the noisy customers and the constant car honks. We obviously didn't have the same noise-tolerance thresholds. I decided to humour him and we were shoved safely inside, away from everything that disturbed him. Perhaps Yaoundé wasn't that peaceful after all. Perhaps it was just me that had become accustomed to the crazy pace of African metropolises.

We got a couple of beers at the supermarket, and some stuff that I'd need to fix the scooter and headed back. Steven's mother and her partner were waiting for us so that we could all go and have dinner at the restaurant of the monastery.

"I just hope there's no rice on the menu!" I said jokingly. Most of the time on the road, the cheapest – and at times the only – choice was rice.

"I wish they'd buy us dinner!" Steven confessed his secret desire.

I was surprised. I mentally replaced his mother with mine and realised that, in a traditional Greek family, parents buying their kids dinner would be a given. As I soon discovered, however, that regardless of their cultural background, all mothers usually have one thing in common: they're willing to offer anything they consider important. The meal was on her. Loaded down with all sorts of goodies, Steven's mother played mum to both of us that day. She'd even brought along some feta cheese, knowing that her son was travelling with a Greek.

In the package that had my name on it, I found all the new spare parts I'd been expecting to arrive from Greece. Costas had them shipped to her address in Germany, so that they'd be delivered to me directly by her, avoiding any unnecessary risks. We stepped out in the yard, each with a glass of beer in our hand, and I started tinkering with the scooter. I changed the shock absorber, spotted the electrical issue that the other day had caused the engine to fail and never start again and, after hours of intensive work, came the moment we'd all been waiting for. I turned the key, I kick-started the engine with determination and... it revved to life!

EASTER

During the brief moments before my parents located the right button to turn the computer off, I pressed the earphones hard against my ears trying to make out a sound – one that would remind me of Easter in my mother's village. Silence.

We talked for about an hour. I made them transmit in detail all the images of the springtime landscape of Chalkidiki, with the poppies and daisies in full blossom. I wanted them to describe to me every smell coming out of the oven in our house; the sweet, spicy scent of mahleb and fresh butter from the *tsoureki*[1] and the Easter cookies. I imagined my father, his hands black from the coal, getting ready to roast the lamb. I thought about my mother, too, who, if she could, would definitely send a tsoureki over here by mail.

Easter was my favourite holiday. How can a kid not love fifteen whole days of vacation in springtime? In Holy Week, my grandma would usually drag us along to church and we'd always get up to some mischief to pass the time during mass. "Shshshsh!", the strict voice of a neighbour would sound when we'd go too far.

When the day of the Resurrection would arrive, I'd feel sorry for Judas who was burning up at the village square for hours – even though he was just a hay effigy. What a custom! On Sunday, friends and family would gather up at the house yard and celebrate as if they'd come back from the dead themselves. We would be somewhere nearby playing. Years went by and I became an adult, and never enjoyed Easter in the village again. Work kept me in Thessaloniki serving coffees with a festive cookie as a treat. Maybe I missed the village. Or was it my childhood carefreeness that I missed the most?

The bells of the monastery brought me back to reality. That year, the Catholic and the Orthodox Easter were celebrated on the

[1] *The Tsoureki is a brioche-like type of sweet bread, with a moist and stringy texture, typically prepared in Greece during Easter, which, among other ingredients, contains the mahleb spice.*

same day. Crowds of the devout, in their most elegant outfits and with their most festive mood, flocked into the church. It was time to take a stroll. I put my laptop in my bag and got up. It'd been two days since Steven and his family rode off on two bikes. The time I'd do the same was approaching. I decided to have a beer at the same place as the other day but this time, I'd sit outside.

As darkness fell, the music at the café pumped up. It had now turned into a bar and the DJ was dancing to the rhythm of the songs he was playing. I made to leave. Before getting on the scooter I turned back and looked at the pizzeria right across the street. That's how I'd celebrate Easter!

With the big carton in my hands, I went back to the tent, put a movie on and tried to remember when it was I'd last had pizza. Then I remembered! It was back in Nouakchott, at the joint of Danny DeVito's double, who made the "best pizza in the world". I couldn't remember how long it'd been. What about Esteban? What had become of Esteban, the Spanish rider who had taken me there? We'd never spoke since then. I fell asleep.

ON THE HIGHWAY

"I showed you all my documents and I talked to the embassy and they told me I don't need anything else" I said and a squeal of exhaustion altered my voice. "I'm completely legal!"

"You're overloaded and I'm going to fine you!" he replied, after thinking it over. It was more than clear that he was desperately looking for a reason to take money from me. Unfortunately for him, right at that moment, a small bike with four passengers on board and a dozen chickens on the rear rack passed by.

"Isn't that bike overloaded?", I asked.

Before he even had the time to answer, another one came along. This time a few sheep were strapped on topsy-turvy behind the rider. The police officer hovered for a moment and, right before a third bike passed us by, he took out his little notepad and waved it at me proudly.

"Don't think that they'll get away with it", he said. "See? Here, I got them all jotted down!", he stated as he flaunted it in the air.

"In that case, you might as well jot me down, too, 'cause I've got no money on me", I suggested. "Or, if you prefer, hand me the traffic ticket and I'll pay it at the next police station I'll run into on the way".

He looked at me. He didn't say a word, just nodded me to leave.

By the time I reached the small town called Sangmelima I was hungry and sleepy. I'd been spoiled by the days I'd spent in Yaoundé and so I was looking for somewhere quiet to spend the night. The little guesthouse with the weird name, "*Kapablon*", caught my eye. The earthen floor of the room and the tin roof justified its low price. I'd grown comfortable in this kind of place, so much that I couldn't even remember what I was thinking when I considered staying at that five-star in Yaoundé. The owner of the guesthouse showed me to the restaurant that was right next door. I was the only customer and sat on a bench. The place looked a lot like a restaurant I had been to in Bamenda, the first city we stayed in Cameroon. I remembered the guy with the dreadlocks who had ripped us off that day. He came up to us and started chatting and, without us realising it, on his way out he told the owner that we were buying. His meal did not cost more than a dollar, but our ego had been trampled nonetheless.

After a twenty-minute wrestle with the hardest chicken leg I'd ever eaten, I finished off the beans dish and walked out victorious. I even managed to do away with the thick, bumpy chicken skin. The cutlery given to me by the female cook did not really do it, so I had to resort to my Swiss pocketknife, which I always kept hidden in the chest pocket of my jacket. Liam – or was it Steven? – laughed every time I pulled it out with a swift move as if unholstering a gun, to use it on one of those unnaturally coloured yogurts we loved so much.

"Cellphone in one pocket and a set of spoons in the other!" they teased me. I'd always been pegged as a trencherman. Back in my teenage years I had a growth spurt and suddenly became the chubby kid who, in the class photo, stood a head above the rest. And yet, I was getting along just fine away from the gastronomic variety of my country. My appetite for travelling was such that it had beaten my appetite for well-cooked food.

The next morning, after a good night's rest, I continued on the

N9 to the border. It was registered in the GPS as the only main motorway and it was only when I fell into the first pothole, deep enough to fit a tractor trailer, that I remembered that I was in Africa and not on some section of *autostrada*. Reality is not just one thing. Here, this was what motorways looked like and there was nothing I could do but accept it.

MARIE-CLAIRE

The jungle was so dense, that there was no way I could find a place to camp. The Chinese paving company had uprooted the centenary trees to widen the roadway, and the red dirt was piled up on each side of the newly laid road. The sun was about to set. The trucks – each of which could not carry more than five enormous tree trunks – had pulled over for the night. I climbed up one of the levees, which seemed firm. On the other side, I could only see a steep slope and a forest. It was the only spot that looked relatively safe, but still, I knew I was in for it. A good rain shower could make the soft soil recede and I could end up rolling over down the slope.

I don't know why, but I preferred to spend that night away from villages and their racket. Besides, there didn't seem to be any villages around. I set up the tent and took out the last, now a bit stale, croissant I'd been carrying since Yaoundé. The bakeries in the capital of Cameroon made the tastiest pastry goods we'd come across so far during our trip. Finding really tasty bread was such an unexpected and pleasant surprise, that Steven and I had loaded a few loaves before leaving. I hadn't made up my mind yet on whether I'd cook rice or spaghetti on my new camping stove – the one I'd bought back in Greece hadn't pulled through – when I heard someone calling me. I turned around and saw two men. They approached and, as they got closer, put their hands together over their heads, to show me that they came in peace. I'd learned that gesture. I used it myself now.

Before I knew it, I was invited by Gasson, the patriarch of the family, to set my tent outside his hut. As soon as the three of us – Gasson, his son and I – got to the village, which consisted of four houses in a small clearing, the women rushed to welcome us. Gasson, in a strict tone, reminded them of their duties. The guest needed to take a bath and have some rest. In the pitch-dark night, a makeshift wooden construction behind the hut, a plastic bucket filled with water and a cup were waiting for me. Unable to see a thing, I washed up, changed clothes and went back to meet the entire extended family. Daughters, sons, daughters-in-law and sons-in-law, grandchildren, nephews and nieces all paraded before me and I greeted them, one by one, by handshake. A little while later, they all vanished, letting me go to sleep. I'd regretted doubting whether I should spend the night near the locals. Cameroonians are among the most discreet people I'd ever met.

The next morning, about ten members of the clan, who'd been up since before daybreak, watched me loading the scooter. When I finished, I joined them for a cup of coffee and conversation. The awkwardness of the previous night, when we were looking at each other unsure about how to communicate, was completely overcome. I took out my map and showed it to them. I was surprised to notice that the northernmost point depicted on it was Thessaloniki, while the southernmost extreme was only a few kilometres away from their village.

"Here, that's where I live!", I told them as my finger traced the course I'd taken, while making a growling sound to imitate the engine. I wanted to explain to them that I had travelled all that distance on the scooter. When I reached the spot where the last big town before Gasson's village was, I hit the imaginary brakes and pointed downwards, to the ground we stepped on.

I was about to put my helmet on when the host approached me in an almost conspiratory fashion. He pointed to where his daughter was standing. Since last night, Marie-Claire hadn't taken her eyes off me. In the souvenir photos we took, she always posed next to me and, every time I needed something, her father urged her to help me.

"She's a good girl and a healthy one, too" he told me. "Take her with you, marry her and go back there", he added, pointing to my birthplace.

I stood there smiling. He meant it. Marie-Claire, a few metres aside, was watching us, waiting for the answer that would determine her life.

BAKA

Alone on the scooter, with the thought of Marie-Claire in my mind and that of her father, who wanted to ensure a better future for his daughter – and perhaps for the entire family – I was travelling the last leg to the border. I was now well into the tropical forest of the Congo, named after the river of the same name. The road was getting narrower. The mud was thick and sticky, but the locals had ploughed parallel paths with their bicycles and motorbikes, which made the passage easier. The sun had a hard time sneaking through the lush vegetation and, on the few green-grass clearings, small shacks cropped up; the peasants who owned them sat at their porches and watched life pass.

I knew I was in the land of the Baka – *the forest people* – who belong to the pygmy tribes. I wasn't really keen on the term "pygmy" and, as far as I'd read, they weren't either. The Baka people – so say the books – lead a semi-nomadic life in southern Cameroon, northern Gabon and the Congo and live off what nature provides them. They hunt, fish and gather their food from the land of the rain forest. They know all about herbs, and all about the secrets of nature that pass on from one generation to another; they speak their own language, preserve their own traditions and live by their own rules of a non-stratified – an *acephalous* – society. However, the Baka people suffer marginalisation and racism. The rest of the ethnic groups in the regions where they live don't accept them. Most of them are not even registered as citizens of a country. As if this weren't enough, deforestation, the construction of a modern road network and the exploitation of natural resources on an industrial scale seriously threaten their way of life. I hadn't run into a single Baka on my way through the area and bearing in mind that the forest people hide well, I kept going, convinced that I'd never see them.

About 30km before the border, right at a turn, a man showed up. His small-built figure made an impression on me immediately. He was wearing an old, tattered grey suit, a colourful jockey cap on his head and a pair of plastic flip-flops. A guitar was strapped over his shoulder. He was walking. I stopped and said hello. He stood and looked at me, and a warm, heartfelt smile was drawn on

159

his time-carved, unshaven face. I pointed to the direction we were both headed with my hand.

"*Congo?*" I asked, trying to find out where he was going. "*Bonjour!*" he said. "*Oui, Congo!*".

"*Bonne route!*" – Have a nice trip! – I shouted from afar and he kept walking. He was going to the Congo on foot. It made no difference to him where he'd cross the border. He, like a forest, couldn't be bound by borders.

I went on my way, thinking. I hadn't gone too far when, suddenly, it all fell into place in my mind. The little children that I saw in the clearing huts, the women that were dressed differently than the rest, the guitar hanging from the small-figured, kind man's shoulder. I remembered a documentary I once saw that said that the forest people – the Baka – are among all other things, musicians.

All these people I'd met that day were Baka people! How stupid of me to think that they'd be dressed in grass skirts and live hidden from the world in a mysterious, untrodden land. Or maybe this was what I hoped for all along: that somewhere, some people continue to live as they actually please.

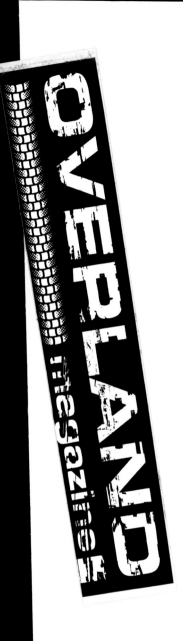

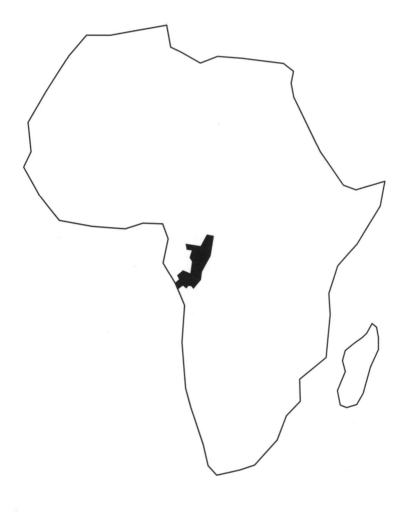

CONGO

RHUM-CAFÉ

My entrance into the border office of Congo was truly spectacular: I slipped and almost fell flat on my back. My boots were caked in mud and I was staggering forward on the clean wooden floor. I approached the immigration officer and apologised for the muddy boot prints I'd left all over the office.

It was the first time I'd ever crossed a border on my own – not accompanied by another traveller – and I was a bit nervous. Who would take up negotiations if I was looked at askance? My fellow travellers and I always followed a very specific strategy: when one of us failed to negotiate or lost his cool in the face of the absurdity of officialdom, the other would jump in and pick up negotiations.

"You're all set, sir", the shiny man on the other side of the counter informed me.

"Thank...uh...thank you" I stuttered, unable to believe that the procedure was actually over. "So... can I go now?"

"Of course" he assured me. "Is there anything else you need?" I asked for some water, as I didn't know how much distance I'd have to travel that day. One of the police officers brought me a six-pack of bottled water. Even more dumbfounded, I took my wallet out to pay.

"No, sir. It's free", he said.

I cast an inquiring look around to make sure that the whole thing wasn't a prank and took the bottles reluctantly. I thanked them and left.

With the bottles loaded in the panniers and sun setting quickly, I was heading to Souanké, the first inhabited area I'd spotted on the map. It'd started to drizzle and the treetops were hidden in a haze. I could only hear the sounds of the birds perching on the nearby branches, getting set up for the night. Further away I could barely make out the moan of the last trucks, racing to their destination before dark fell.

The road was narrow; it could only fit one vehicle, and on its sides the dense vegetation rose as thick as a wall. I rode up a smooth slope and as I started to go back down, the truck that I believed to be far away, showed up in front of me, out of the blue. Gliding through the mud, with its wheels wobbling from side to side, it was running up to climb the slope. It was coming head on towards me!

The driver signalled with his headlights, letting me know that he had no intention of stopping. I made a sharp turn to the right and threw the scooter straight into the wall of vegetation. I fell on top of it, sticking to the side of the road as much as I could. The truck, without slowing down at all, just scraped past me and vanished into the jungle. I got up, dusted myself off, and trying to pull myself together, I moved the scooter back to the road and put it on the centre stand, to take a picture. I turned around and took a few steps away. Before I had time to get far enough, the poor bike fell back into the mud. I picked it up and rode on until I bumped into a small settlement.

"There's no way this is Souanké", I said to myself. It was late and I was exhausted. I stopped and asked to see the village chief, the *"chef du village"* – as I had learned to say with my hilarious French accent. He showed up, and the entire village followed. After the customary handshakes, I was granted the necessary permission. Not only was I allowed to camp there, but I also got invited to his house for dinner. I stepped into the dark hut with the straw walls and the hay roof. The only source of light was a gas lamp sitting in the corner, which gave out a faint glow. I sat on the ground, next to the man who was expecting me. His wife brought two plates for us to fill up and some pots. The menu consisted of rice with tomato sauce and that pale, lumpy, dry puree made of cassava or some other kind of flour, which is typical everywhere in Africa. Usually, everyone dips their hands into a big receptacle, cut up a piece of the dough-like mixture and shaped it into a ball, before pouring some sauce on top. I tried it once and I found it completely insipid.

After we finished our dinner and washed our hands in the little basin my host's wife brought, he took out something very special and offered it to me. It was a sealed plastic sachet that contained a portion of alcohol. "*Rhum-Café*", read the tag on it. We tore the upper side of the packaging open with our teeth and started drinking. I'd seen plenty of empty sachets like that tossed on the road, even at the most remote places. Strong, sweet-tasting alcohol, with a pleasant scent of coffee. Was its sale controlled in any way? I'd once read that alcoholism was the greatest threat to the Baka people.

A couple of sips of *Rhum-Café* were enough to loosen me up. I looked around me. We're usually unable to perceive the greatness of a moment until after it's passed, however that night, I was fully aware of how lucky I was. The woman had disappeared into some dark corner of the hut. She hadn't joined us, or had dinner. I was talking with her husband; how many children he had, which members of his family lived in the houses nearby. With a little bit of effort, we managed to understand each other. They were Baka, too. I could now distinguish their features. Besides, their short stature gave them away.

Before drifting off to sleep, I remembered the man with the guitar that was walking his way to the Congo. *Did he get where he wanted to go?* I wondered.

MACHETE

Around three in the morning, my sleep was interrupted by a completely unexpected violent downpour. Torrents of water whipped the earth and my brand-new tent began to float almost immediately, making me feel like I was lying on a water mattress. It was delivered to me some time ago, in Bamako, by my friend, Kosmas. He worked at a courier company and when I explained to him that the old one was useless, he willingly offered to send me the new one, which I had already ordered. Now was the time for its efficiency to be put to the test.

Before the break of dawn, I could already hear the voices of the villagers around me, but the heavy rain went on falling and the tent remained dry which provided the ideal conditions for lazing in bed for a little longer. Around 11, when the rain let up, the sound of the tent's zipper drew the attention of everyone nearby. The first to approach was the eldest member of the family, my host, who, concerned, asked me how my night had been. I showed him the interior of the tent, where not a single drop had gotten in. His eyes rounded and he let out the characteristic shriek-like sound that all Africans I'd met so far made to express their surprise or excitement. Within a few minutes, one by one the heads of all the villagers popped in, staring in curiosity at the miraculous fabric that prevented water from soaking through. They explained to me that, when they went hunting in the woods, they could be out there for days and that a tent like that would come in really handy. I didn't quite know what to say. Perhaps they could get one in Brazzaville, the capital. But then again, maybe they wouldn't be able to afford it. How much would it cost? How much could they spend? My suggestion was totally useless to them, but they still listened to me carefully.

If I had paid the same heed to their advice not to leave until the ground was dry, my trip would have taken a completely different course, but I packed my muddy belongings and set out. Within 50m I fell flat on the ground and into the sludge. I got up. A few more metres further and back down; a few more and yet another plunge. The mud was building up under the mudguards, preventing the wheels from spinning. I tried to cheer poor Kitsos up (I always remembered his name when things got tough), but the white smoke and distinctive smell that came with it made me give up all efforts. I'd burned the clutch. I held still next to the silent bike. For the first time, we'd broken down in the middle of nowhere. Ouésso, the next nearest town, was 300km away and I was still in the heart of the jungle. For a minute, I lost it. What was I to do?

All of a sudden, a man emerged from within the dense vegetation holding a machete, a tool that's associated with the most gruesome images. Machetes have always been used by Africans to massacre each other in civil conflicts and war. We looked at each other. He wasn't young but seemed strong. Wielding the machete, he walked towards me and when he got close to the fallen scooter he stooped down over it and started to clean the mud off. I smiled and took his queue. We pulled the wheels out of the mud and managed to push it all the way to his house. It was a bit further away, on a small mound at the side of the road. The young men of the family were away and the women, scattered here and there, were looking after the children and doing the house chores. I stood there and looked at the huts, the colourful laundry hanging outside, the chickens and two or three puppies playing with the little kids. I was in heaven! What was I worried about? I would set up the tent, meet this family and, at some point, someone would show up and help me. I was in no hurry.

BEYONCÉ

I'd barely had the time to get to know my new hosts, when I heard the engine of a car approaching. I ran up to the middle of the road and stood right in front of it. It would stop anyway since, as it turned out, it was the "taxi" of the area. A pick-up truck loaded with food, furniture, people and animals, it travelled the same route daily. On that particular day, it would go to Souanké, about 15km away from where I was. The driver asked for two dollars and with the co-driver loaded the scooter on the back of the truck right away. After ceaseless skids, lots of over-steering and absurd speeding, we soon reached our destination.

Outside the liquor store at the entrance to Souanké, I set the tent back up and started to tally up the damages: one crooked headlight, all turn signals broken, and countless scratches – that was the count. I dumped everything as it was and headed into the city on foot, in search of something to eat.

At the shack that resembled a restaurant, the menu was predetermined. I took my plate, filled with overcooked pasta and drenched in oil from the sardine can that the cook had emptied on top of it, and sat at one of the counters. While eating, I started to observe the place. Its wooden walls were cluttered with posters.

Cheap glossy paper like the pages of a newspaper supplement, with pictures of movie and football stars. All the faces posing were renowned members of the show-biz glitterati. And what they all had in common was their African ancestry. Above my head was Beyoncé and right next to her the picture of a pink Bentley and a pink mansion. It was right at that point that the conceptual motif of the decor unveiled itself to me: a celebrity, their car and their house. The dream of the young cook in Souanké had materialised, albeit mentally. Surrounded by successful – by the standards of the Western society – Africans, he kept serving sardine pasta.

I engaged in a chit-chat with the restaurant owner and explained to him that I was trying to get to Ouésso, 300km to the east. As soon as he understood what I was saying, he told me that a car was to set out right at that moment from the liquor store at the town's entrance.

"Right now?", I asked again.

"Right now!", he assured me.

I darted out and sprinted hell for leather back to the exact spot that I'd left my stuff about half an hour earlier. Indeed, the pick-up truck that was parked outside the liquor store was being loaded and a small crowd had gathered around it.

"Got any room for me?" I asked as I was packing the tent back up.

"Sure!", he replied. "That 'll be 300 dollars!".

Immediately, I took out my calculator and got ready to barter. While dashing my way there, I'd made some quick calculations that gave me a rough idea of a reasonable fare for the trip. I calculated the distance, gasoline, the amount of money I'd have to spend to get there by myself and the amount that seemed just for the driver. I added it all up and – in my mind at least – the total was not over 30 dollars.

"I'll give you three!", I told him grittily.

"I'll take you for 100", he answered completely unsurprised by the price I'd proposed to him.

"Want five?", I asked, prepared for the upcoming rejection.

"Give me ten and you're on!"

I'd just driven the most surreal bargain of my life. I looked at him bewildered, and accepted. I thought that maybe the colour of my skin had him believe that I was rich. The amount he asked for seemed completely arbitrary. However, a Western traveller was likely to actually pay those 300 dollars without thinking it twice. With no further delay, I sat in the free seat in the cabin, along with the co-driver and a female passenger, who kept babbling throughout the entire trip.

WC

First overnight stop: Sembé. Darkness had fallen before we got there and the trip took an even more nightmarish turn. The road was getting worse, with tons of mud piling up on its sides and heaps of freshly dug dirt forcing us to take detours through fallen branches and potholes full of water. The driver stopped every once in a while and one of his assistants jumped off the cargo area and pulled the lever that shifted the motion mode of the vehicle. The car, an old Toyota 4×4 geared up with iron racks and bullbars, moaned and groaned as it floundered its way along what only resembled a road network on the map.

At an uphill slope, we ran into another vehicle, a mini-van coming from the opposite direction which had become stuck. We all got off, tied it up with a wire rope and started digging and pushing in an attempt to tow it along. When we finally managed to pull it out, the driver of our vehicle advised his colleague to turn around. The road would be impassable for the mini-van.

Covered in mud, we got back in and continued our way. That was life here, in the forest of northern Congo: fighting against mud in the daytime and at night watching soap operas at the neighbourhood joint, with the buzz of the power generator covering up the sounds of both nature and the TV.

The hotel where I was practically forced to spend the night at Sembé was owned by the driver's sister. I didn't want to disoblige him. Besides, it was so cheap that the experience of staying in one of its rooms alone was more than worth it. Each of them was an independent shack with ramshackle, half-plastered walls and a tin roof. There was no floor. The bed was grimy, with a perished mosquito net hanging over it. On the opposite wall, written in red paint, the price for a night's stay, along with the only term of payment: *"Payer avant de dormir, 3,000F"* – *Pay before sleep, 3,000 francs.* Next to it, a blurry mirror.

I'd dumped my belongings in the car of a stranger, who had given me his word that he'd come back the following morning. I only had the sleeping bag and the top case with the laptop and the camera. I'd thought it through: if the driver disappeared I'd continue on foot, until I'd find a new bike. I was convinced that, no matter what happened, there'd always be a solution.

The next morning, as I got out of the "toilet", I saw the driver gesturing from a distance. Of course he'd come back. Before following him, though, I reached into my bag for the camera. The shed with the "WC" inscription on it was the most well-kept of all the toilets I'd come across. At the top of the pit, right where the drop-hole leading to the abyss lay, a truck tyre was placed, which was meant to be stepped-on by anyone using the latrine. This way, the filthy sludge that I usually saw in other latrines, and which made my stomach turn, was significantly less. Before the perplexed eyes of the driver, I took a picture of the "WC" and got back on the old Toyota.

DISGUSTED

Relaxed, I watched the driver from my seat. At every stop, he'd open his ledger and take notes. He had everything in there: debts, payments, orders. When we'd reach a village which, despite consisting of no more than six or seven huts, had about fifty children, the women would run up to us and start transactions. The old Toyota was the only means through which all kinds of necessary things could get there.

My tranquillity, however, was interrupted abruptly when, as we were leaving a slightly bigger settlement, the insistent sound of a honk made us stop. A small motorbike with two police officers on it stopped right next to us, and they started talking to the driver.

"You have to follow them", he told me. One of his assistants came along with me, to help me out with the communication, although he didn't speak a word of English. As soon as I got into the police station, the chief started to bark out unintelligible words, his only aim being to scare me. His subordinates were

170

secretly laughing at the situation and I, with my palms stretched forward and the most witless and bewildered look in my eyes, insisted that I couldn't understand a word he was saying. The whole situation looked like a scene from a sitcom. "You passed through the roadblock" the other, calmer, officer tried to explain to me. He was playing "good cop".

"You have to pay a fine because you didn't stop to be registered". I unflappably explained, with a lot less French words than those I actually had learned, that I was broke and that my bike had a failure. What's more, I wasn't driving the car and so I couldn't have known there was a police check. I was sick and tired of policemen looking for a chance to rip people off! These two had nothing to do with their polite colleagues at the border, who probably were the exception to the rule. I waited indifferently to see what would happen next.

In a little while, the chief changed the tone of his voice. His wild barks turned into pleading meows begging for a "little gift", as they liked to call it every time they saw their hopes evaporate. I refused. As we walked away, the driver's assistant, who was probably ashamed of what had just happened, started to apologise and complain about the corrupt police force. I gave him a consoling pat on the back. We got back in the car and moved on.

The road was getting wider and there was finally asphalt for the most part of the route. We were about to go past the great junction of Ketta and turn north to Ouésso, when we came face to face with yet another roadblock. We pulled over 20m ahead and our driver solemnly asked the passengers for their documentation. I saw each one of them tack a bill of some value between the document sheets. They had no choice. All together, they walked towards the police officers, who stood there aloof with their bullet-proof vests on and their machine guns in hand. I stayed back in the car. One of them came up and knocked on the window glass and I showed him the passport and the rest of my papers without letting go of them. Another one came up. He approached me rubbing his thumb against his forefinger, in a gesture that, all over the world, tends to mean the same thing: money! I didn't even turn to look at him. I was really irritated. Then a third one came, who shoved his arm through the window reaching for a piece of stale bread that I'd left on the dashboard. He also took an empty jar of chocolate-hazelnut spread that was lying next to it. He tried to open the jar. Although it was pretty simple to unscrew the lid open, he wasn't able to do it. Embarrassed, he tossed it back inside and walked away.

An hour had passed until my fellow passengers came back and we could finally get going. We had barely moved when we heard the wail of the police siren and saw in the rearview mirror three policemen running towards us, wielding their guns. They started yelling at the driver, who explained to me that I had to go back to the roadblock. I walked slowly, in an attempt to buy myself some time to calm down. The chief was waiting for me in the monstrous 4×4 with the tinted windows. He was sprawled all over the driver's seat, surrounded by a bunch of his disgusting henchmen. With the most appalling look on his face, he started to bark at me. I smiled politely, pretending that I had no clue what he was asking of me. However, I knew perfectly well what he was up to. He wanted me to go back to the car, unload all my stuff, and then carry it all the way back and lay it at his feet. He also wanted me to get the scooter off the truck, too. And, finally, he wanted me to pay the fine, for refusing to show my documents. At the same slow gait, I went back to the parked car, where the passengers were waiting concerned. I told them what was going on to ease their worry. I went back to the chief mobster empty-handed. He sent me back again. I went back and then came back over again.

Time went by and the corrupt policeman was putting my patience to the test. I'd started to feel guilty for my fellow passengers, who were being stalled without good reason. In the end, I decided to do what I hated the most: to use a fake identity, a sham status, which would pull me out of the tight spot I was in.

"I'm a journalist and I work for an NGO" I stated boldly with a straight face.

"I collect data for a study about Congo" I added boldly. "Please excuse me for not speaking French so well".

All of a sudden, his eyes popped out of his sockets and he jumped up. With the slimiest smile and the phoniest mellow tone in his voice, he reached out for a handshake.

"I apologise for the delay sir" he said. "Welcome to the Republic of Congo."

I was utterly disgusted.

I'M ALIVE!

"I'm alive!" read the first text message I sent to friends and family in a long time.

I was in Ouésso, at an upscale fuel station, one of those that cropped up unexpectedly in poor cities. My main priority was to let everyone know that I was OK. I also had to reach Costas, the only person who could repair a Vespa over the phone. When I was done, I went over to the market to look for the tools I was missing to start tinkering with the bike.

Where on earth are the thirty thousand inhabitants? I wondered as I walked the deserted dirt roads, along the bank of the river Sangha. Built in the middle of the forest, Ouésso, with its low houses and the wide streets, is the biggest city of the area.

Holding the bag with the tools I'd just bought, I sat in the shade of a tree looking out to the brown water that was rippling peacefully, rocking the moored pirogues gently. People passed by on their bikes loaded with all sorts of greens and small animals which they'd killed in the forest. They looked like big rodents, but I didn't bother asking. I was thinking about the experiences of the past few days. My clothes were still stained with red dirt; my beard was tangled up in a massive knot that no comb could straighten out. My glasses – the ones with the old, damaged lenses – had more scratches than before.

Where was I? I'd sat beside some people who willingly shared their scarce goods with me. I'd managed to communicate with them, had made them laugh, had listened to them as they said a thing or two about their lives. I'd drunk alcohol from a little plastic bag, with an elderly pygmy. I'd avoided an arranged marriage with a local girl. I'd hoisted little kids on my shoulders and heard them laugh to tears, but I'd also seen the flip side of the coin. Those human parasites that abuse their power in the worst possible way, giving their fellow citizens and me a hard time. What the hell, people are the same everywhere! I reminded myself.

The sound of Kitsos' engine disrupted the silence of the night, as I rode across the city and headed to the N2 highway to Brazzaville. It was Sunday before dawn and I'd already left the hotel where I'd spent the three previous nights, while getting the bike up and running again. I'd deliberately chosen the day and time to avoid the roadblock on the big junction.

"Hush now, Kitsos, or they're going to hear us!" I urged the noisy engine and closed the throttle. We were getting close to Ketta where, a few days ago, I'd experienced the utter absurdity of the corrupt police officers. As I rode past the deserted roadblock, I turned around and cursed. Just to let some steam off, and even though I knew there was no point in doing so, I needed to curse this morbid situation, which would definitely carry on, regardless of what I did.

The sunrise caught me on the highway, with my helmet open, enjoying the morning breeze. I had 1,000km left to reach Brazzaville, the capital of Congo. I wanted to stop over at Makoua, where the imaginary line of the equator lies, but the weird noise of the engine forced me to stop much earlier. Moyoy – or something like that – was the name of the place I chose to stop to look into the new mechanical issue.

A little girl with skinny legs wearing a pink T-shirt, received me and stayed with me the entire time I spent checking the carburettor. I was sure that the problem came from there. I saw the disappointment in her eyes when I started the engine and rode off; however, she seemed to be in luck, as the scooter went quiet again a few metres away, leaving me perplexed. "I did everything right, why isn't it working?", I wondered and my bewilderment was soon accompanied by cussing. The little girl followed me to a shack nearby. The man who occupied it, eagerly allowed me to set up my tent right next to his home.

I eased up for a moment and chatted with him, before I tried starting the engine back up, more concentrated this time. I wouldn't find peace unless I discovered what caused the interruptions. And I soon did. A weld made by a mechanic back in Yaoundé, a month earlier, had been displaced. I was happy about my diagnosis. I'd be off next morning. I tried to crank it again. Tough break...

Around evening, the power generator behind the shack was turned on and the only lamp lit up. With it, the TV set, tuned into the soap opera network. One after the other, people that to me seemed to pop up out of nowhere, gathered around it and quietly watched the entire show. In the same mysterious way, when the generator stopped, they vanished, and the whole place plunged back into darkness. I even lost sight of the little girl in the pink T-shirt. I surrendered myself to a dreamless sleep, worn out and downhearted.

The next morning found me drinking coffee from my metal cup while planning out my trip to Brazzaville. Sure enough, a truck would come by at some point during the day. I would ask to load my belongings onboard and head south. I packed the tent and walked to the scooter. I landed an angry gaze on it for betraying me and then had a flash of inspiration. The previous afternoon, while trying to fix it, I turned the fuel tap off. I cranked the engine to get going, but I forgot to turn it on. So, after using up all the gasoline that was left in the fuel line, the engine died out. I bent over, turned the lever and the engine started to roar at once.

"I'm such a dimwit!" I yelled as I entered the highway.

THE CONGO?

The heavy cloudburst had turned the streets of Brazzaville into rushing cascades within minutes and the roadside ditches into death traps. I'd travelled all the way to the capital completely dry, but the menacing black clouds that were mustering overhead as I entered the city were an ill omen. I was straying around the streets of the outlying neighbourhoods looking for a place to stop and followed the traffic, without wandering off. I was afraid of the ditches, which gaped hidden underneath the water. The exhaust pipe of the scooter was submerged most of the time and the muffled bubbling sound it made was both funny and unsettling. All around me people were rushing to find shelter from the rain. Garbage and rotten vegetables that floated adrift in the streams, got trapped on my boots.

Right on the verge of despair, I saw a neon sign blinking right at me. The bright letters read "*Pizza*" and made me notice the small restaurant behind it. I propped up the scooter against the concrete curb and stepped inside. I was completely drenched, but Hassan, the owner, gave me a warm welcome. I don't know if he changed his mind when he saw the mud-spattered bathroom sink, but the pizza he made me was delicious.

I finished up my beer, my well-deserved reward for having travelled all the way to Brazzaville, and contacted Steven. I was certain that he'd have already done a web research on the cheapest accommodation in the area. I was right. In a little while I was at the hotel of a French guy, an avid traveller himself, who offered his yard with no charge to overlanders. This was his way of repaying the hospitality he'd received as a traveller over the previous years.

The days went by peacefully, waiting for Steven to arrive to sketch out the crossing of the other Congo, the big one. It wasn't long before he showed up along with Katrina, the Slovene cyclist, Francis, the weird Frenchman on the GS and two more travellers who I hadn't met before: B. from the Netherlands with his dog Simba, a Rhodesian Ridgeback born and bred in the African continent.

Lost in the streets of the city centre, discovering the *boulangeries* – the French colonists' legacy – we talked about our experiences until our arrival in Brazzaville. We took similar routes, depending on our time, mood and luck. My mind went back to Liam, who was still stuck in Ghana with no passport. Our hopes of meeting again on the road had been dashed. I remember when, back in Ouagadougou, we were planning our trip to Nigeria drinking *Brakina* – the local beer. I'd told him and Steven that I'd probably not go to the big Congo, the DRC. Liam's shock was such that it made me reconsider.

"*The Congo?*" he had exclaimed, his eyes rounded with surprised. "*You should definitely cross The Congo!*" and his enthusiasm was enough to convince me. And there I was, getting ready for *The Congo* without him.

Katrina came back almost crying, just a few hours after her attempt to cross the central border checkpoint. Kinshasa, the capital of the Democratic Republic of the Congo was right across the huge river, after which both countries were named. She explained that she had been forced to deal with hordes of *fixers*. The "processors", who we stumbled upon everywhere, are self-appointed, pestering factotums that congregate at the border and forcibly – for a convenient fee – take charge of the travellers' bureaucratic procedures. However, they were so pushy that she didn't know how to handle them. She'd also had to tackle the most corrupt police officers, who'd asked for 500 dollars to permit her to take her bicycle along. They subjected her to all sorts of coercions with the aim of screwing money out of her, and so she decided to come back instead.

We listened to her story carefully. The only solution was to travel further south, until we'd find a quiet passage.

COBRAS AND NINJAS

Three bikers, a cyclist, a car driver and a dog made up the team. It was our last day in Brazzaville and we couldn't wait to set out for the Democratic Republic of the Congo. After my solo trip to Cameroon and the Congo, I'd be travelling with company again.

I was wandering around the downtown, gazing at the skyscrapers of Kinshasa on the horizon. The sultry heat made the atmosphere stifling and a faint cloud had gathered in the sky right upon the neighbouring capital. The air smelled like rain. I turned around and started to walk back towards the hotel. Contrary to the *black neighbourhoods*, the city centre that was originally reserved for white residents only, was relatively quiet.

It was hard for me to imagine that it was barely fifteen years ago that the civil war, which cost the lives of so many people, had ended. The whole decade of the '90s was a turbulent period in the history of the Congo. From 1997 up until early 2000, the clashes on the streets of Brazzaville between paramilitary groups, supporting either the government or the opposition and forces from foreign countries and international organisations that intervened, left behind thousands of dead, injured and displaced, in a situation that would be almost impossible to reverse. I could hardly remember what part of all this had actually reached the ears of the Western world. The havoc, starting from the outskirts and extending to the capital, spread over to the poor districts of Poto-Poto, Bacongo and Makélékélé, and various militia under names such as the "Cobras" and the "Ninjas" slaughtered innocent people in the name of democracy and peace.

The first thick rain drops got me right at the doorstep of the hotel. The storm that followed simply obliterated any other storm I'd ever seen to that day from my memory. The sky gave in and the water that was pouring down no longer had the shape of drops. Its flow was so dense it looked as if someone had climbed up on the roof and was throwing buckets full of it just to pull a prank on us. We sat in the big lobby and watched, unable to go back to our tents and save anything that could be saved. When the clouds finally decided to change their ominous dark colour for a lighter shade, the rain let up and we were finally able to get out. In the yard, the sight was disheartening. The wind had lifted Katrina's tent and had thrown it on top of the rest. Some of my cooking pots had vanished, while others were floating around here and there. We rushed to the bikes; they were still standing!

The morning broke with not a single cloud in the sky. The weather always gets better if you wait long enough.

"Ready?" I asked Simba, who was watching us pack wagging her tail. That sunny morning of May, three bikers, a cyclist, a car driver and a dauntless dog set out for the other Congo. The big one.

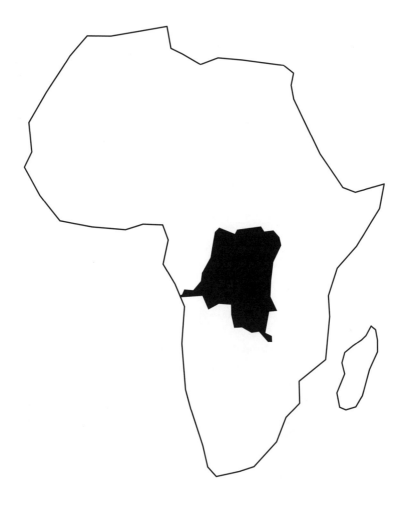

DEMOCRATIC REPUBLIC OF THE CONGO

FRONTIÈRE CONGO BELGE

The stone plate still stood almost intact, indicating the borders of the old colony. *"Frontière Congo Belge"* it read; a remnant of another time, which was meant to leave its indelible mark carved for good in every inch of this land. Apart from the plate, the only indication that we were now in a different country was the dramatic deterioration of the state of the road. About 100km south of Brazzaville, while we had got off the highway, the asphalt suddenly disappeared, and a strip of dirt took its place. Weathering pits and potholes made riding an arduous task, which demanded extreme caution and concentration.

B. with his dauntless doggy occupying the front seat, soon needed help. A truck had become stuck and blocked his way. It looked as though it'd been there for days, relieved of its burden, and without a single soul around. We stood there scratching our heads, trying to figure out what to do. A group of locals that happened to pass by gave us the solution. A bit further ahead, there was a hidden junction that led straight to the first village after the border, Ndalatando. The road to Lwozi, the point of departure for all kinds of vessels that set out to cross the Congo River, was not more than 50km away. However, we were so exhausted that we spent the night next to the police station of Ndalatando. There, on the following day we got our passports sealed, without complaining about the completely needless three-hour delay. None of us really cared about the time that went by.

We got to Lwozi relatively late and looked for the Catholic mission. It wasn't difficult to find. It seemed like a place used to receiving travellers. Most of them, though, continue south towards Angola, thus avoiding the rickety road network of the DRC as well as the country's bad reputation. We set up our fabric makeshift camp on the thick lawn of the yard, rejecting the luxury of rental rooms.

It was a feast day in the town and the locals, along with attired members of the Red Cross and a few more organisations, had flooded the streets. We mingled with the crowd and soon, unaware of what was actually being celebrated, we became part of the merrymaking. People followed us as if we were right under an invisible spotlight, and didn't let us take a step without giving us a handshake first.

Lwozi was a somewhat scruffy but colourful town. The mudbrick houses with tin roofs were all painted in the colours of some cellphone carrier, adding even more colour to the landscape – as if the women's multicoloured dresses weren't enough. At the market, huge piles of coffee, sugar and rice were stacked up in plastic pots. The only way sugar could be distinguished was by the thousands of flies sitting on it. We found a restaurant that stood out from the rest. Bigger and more attractive to the eyes of the foreigners – perhaps even the locals – but without a trace of luxury. We had one of the most disgusting river fish that I'd ever tasted and went back to the mission.

On the following day, we'd get to Kimpese and there, B. and Simba would go their own way. The night caught us talking. The Dutchman offered us cold beers from his fridge and Simba became a pillow for Francis' dizzy head. What an amazing companion a dog is! They're magical creatures, able to comfort people by their mere existence.

"What meds are you on for malaria?" B. asked. We all had our arguments to justify our decision not to pop any pills: either it was the terrible nightmares, probably their worst side effect, or the belief that, since we'd be spending a long time in Africa, we'd better not strain our kidneys for no good reason. B., meticulous and formal, never missed a dose. We turned to Francis, who had spent half his life in the long-suffering continent. With his eyes half-closed and his beer in his hand, lying on top of Simba, who seemed to enjoy the human weight on her back, he was ignoring us.

"What about you, Francis? Do you take any pills for malaria?", I asked him.

He opened his eyes, turned his head lazily and replied, nonchalantly with his markedly French accent, as he stroked the well-muscled haunches of the Rhodesian Ridgeback: "*Of course non!*"

Our laughter echoed throughout the entire mission. Only B. seemed startled at the recklessness of this guy, who was his own age.

WILDCAT STRIKE

"What do you mean 'the boat is not leaving?'" Francis repeated his question to the captain.

"We're on strike! A work stoppage" he answered and we had no choice but to respect the decision of the port employees to defend whatever rights they were fighting for. We headed back to the shack that was nearby. The Congo River in front of us kept flowing, oblivious to the human problems. We ordered some tea and found a shady spot to sit while waiting. The first sip brought the nauseating taste of a warm, rotten fish-smelling liquid to our mouths.

"It tastes like dish-washing wastewater!" I observed, spitting it out.

The strike was soon over. We got on the vessel with our vehicles, and along with some locals and animals that would probably cross the river for the last time. The tricky part awaited us at the opposite bank. The ramp of the ferry hinged open, but the distance to the concrete dock was suspiciously large. The brown water concealed a mystery under its murky surface. "Off we go, Kitsos!" I yelled as I ran up to take the plunge, throttle wide open and with the shock absorbers severely abused by the excessive weight. The scooter groaned and got up the mound, making me proud, but a bit further ahead, it took a little help from some men to get me pulled out of the mud. Francis' bike, due to its powerful engine and the momentum it had gained, ended up ramming into the bumper of the car ahead, which didn't have time to move forward. Steven on his light XT, marched off high and mighty like a conquistador, without the slightest effort. Without further ado, we set out for Kinshasa.

The little flags in the colours of the DRC were flapping, pinned on all the vehicles that made up our odd caravan. At Kimpese, we said goodbye to B. with a heartfelt handshake and to Simba with a few gentle strokes on the head and our paths parted. With Katrina's bicycle loaded on Francis' bike and herself riding on Steven's back seat, we moved on.

DAYS OF REARRANGEMENT

I was riding towards the hotel that we'd set as the meeting point with the rest of the group, in case we lost each other on the way. The boulevards of Kinshasa, completely jammed with an utterly chaotic and disorderly traffic were a genuine nightmare to me. *How the hell am I going to get out of here?* I wondered. The vehicles didn't follow any kind of rational order and looked as if they were abandoned in a huge, wildly absurd parking lot. Many drivers got off the road and tried to cut through the empty building plots that extended either side, ignoring the pedestrians and merchandise stands that were there. Honks and a lot of tension reached its peak when, right ahead of me a tall 4x4, in order to take revenge on a small bike that had made a sloppy pass, pulled up sharply and bumped against it, knocking all three female passengers off. The car driver and the rest of the passengers burst into laughter, until they got stuck in traffic, 5m ahead. Enraged locals gathered up from the surrounding area, and I, with desperate manoeuvres, managed to get away from there.

I felt so relieved when I reached the hotel. It wasn't long before the others showed up, too. The four of us, a shabby dissonance in the luxurious, baroque lounge, talked about how long we should stay in the noisy capital with the tall, modern buildings and the slums extending over kilometres at its edges. We didn't feel like spending too much time there; just a few days to rearrange ourselves. We looked forward to setting wheel to dirt again and getting lost within the green tropical forest.

Our host in Kinshasa was a French teacher, who we'd contacted online. Every afternoon after getting off work, he helped us find spare parts and everything else we needed for the bikes and ourselves and then we had dinner with him and a friend of his, a local woman who often stayed over.

One of those nights, as we were all sitting at the dinner table, the mysterious friend told us her story. Maybe it was the wine, or it might have been the fact that we were passers-by that made her trust us and pour her heart out to us. She came from a village in central Congo and it hadn't been long ago that she'd managed to arrive in Kinshasa in search of a better life. Her voice lowered as she quickly went over her adventures, without much detail, skipping to the part when she settled in one of the slums which, like mazes, surround the city centre. She finally got a job. Poorly paid like all of them and kilometres away from her home – a squalid room where the rain water leaked in and without power, running water or a toilet. With her salary, she had to pay for rent and food, as well as to send money back to her family, so that they could get by. The rest of the money was spent on transportation.

"You know, when the Congo was under Belgian rule, the locals weren't allowed to live in the city" our host told me. I knew that. I also knew that they still aren't. Now, however, the ban is unofficial and only stands for the underprivileged, in other words, the poor.

DAYS OF DISARRANGEMENT

"That's it! We'll go via Ilebo!", ordered Francis, probably fed up with our ceaseless yapping about what route we should take. I wasn't particularly stressed either, but I enjoyed getting into supposedly serious conversations with the well-organised Steven. The central road, which cut across Tshikapa and joined all the major cities of the country, was teeming with trucks which, due to the road's bad condition, regularly got stuck causing a headache to the rest of the drivers. We assumed that police checks would be more frequent along this route. So taking a northern detour, before heading back south to Lubumbashi, seemed like a good idea.

"Ilebo!", the three of us shouted, clinking our beers cheerfully. We were sitting in the bright yellow plastic chairs at a restaurant in Kenge. We didn't know when we'd meet Katrina again. She'd stayed back in Kinshasa to plan out her own route. I looked at Francis. He was as old as my father and as strong as a thirty-year-old. He didn't talk much about himself and seemed completely stress-free. From scattered, drunken chats, I'd inferred that, one fine day, Francis stopped stressing because stress nearly killed him. He travelled to get away from something, but it was no business of mine to figure out what. I turned to Steven. He was my age, dreaming of riding around Africa and – why not? – the whole world. He was weary of the German discipline and yet so imbued with it. And me, the bearded waiter from Greece, I was naively enthusiastic though wary of anything taken for granted. I couldn't tell whether it was the cold alcohol or the enthusiasm, but I felt my heart pounding every time I thought of what we were about to do. I had no illusions of us being extraordinary explorers, or that we had any special abilities whatsoever. It would be ridiculous of me to think that, when the locals' daily lives consisted of undertaking what many foreigners considered achievements worth bragging about.

"Back in '95 lots of people died of Ebola here", Francis told us at some point, and we laughed. We thought he was trying to make a joke out of the situation following the epidemic of the virus that had broken out a few months ago in western Africa. Ebola seemed to be hot on our tracks. Every country we crossed, shortly after our passage, entered the list of the afflicted areas and we exchanged jokes, in an feckless attempt to rid ourselves of the wretched reality of the people who died helpless, away from any sort of health system structure. Steven had once read that the deadly disease was named after a river somewhere in the north of the Congo. How sad it was that even that information was meant to add to the already bad reputation of a country that seemed so special!

Kikwit, about 500km east of Kinshasa, was the last time we'd lay wheels on asphalt.

"This is sand!" I realised in anger, while sinking. At first, riding on a path through the forest, a path which the map called a highway, was fun. But as we moved on, things were going from

186

bad to worse. I couldn't understand how vegetation so dense could grow on sand as fine as powder. I couldn't believe that, although I'd only moved a few kilometres, my arms and back hurt so much. At some point, the path widened. From then on, we had to remain in two parallel furrows, left behind by passing-by trucks. That was the road. Francis was groaning, erect on his bike, struggling not to fall off. I no longer felt like messing with him about his heavy GS. I was gasping so hard, I could hardly speak. Steven on his enviable XT, had the same trouble keeping his balance on the frail ground.

"Oh, for FUCK'S SAKE!" I screamed in my mother tongue. I knew that, although they didn't speak Greek, my fellow travellers understood exactly how I felt. As I lay on the ground, with Kitsos tilted to the opposite side, the deep wheel-ploughed ditch seemed like a bottomless gorge. The panniers bumped the sides and at the first swerve I'd lose control and fall flat on the fluffy sand. My pouring sweat stuck it to my skin and made my eyes smart. Steven, every once in a while, had to dump his own bike and come pull me.

At some point, as we were sitting in the shade of a tree to catch our breath before throwing ourselves back into the struggle, I spat it out. My voice got low-pitched and dull and my eyes lowered. I wiped my muddy face clean with my scarf.

"Screw this, I'll turn around and head to Angola!" I said and at once turned my eyes away, to avoid theirs.

"*No!*" their opposition resounded in unison.

"There's no way, man, *there's no way!*" I dared to utter but I immediately regretted it. I was the one who always said that everything is possible.

It was right then that I realised the importance of travelling with those two. Interrupting each other, without stopping talking at the same time only to say pretty much the same thing, they were trying hard to dissuade me.

"We're a team!" one of them said.

"We won't let you!" the other one added.

"Plus, we've placed a bet that we'll get whacked!", they teased me.

"We want to see your scooter fall to pieces!"

With a round of both hilarious and serious arguments, they got me to come around. I looked at them and smiled.

"Fine, but I'm just doing it for you" I told them jestingly. We shook hands and got up.

LOOKS LIKE HE'S WASTED!

"Looks like he's wasted", I told Francis, pointing at Steven stumbling around, bottle of whiskey in hand. I was sitting on the floor. In front of me, a bunch of pasta – both boiled and raw – was spilt on the concrete floor. Huge crimson stains went along with it and I was trying to stir the remainder in the pot, avoiding further casualties. My forehead burned. Now and then, I would sweep the sweat off the tip of my nose; when I was too slow, it would just drip into the boiling pot.

"And you're sober, right?", Francis replied. I sure wasn't! After an entire day's riding we'd barely moved 100km in the most incredible conditions we had experienced so far. The three of us had been struggling to help and cheer each other up, with our feet slipping on the fine sand and our heads at the mercy of the scorching sun.

It was getting dark when we finally made it to the mission where we'd spend the night. We didn't get into the city centre; our quick passage by its edges barely showed us any evidence that it was inhabited by sixty thousand people. Each shack had its own yard and plenty of green, enclosed in a wooden fence. The layout of the neighbourhoods was cut up and measured, as if with a straightedge, into squares. Square houses, square yards – all square. The thick vegetation and the earthen alleys, some of them only wide enough to fit a bicycle, made Idiofa look like a tiny village. Only the engines of our motorcycles disturbed its peacefulness, startling the heck out of a few chickens that were carelessly pecking around.

Like a buzzing beehive, the kids surrounded us at the yard of the mission and I, as usual, mustered up all the courage I had left and spent some time playing with them. I'd always get worn down by children's inexhaustible energy and, though it had never crossed my mind to have some of my own, these little fellas, with their gurgling laughter and the sobriety of an adult that their eyes emitted at times, made me want to hang out with them.

"Stop talking to them, I have a headache!" Francis complained and, as a good teacher, got up and told them off. The caretaker of the place rushed in to help out. He closed the gate of the fence and had a serious talk with them in *Kikongo* – the language spoken in the area. As gritty as usually kids their age are, these little rascals took advantage of the lack of fencing in the back; they were soon back in and started poking me. How could I possibly ignore them?

When their parents' calling made the last of them disappear, I reached into my bag and took a couple of whiskey bottles out. We'd bought them a few days earlier, just in case. We were exhausted, but the feeling of fulfilment after reaching our first goal – just to withstand – gave us energy.

"Let's celebrate!" I said and opened the first bottle. The level of the strong liquor soon went down. Our flushed faces and our uncontrollable laughter caught the attention of a chaplain, who cheerfully joined us for a slug. I don't know if I was speaking Greek, French or Kikongo that night. The only thing I can remember is that I kept laughing.

A HELPING HAND

The following dawn, Steven was good to go, I was a bit sluggish, and Francis sound asleep, half his trunk and his feet hanging out of the tent. A strong coffee and a bucket of water was all it took to sober up and within a little while we had loaded the bikes. We had no expectations of the road network getting any better, and our attempts to collect any information from the locals were in vain since, for some reason, every person we asked told us what they assumed we wished to hear.

Another day of plunges and falls, exhaustion and cursing and the amazing feeling that, despite all hardship, we were in one of the friendliest places ever. Countless times, while trying to pick the scooter up, someone would show up out of nowhere and come to my rescue. People would stretch their hand out to wave hello, to help me up from the ground, to offer something. Nevertheless, the gruesome stories from the time of the colonists and afterwards, when various warlords incited inter-ethnic hatred, were going around in my mind. Looking at the Congolese, I couldn't believe that it was a helping hand they stretched out – but it was!

Late that night, we arrived at an anonymous village, wiped out. After a meal consisting of rice and antelope skin, which I was the only one willing to chew on, I went straight into my tent, longing to fall asleep. Outside, there were breaths and whispers of the children who just wouldn't go home. Amidst the haze of exhaustion and the kids' mumbles, I started to reflect on where I was. I was in a country which, up until the early 20th Century, was private property of a single person: King Leopold II of Belgium. I couldn't believe my eyes when I saw the pictures of the "savages'" mutilated hands – victims of the king's personal army. The hands that willingly stretched out now belonged to the descendants of those who, one hundred years ago, posed sadly for the camera with their forearms hanging like branches and their generous palms chopped off.

THE LAST CLUTCH

We were about 150km far from Ilebo, but every day that passed, our speed reduced.

"Right, now some rain to top it all off!" I gave the dark clouds above us a piece of my mind. The tropical vegetation there was not dense enough to hold back, even the slightest bit, the torrential streams that flowed over to the road. The two parallel ruts left behind by the trucks, were overflowed with water, and in no time our bikes were drowning.

"It's impossible to move on", Steven observed. Without second thought, we dumped the bikes half-submerged right where they had tilted, and took refuge under a broadleaved bush in an attempt to save ourselves from the downpour. I don't know how long we had to wait exactly, but at some point the rain finally stopped. As if by magic, the thirsty sand had absorbed the water thus creating a somehow harder surface, which seemed safer for us to step on. The bikes didn't sink as easily into the wet, compact ground either. We seized the opportunity that had shown up before us and, before the road got completely dry, set forth. We were careful not to lose eye contact with each other and, every time one of us fell, soon someone went up to help him get back up.

Over the last few days, our mood had been constantly subject to successive swings, which we were unable to manage. One moment, when exhaustion beat us down, we'd sink into deep depression, almost despair. And the next, when we reached some village and were received with smiles, we felt high as a kite. Our sore bodies and ceaseless mood swings were so tiresome, that at night we'd collapse in our tents and drift into a sound sleep, as if we'd been pharmaceutically sedated.

When I saw the slope ahead of me, I knew it would be hard. I started in first gear, controlling the throttle and with my hand on the clutch. My feet pushed along digging in the sand that was dry again and, with extreme concentration and caution, I started to ascend.

"Ah, you BURNED them, you idiot!" I uttered with frustration, when I smelled the distinct aroma of the half-burned clutch-plates. Immediately my disappointment at myself flared up into a crescendo of rage. I tossed the helmet, cursed about the tangled cable of the camera microphone, stomped the ground angrily and crouched down beside the scooter, trying to pull myself together. Shortly after, my fellow travellers showed up. We decided that they'd move on, to scout around the area and then come back for me. The discs were not entirely burned but the clutch had reached its limit. I then realised that it was the last straw. I'd miscalculated the supplies I'd have to ask my mechanic for, and when the package from Greece got to Kinshasa, along with the spare parts and the good-wishes cards of my friends, unfortunately there was only one valuable set of discs.

"Poor Kitsos, hang in there!" I started talking to the exhausted, inanimate metal pieces. With lots of sand stuck on my bald scalp, grazing it every time I wiped the sweat off my head, I started unloading the scooter. I carried my luggage all the way to the top of the slope, pushed the bike along to the same spot and stretched out under the shade of a tree. It was one of those rare times that the passers-by were scarce. Three hours would have passed, when, while in a state of drowsy alertness, I heard the sound of a motorcycle. I was dreaming and my dreams were blended with blurry memories from Greece. I might have dreamed of my home, too. However, it all faded away when Francis showed up. A few kilometres ahead, they had bumped into an hospitable village, where they'd offered us their church to spend the night in. The lads had unloaded, put their stuff in and then Francis came back to get me.

NICE PEOPLE

The village church, a building made with sparse planks, thatched roof and mudbrick walls that didn't reach all the way up to the roof, had become our temporary shelter. Along the horizontal beams that supported it, we hung our clothes which was a quite funny sight. The rain and the sweat, which had dried up on our bodies repeatedly, gave them a foul mouldy smell. From the earthen floor, Y-shaped pieces of wood were placed vertically, so as to support the two extremes of the reed trunks which, fixed horizontally onto the wooden brackets, formed some really uncomfortable benches. We were about to cook dinner, but Francis hadn't shown up yet. When he came to get me at the top of the damn slope, we loaded all of my stuff on his bike and I rode ahead, with the unburdened Vespa moving with relative ease for the first time.

"How long has it been?", I asked Steven, concerned.

"Long enough", he replied.

We suspected that there was something wrong. Steven got on his XT which, without any luggage could now move almost without any trouble on the road, and sped off. I started to order our stuff nervously. I needed a distraction while waiting for the two of them to get back safe and sound. In the end, they showed up, standing on their motorbikes. I rushed out and before they even had time to dismount, I started asking. Francis, cursing, explained to me that at some mound his bike turned over and fell right on his leg in such a way that it was impossible for him to get up. He wasn't seriously injured, but no one happened to pass by and help him, until eventually Steven appeared.

"Poor gramps!" I told him jokingly, "I told you that the GS is no good for stunts like these!" He smiled, let out some swearword in French and, leaning on our shoulders, led us into the church.

"Tonight's drinks are on me!" he promised and took the last bottle of wine out of his bag.

The entire village had surrounded the church. The kids stuck their little heads into the spaces between the mudbricks, which looked like crenels, and watched us unwaveringly. Every time I lifted the camera to take a picture of them, they cracked up and at once, all the "crenels" became frames for smiling faces that posed cheerfully.

The nocturnal tranquillity was succeeded by a noisy morning, and two of the eminences of the village came up to greet us. We offered them tea and they told us that it was a great honour for them that we had sought hospitality in their village. It was the first time they'd received white people and all the villagers were elated. We thanked them for everything they'd offered us and we shook hands. How could we explain to them that it was a great honour for us too, to meet such nice people?

BRIDGES

"Only 120 more kilometres left and we're there," I said, laughing sarcastically. Ilebo was nowhere to be seen! The area through which we were struggling was full of rivers of all sizes and the tropical vegetation had become prolific once again. Be it small streams or the great Kasai River, the last water barrier before Ilebo, we always had to work out ways of crossing. I'd stopped counting my falls and those of the others. The big jerrycan filled with fuel, which I'd placed on the floor of the scooter, rolled off at every jolt, forcing me to stop and lift it back inside all the time, cursing. I fell, and as I got back up and pulled the bike along, I lost my balance and fell flat on my back again at the opposite side. I laughed, cursed and move on. At sight of a decent, if only relatively, dirt trail I cried in joy, until the next turn, when the harrowed sand appeared again and the nightmare resumed. The constant shifts – from heaven to hell – were driving me nuts. I wasn't thinking about anything, just kept looking straight ahead so as not to lose my grit. At some point, the ordeal would be over.

We'd hoisted and pushed each other countless times, until we got to Loange River, a tributary of the Kasai, with plenty of water but a relatively smooth flow. On the map, it looked like a tiny, barely perceivable line, but in real life, this couldn't be further from the truth. We headed to the bridge. We'd crossed tumbledown bridges before, but this particular one, an iron carcass with sparse boards and two metal rails in the middle, did not seem safe at all. Our only option was to load our bikes on the little dugout canoes that crossed both people and merchandise over to the opposite bank. The boatmen skilfully pulled the XT and the Vespa onboard. My heart was pounding in terror. The dugouts were so narrow that the slightest sway became a dangerous abrupt see-sawing and I dreaded that Kitsos might fall into the water. Francis' GS, though, was way too heavy to be loaded on the flimsy vessels. He had no choice but to leave it in the hands of the experienced porters, who would balance it pushing it along one of the two rails of the bridge.

"One bag less to carry!" he said as he unloaded his luggage off the bike and hoisted it on his shoulders. Something was missing from his equipment. He'd dumped one of the panniers. The day before, the plastic, rigid case had been caught on a big branch, making him lose his balance and fall off. He nearly got seriously injured. Furious, he tossed it onto the side of the road and moved on.

From the dugout, I watched those who were crossing the bridge. With acrobatic wobbles, they were trying to stand on its scattered boards. Women with suitcases and all sorts of packages on top of their heads hopped from one board to the next, until getting to the other side. Was this bridge ever in good shape, or maybe its construction was left unfinished? There were so many things in Africa that seemed incomplete. They were either abandoned to their fate, with no sign of maintenance, or down right unfinished. In the Congo, as if fleeing hastily in the dead of night, the Belgian colonial regime seemed to have ditched everything as it was. Infrastructure, buildings and road networks lingered on in abandonment. But people were still there and life moved on, with whatever was left.

KASAI

I can't even remember how I travelled the last 90km to the bank of the Kasai River. Past the Loange River, we left the Bandundu

Province behind and entered the Kasai District – yet another region named after the main river that flowed across it. It was late in the evening, and the big boat that would take our bikes and us across the river had been moored at the opposite bank for the night. It was to resume its itinerary the following morning.

The river water rolled idly in such a way that, as I watched it while sitting under the shade of a tree, I felt hypnotised. The calmness was now and then interrupted by a child's voice or the engine sound of some boat that passed by in the background. A woman, with her curly hair woven into antler-like braids, was washing clothes in the river and her baby's little head peeped out of the piece of cloth that was wrapped around her back. With my eyes half-closed, I tried to remember when the last time I'd thought back to my life in Greece was. It was as if I no longer was the same person, as if the person I was before had never existed. And yet, the next moment I felt I was exactly the same and that nothing had changed about me, except for having adapted to the new conditions I came across every day. None of those plunges into the sand made me want to go back. Not once did I reminisce about the past. *How strange!*

I got up and headed back to the village on the riverside. It only consisted of a few shacks. Mudbrick, with thatch roofs, they lay amphitheatrically on the slanted ground by the water. Two or three of them looked like little stores that probably served cooked food. I smiled at the people around me and they smiled back, whatever it was they were doing at that moment. They were either cooking or carrying a sheaf of wood. None of them refused to pose for my camera. The men put on their most solemn look and stood straight and proud. The women had a stern look on their face, which however wasn't enough to conceal their desire to be photographed. Some of them summoned their children up and hugged them, to show what loving parents they were. It reminded me of my father, in those photos back when I was a toddler and he held me in his arms. Back when his moustache was still black and whatever was left of his hair, brown. Back when life hadn't worn him down just yet.

"I wish you were here to talk to me about colonialism", I told him, though I knew he couldn't hear me.

The night went by peacefully and we enjoyed the sunrise, spurred by the cockerels which had started crowing enthusiastically.

"I'll go order some breakfast", said Francis, who, as the French speaker of the group, took charge of most of our communication, sparing us the trouble. When the blue plastic tray with the matching jugs, little dishes and cups arrived, we burst out laughing.

"That's all we needed, a full breakfast set!" said Steven and tore the instant coffee and powder milk pockets open.

"I just hope the water doesn't smell like fish!", I replied, reminding everyone of the disgusting beverage that we were offered while waiting to cross the Congo River, some time ago.

The boat that would take us across the river soon showed up. It was a dugout canoe like no other of its kind. A huge tree trunk floating on the river, big enough to fit the three bikes and a dozen men together with their luggage. The trip wasn't too long. When the opposite bank came into clear sight, the industrial facilities of the port emerged through the palm trees. Ilebo, once named *Port-Francqui* by the Belgians, in honour of some prominent compatriot of theirs, was an important commercial hub in the 20th Century. Copper and other ores from the rich mines of Katanga, in the southeast, arrived from Lubumbashi via railway. At the port of Ilebo, they got loaded on ships and sailed down the Kasai, up to the point where it meets the Congo and, along it, they ended their voyage at Kinshasa. However, the turbulent history of the country, the problems and the inadequate maintenance almost led to the closure of this passage and today the main bulk of the mineral wealth of the Congo, before reaching every corner of the world, travels to South Africa by road first.

The dugout was ready to berth, when a group of about twenty men that were gathered at the dock caught our attention. As soon as we tied up, they rushed onboard and started unloading our luggage and our bikes. They were all young and strong, raggedly dressed. Their faces, rough and tired, bore witness of the hardships of their everyday life. Their bodies were so muscular, that they'd stir the envy of all Western fitness freaks that spend hours on end in urban gyms. They claimed a tip for the porter services they offered and, whenever someone else barged in and got it out of their hands, they shouted angrily and raced to the next piece of luggage. In the battle for survival there was no room for smiling.

HÔTEL DES PALMES

I stepped out to the balcony. Francis, sitting in the plastic chair, cigarette in hand, was gazing at the view. In front of us spread the weedy hotel yard and beyond, the tumbledown fence. A tilted lamp post, which probably illuminated the entire lot once, dominated the space. Next to it, two satellite dishes with no apparent reason of existence. Beside the French guy, I noticed – standing on the tattered floor – a bottle of banana liqueur.

"How can you drink this stuff?" I asked. As I brought it up to my nose, the alcohol fumes burned my nostrils.

"Do you know when this hotel was built?" he replied, changing the subject.

The faded inscription on the facade was barely legible: "*Hôtel des Palmes*", it read. Its size was imposing, compared to the other buildings around it, and its location, at a beautiful and quiet spot of Ilebo, was privileged. As we crossed the door sill, the cool breeze that was captured within gave us goose-bumps and the chess-patterned floor made us dizzy. At the reception lobby sat two tattered burgundy red velvet couches. Right behind them, in a showcase, a few African art statuettes were on display and among them stood a white Virgin Mary looking at them condescendingly. Opposite the entrance, stood the heavy wooden staircase, which led to the first floor. Halfway there, it split in two, forming a landing step. I went up the squeaky stairs. I stopped and turned around to look at the ground level again. The sun, streaming through the window behind me, cast its rays on the round, rustic chandelier. It was so big, it seemed like it took all the wood from an entire tree for it to be made and it hung right in the middle of the ceiling. "*How did we end up here?*" I wondered.

The doors of the rooms on the first floor – the ones that were still in place – surrounded the indoor balcony with the elaborately carved railings. The attendant, who spent his day lying on the couch, made clear to us that we didn't need any keys. Everything looked long abandoned to its fate. The furniture was dusty and moth-eaten. There was a filthy mattress on the double bed and a shabby bathtub standing pointlessly in the bathroom. There was no running water. Or power. If we wanted to take a shower, one of the women should bring the bucket upstairs. As usual, we'd charge our cellphones and laptops at one of the stores in town, which offered that service.

I learned about the story of the hotel and started to visualise the glory of its past. In the early 20th Century, when Leopold II decided that he had no choice but to render the Congo – which until then was his property – to the government of his country as a colony, Ilebo was already a very important city for the sectors of commerce and transportation. A few years later, his heir to the throne, Albert I, found out about the atrocities perpetrated by his predecessor, which had reduced the country's population by half. Being a good Christian, he began to care a bit more about his "savage" subjects, who were being decimated. He travelled all the way to the tropical forests of the Belgian territory and in 1928 arrived at Ilebo to inaugurate the railway and coastal navigation routes, which connected the inexhaustible mines of the South to the Atlantic Ocean. It was then that the *Hôtel des Palmes* was built, since the reception of the king should be made with pomp and circumstance.

"I guess we'll sleep on the same bed as Albert!" I said, looking at the neglect and decay around me.

Waiting for Francis and Steven, who had decided to set their tents on the floor and sleep there instead of the royal beds, I walked out in the yard. I looked at the two-storey building. Painted white, with blue details and wooden window shutters, wrought iron railings on the unified balconies and a slanted roof with flat, dark-coloured tiles, it had been standing there for almost a century, waiting for someone to stay in its luxurious rooms, now eaten away by neglect and woodworm. *We're its only guests – go figure!* I thought and felt like I was playing a tiny part in the history of this place.

IL-EST-BEAU!

"*Il-est-beau!*" – It's pretty! – I spelled out the name of the town that had accommodated us for the past three or four days, feeling proud of myself for this French wordplay. Francis looked at me.

"I said it right, didn't I?" I asked.

"You're getting better!" he assured me. We were sitting in the shade, leaning on the wall of a store painted in the colours of Brasimba – the historical Congolese brewery, founded in the '20s. As I was sipping on my cold beer, I decided to share some of my knowledge with my French friend.

"Somewhere around here Lumumba was arrested in 1960", I said. "Who knows what this wretched country would look like if they'd let him govern!" I added. He clenched his lips together and puffed some smoke out indifferently. He had those huge, ridiculous sunglasses on, the ones we bought when we first got to Ilebo and I found it particularly hard to look at him and not laugh. We'd bought one pair each and thought we might make a skit video wearing them, a parody of the serious looking, heroic travellers with epic achievements and grandiose titles. We'd already pictured the shooting process, and we couldn't wait to take our own epic dives into the dirt, always with a haughty look and impeccable style!

I turned to the waiter and asked for two more beers. He smiled and vanished to the end of the street. I looked at Francis, bewildered.

"He has only two beers in stock" he said. "How could he keep them cool with no power?" As we waited for our beers, another customer came in. With slow, almost ritual movements, he pulled a chair into the shade. He took a transistor radio out of the pocket of his jacket and started zapping through the stations. Soon, among the interference, Congolese rumba burst into the place, touching the thoughts and movements of everyone. The chubby ladies in their colourful skirts holding their parasols, walked as if dancing. The well-built men that passed by on their overloaded bicycles seemed to be moving effortlessly. The children in their school uniforms tapped their fingers to the rhythm and suddenly the chores awaiting them back home seemed less dull. A truck full of workers was honking and the passengers onboard started whistling and waving.

"I want to live here!" As soon as these words had come out of my mouth, I knew I meant them more than Francis actually thought.

"You've had too much to drink", he replied.

TYPHOID FEVER, MALARIA AND MENINGITIS

We were headed back to the hotel. We'd been out almost all day and looked forward to getting back. The doctor would arrive any minute. Poor Steven; he hadn't had much time to enjoy the strolls around the markets of Ilebo and the cold beer. As early as the second day, he started feeling bad and, within only a few hours, fever and malaise had him bedridden. When the doctor, along with the male nurse, walked into the *Hôtel des Palmes*, we were already there, waiting on them impatiently. Steven, lying on the rickety bed, was sweating and silently enduring bone and joint pain. Through the IV catheter that pierced his vein, the physician poured a bunch of antibiotics and other medicines, the names and active ingredients of which we tried hard to figure out by looking them up on the internet.

"It doesn't look like malaria", the doctor assured us. "Typhoid fever, perhaps".

"But he's had the shot" answered Francis. "Haven't you?", he turned to Steven, who flinched with pain.

"It says here that these cure meningitis and lots of other bacteria too", I cut in pointing at the box. "And gynaecological issues, as well!" I cracked a clumsy joke in an attempt to make them laugh even a little bit.

I'd never been interested in drugs and illnesses. Right before setting out, I went to the local hospital and got all the vaccines that were recommended to me. I didn't want to push my luck.

Francis went out with the doctor and I stayed a little longer with Steven. He soon fell asleep and I decided to head out for a stroll. The bar Francis and I used to hang out in was not far from the hotel, but that day I felt like walking a little. In the city, cars were hard to find. A couple of 4x4s with the badges of the United Nations and the Red Cross passed by now and then. Maybe a couple of trucks, too. The locals either walked or rode their bicycles to get around. A few of them had motorbikes, which were the only vehicles disturbing the tranquillity of the place somewhat more often.

With the camera always hanging from my neck, I walked around the market. Smells of food mixed with the reek of the open sewers had my appetite confused. A woman stood beside me for a moment. She was holding a basin on her head, full of desiccated animals. A few monkeys and some rodents jutted out from the edges of the plastic container, dusky and stiff, making me sick. *Everything is edible here!* I realised in amazement and went on my way in search of my own sustenance. I thought I might cook some rice on my stove, but the prices at the market were really tempting. I could gorge myself for less than one euro and I needed about the same amount for a big bottle of beer. I hunched over a plastic basin, which apparently contained something edible. I saw some plump caterpillars, served on skewers. The woman who sold them laughed when she saw me take a startled step back. I'd seen caterpillars as snacks in markets before and although these were chubbier they looked just as disgusting.

The splendid smell of grilled meat met my nostrils; I had no idea where it came from, but I followed its trail and bumped into Francis. There he was, sauntering around with his brand-new gloves on and joking with the locals.

"Let's go grab a bite," I suggested and he followed, holding a cob of boiled corn he'd bought to go with his beer. Eventually we got to the source of the majestic smell. A woman was standing behind the grill. We took a better look. The grill in fact wasn't a grill; it was the set of metal coils found in the rear of a fridge which had been imaginatively re-purposed.

"Don't ask what kind of meat it is, just grab it and let's go!" Francis advised me.

"I had no intention of asking", I replied, with my mouth full.

ANOTHER WHITE MAN!

That morning, one of the employees of the hotel told us that we were the first white people to set foot in Ilebo since 2014. It was nearly June and they hadn't seen any other white men in town. For the first time in four days, the three of us went out for a walk downtown. Steven was finally off bed rest, strong and feverless. We visited one last time our favourite beer joint, right across from a low building that housed the local bank office. We'd leave the following day and we wanted to say goodbye to the man with the transistor, whose music kept us company, and the kind waiter who took long-haul trips to bring us the next round.

"I seriously thought that the second shot would make my heart stop!", Steven confessed after ordering his beer. "It reminded me of that time in India when I got sick and they gave me cow medicines!"

We were sitting languorously in the plastic chairs when a bicycle ridden by a white man emerged before our eyes.

"Hey look! Another white man in our town!" I yelled and jumped off my seat. It was a Scottish cyclist. He'd taken roughly the same course as we had, but he was exhausted and regretted having loaded his stuff on a trailer, which he had to tow along at all times. He was looking for another way to get to Lubumbashi, which was still more than 1,500km away.

The Scot went on his way and the three of us walked among the shacks and the tall grass, heard once more the little kids who were chasing us shouting *"Le blanc, l' argent!"* – White man, money! – and got back to our beloved *Hôtel des Palmes*. The guard, armed to the teeth but with a relaxed and a leisure gait that did not fit at all with the machine gun hanging from his shoulder, greeted us. And so did all the employees at the ghost hotel.

The following day we got up early. Dawn was breaking and the clouds were a pale pink shade. The morning dew made nature look greener still. We were getting our bikes ready to leave the town we'd made our home for a week.

"What if you left me here?" I said jokingly. "I'll live in a palace, with internet, I already know my way around...". Steven and Francis laughed. They didn't realise that Ilebo and its hospitable inhabitants had found their way into my heart. I was sad to be leaving.

COME ON, GRAMPS, YOU CAN DO IT!

Less than 10km past Ilebo, the road went rough again. The locals, without being aware of the state it was in, had assured us that it wouldn't be that bad, but what we saw once we got out of the city, took us back to the nightmare of the previous days. Francis looked exhausted. He had more trouble getting back up after each fall.

"Come on gramps, you can do it!", I tried to cheer him up. "You're only 62!" I shouted to him, admiring his stamina.

Even Steven had more falls now. I, on the other hand, found it easier to count the times I managed to stand, even for just a minute. I tried to keep the handlebars straight with all my strength and "scanned" the road for bicycle tracks, which would lead me to more solid ground. I remembered when, right before getting to Ilebo, I was lying flat on the road after a good fall and, as if nothing had happened, leisurely asked the women who were looking at me for directions to the nearest town. This was how familiar I'd grown with lying on the ground.

On the following day, Francis' GS had had it. With its clutch burned out, there was no way he could continue; he had to load it on a truck and either go back to Kinshasa, or forward to Lubumbashi. His wit and good spirits were gone. Frustrated, he sat on the side of the road, soaked in sweat and with a backache.

"Guys, I'll stay here and wait for a truck to pick me up" he said determinedly.

"Will you be OK on your own?" I asked, not keen to leave him.

"I'll be fine, you go ahead", he assured us.

Maybe this breakdown was what he needed. He was exhausted, but he didn't want to give up. Now he had to. I gave him a bottle of water before we took off. Francis didn't carry much stuff with him. Whenever he was hungry, he ordered a portion of anything available. Whenever he was thirsty, he always found a beer. As he used to say, by avoiding drinking water, he avoided getting water poisoning. We gave each other a hug. As I honked goodbye, Kitsos' honk sounded loud and uplifting.

KINSHASA – LUBUMBASHI: THE END!

At the mission of Domiongo, the only thing that could be heard in the dark was the crickets. After filtering some water to drink, we took a bucket bath and went to bed exhausted. On our way out the next day, we got some bottles of gasoline. We struggled to convince the attendant that the quantity of one litre – for which he already charged us too much – was one finger below the neck of the bottle instead of two thirds of the entire bottle. He didn't seem to want to rip us off, but his insistence was testing my patience. I was about to burst with anger. Steven with a strict look on his face, which he rarely recurred to, proved to be more patient than me and in the end he convinced him.

"This is what I like about us travelling together", I told him as we left. "When one of us gets mad, the other steps in and saves the day".

A bit further ahead, at the police road-block we stumbled upon, it was Steven's turn to nearly blow up in rage. While I was talking to the police officers, he remained quiet, as his patience had already been used up. We weren't able to go past the control in question pretending that we hadn't noticed it, so the cookie jar game which I started playing with them went on for quite a while. They wanted to make us unload the bikes, supposedly to search through our stuff.

"What you ask of us is really difficult"

"No, it isn't"

"It is!"

"Is NOT!"

They realised that the whole thing was pointless and that we weren't willing to pay them to let us go, either. Finally they let us through. Our joy, however, wasn't meant to last. The nightmarish road, full of sand and relentless slopes, went on and all hope of it getting better had vanquished. About 100 sweaty kilometres after Domiongo, the last threadbare clutch discs were burned. Kitsos went silent and I could do nothing about it.

"I'll be fine, you go ahead" I echoed Francis' words just the day before, and Steven left honking.

THERE ARE REBELS HERE!

I'd been dozing off for over four hours at the side of the road. At the slightest noise, I jumped up hoping that I'd see a vehicle.

"Don't stay here, there're rebels in the area and you're in danger!" the few passers-by warned me, but I refused to believe them. Throughout the ill-fated history of the Congo there had always been groups of rebels violently claiming their rights over territories, wealth or, simply, food. I'd heard about massacres, pillage, rape, kidnappings and many more atrocities. Sometimes, it is nearly impossible for the human mind to conceive how people can become, from one minute to the next, either victims or perpetrators. Two months earlier, a little while after I'd reached Cameroon, I heard the news about yet another kidnapping of three hundred female students by Boko Haram, in a town called Chibok, in the north of Nigeria. Nobody knew whether they were still alive, and I feared that the raising of awareness in the Western world of this issue was, as always, ephemeral.

What if I'm in for trouble? I thought.

When the night was about to fall, I decided to trust a man that was passing. I asked him to help me push the scooter all the way to the nearest village. Tough break! My feet, at the slightest effort, would dive into the soft sand making me lose my balance. It was impossible to lift any weight off the loaded bike and, no matter how used Guillaume was – the thoughtful peasant – to walking on this kind of soil he ended up gasping for air just like me. Erique, a young man that we happened to run into, eagerly offered to help us, and when Guillaume asked yet another passer-by, Besame, for his help, pushing the scooter turned into a fun business! I kept stumbling in a hilarious way, while at the same time I commended them for their skills and they laughed hard.

We reached the edge of the next village, about 5km away, and a few villagers came up curious to find out more details about our arrival. Without giving it much thought, I bought some puffy fried doughnuts from the first woman with a food stand I saw and offered them to my companions. Right before they left, I also decided to give each of them one dollar. I was embarrassed. Although I knew they didn't expect any money in exchange for their help anyway, the amount still seemed too small. I called them up and gave them the money. Their faces brightened up and their eyes glowed with joy. Then I remembered how much the average wage of a worker in the Congo is and I understood...

HELLO MISTER, WHAT IS YOUR NAME?

The news about the arrival of a white man spread like fire in a pine grove, and the first few curious villagers were soon followed by the entire village. Just as everywhere else in Africa, where life expectancy rarely exceeds 60 years and the customs along with necessity, lead to the birth of many children, countless schoolkids gathered around me. "Hello mister, what is your name?" they asked me all of them, one by one, showing off their knowledge of English. *At least there is a school in the village!* I thought. I patiently repeated the exact same answer over thirty times. I didn't want to displease any of them. But children are tireless! As I closed my eyes to go to sleep, I felt their breaths barely a hand span away from my face. They saw it as a game and, every time I opened one eye and made as if to grab them, their laughter resounded around the perimeter like a blast wave.

It was past ten when I heard the menacing moan of a truck through the woods. Soon, I could make out its headlights, too. The previous truck that had passed, asked for an exorbitant amount to take me 200km further, to Kananga, and I simply refused to get on. I jumped up and signalled with my flashlight. It stopped. After some bargaining to come up with a fare to Kananga that would be just for everyone, the driver and five of the passengers, apparently his assistants, grabbed my stuff and the Vespa and loaded them on the cargo area. We'd seen many rolled-over vehicles lying around dishevelled on the sides of the road and the image haunted me, but there was no other choice. Around midnight, the driver hit first gear and the engine set the axles in motion with a roar. *Off we go!*

ANY MOMENT NOW

"When are we getting there?" I asked the driver, who steered the wheel with ample movements, to avoid getting stuck in the sand.

"Any moment now" he assured me, but until we reached the truck station on the outskirts of Kananga, 72 hours passed. The minute I set foot on sub-Saharan Africa, I tried to adapt to the way locals perceive life by observing their daily routine. I wanted to strip myself – as much as possible – of all those pre-constructed images, so attached to the specific setting that we grow up in. I wanted to accept everything new that came my way, without being judgmental. There was no point in carrying myself around unchanged, unable to see the life unfolding before me. So I started getting a better grasp of the Africans' relation with time. The truck driver gave me vague answers, because he didn't know either when we'd get there and he didn't really care. *We'll get there when we do!* I thought and finally calmed down.

On the first night, after a day of constantly getting stuck in the sand, we stopped at a settlement to get some sleep. All the passengers jumped off the cargo area of the truck. Those who were quick enough laid some tarps underneath the truck, and went to sleep, protected from the dampness of the night, while the rest vanished in the darkness. I stayed put, unable to decide on where to lie. In the end, I lay at a little nook on the ground. First it was the dampness that pierced through my bones and made me quiver; then it was the mosquitos' turn. They kept buzzing around my face and some of them had decided to spend the night in the cosiness of my nostrils. After that harrowing night, I never slept outside again. Despite the pain in my joints from the uncomfortable posture, the truck cabin became my bed.

The following day wasn't much easier. The Vespa, all tied-up with straps and ropes, was still hanging outside the truck. I thought I kept seeing the same half-demolished bridges and the same decrepit roads – like a leitmotif – and felt like I'd lost all sense of space and time. The woods, the streams, the food; the way that, like a well-oiled machine, the assistants worked together to pull the heavy, small-wheeled *Iveco* out of the sand. Over and over again. Each time we'd sink, the robust assistants would jump off, take the shovels to level the sand, place the tree trunks – always available on the truck – in front of every wheel and, as soon as the truck was unstuck, grab them and throw them back into the carriage. Then at once, and while the vehicle was in motion, they'd jump back up.

There were times when we moved so slowly that the women with the plastic basins on their heads walked beside us and had enough time to sell us ready-made snacks. Arms were stretched out of the truck, money in hand, and little bags with food hurled towards them. How had I not realised earlier that the hundreds of passers-by on the road did not just happen to be there? They were perfectly aware of the needs of the travellers and were always around to provide them with the necessary supplies for their long journey. The menu was simple, consisting mainly of nuts and predominantly dried fruit: bags of peanuts, banana, papaya, sweet potato, all of them costing no more than a few cents. The rice with tomato sauce was a luxury that we could only enjoy in villages. Until we reached Kananga, the driver and the polite co-driver, both of whom were kind enough to make sure I was OK throughout the trip, taught me how to properly crack the coconuts open. The contrast between their rather insipid taste and their rich fragrance, which reminded me of my mother's oven-baked desserts, was truly impressive.

An anonymous village, one of many along the way, with a few thatched huts and a clearing where the locals gathered in the evenings, was our last stop before reaching Kananga. I turned down the insipid fufu – the local name for the sticky, white mass made of cassava flour. I didn't want rice either; I chewed down some fruit and went to bed.

At the break of dawn, with the morning mist still covering the rainforest and the first birds reluctantly starting their early twitter, the driver knocked on the window.

"Want coffee?" he asked and before he had time to blink I dashed out of the cabin. I'd really missed coffee. We took a few steps away, to the hut where the co-driver was waiting for us. With his driver's log in his hands, he jotted down the expenses and payments of the previous day. We sat outside on a bench leaning on the earthen wall. Right next to it a woman was stirring her pots and the smell of burned wood tickled my nostrils. She'd lit a fire to heat some water. The strong coffee straight out of the cloth filter, sizzling and full of dregs, soothed my throat and soul. I sat there, with the cup in my hands, watching the sun emerge among the high treetops. At last, my mind was in tune with life at the heart of the Congo. I no longer cared about what I'd find ahead.

BALUBA

It was high noon when we got to Kananga, which looked bigger than any other city we'd passed by so far. Due to its geographical position, it was an administrative and economic centre, but because of the immense mineral wealth of the area, its history has been blood-drenched.

"One and a half million inhabitants!" I said astounded, to the co-driver, who had also become my personal tour guide over the past few days. I looked around me in bewilderment and wondered whether I'd ever get any better at calculating the size of African cities.

"Tonight we'll hang out at a bar nearby", he told me. "Why don't you come along? This way I can tell you more about my country".

It wasn't dark yet. The driver locked up his truck, covered the merchandise with a thick tarp and we headed for our night out. As we got further, I turned around and took a last look at the vehicle that was carrying all of my belongings on it.

"Nothing will be stolen here", I heard the driver's assuring voice, as if he'd read my thoughts. I felt more comfortable now about leaving my stuff unsupervised in the villages, but it was the first time I'd done the same in a big city.

The bar where we went was outdoors: just a yard really, with gravel and thatched parasols. Beer, music and grilled meat; that was the menu. "Mitshopo" was the name of the little chunks of grilled meat served with onions, chili peppers and "kwanga", a bread made with cassava flour. I was with the driver, the co-driver and another local, and then two girls joined us. We drank and talked about their ethnicity. They were all *Baluba*, one of the ethnic groups that live in the DRC. Having a reputation of being hard-working and smart people – which eventually led them to be massacred in their thousands – the Baluba once tried to have their own independent state. For a short period of time, in 1960, their region, the province of Kasai, became a semi-autonomous administrative entity. With the support of the Belgians, who didn't want to abandon the area without finding a way to keep exploiting its inexhaustible diamond mines, the province of Kasai, along with that of Katanga, became independent for a while. However, from the initial turmoil that broke out at the wake of the declaration of its independence up to now, Kasai never stopped facing problems.

To prevent the mood from getting even heavier, I thought I'd change the subject and asked them about their language and customs. When they told me that they spoke *Tshiluba*, the alcohol had already set the right tenor for my jokes. "You're *Baluba* and you speak *Tshiluba*!" I told them giggling and they, knowing that my intentions were good, started laughing back and teasing me about my white skin and my funny facial features. They asked me why I wasn't married and then blamed it on my physique. They said, jokingly, that I'd never find a white woman or a black one.

The driver and I went back to the truck, which was my bedroom. He said goodnight and left. I got into the cabin and, still under the influence of our talk that night, I started thinking. It was weird, but, although I'd met beautiful women along the way, it had never crossed my mind to get involved with any of them. I was constantly on the move and never had the time to get to know anyone a bit better. And, though I didn't want to admit it, the long shadow of AIDS and other diseases that rage across Africa had a deterring effect when it came to relationships, even fickle ones. I couldn't even remember when the last time I'd considered that issue was.

SHE'S NEVER SEEN A WHITE PERSON BEFORE

Any moment now, we'd be on our way and as I'd learned what that sentence actually meant, I hung the camera's strap around my neck and went out for a walk near the truck station. I thought I might buy some bottled water for the road, but I laughed at myself the next minute. The clean water that I had with me, had been over already on my second day there and, I'd been filling my bottles at the creeks, together with the locals ever since. I merely tried to stand at the top of the stream, so as to avoid drinking at the same spot where we washed ourselves. I put my six-pack of bottled water down and immediately thought of Liam. He used to tell me that, before setting out on his trip, he wanted to adapt to the poor hygiene conditions that he'd have to face later on. So one fine day, he decided to drink water from a canal in the UK. The only thing he achieved was severe poisoning. And quite a few more followed since then. I, on the other hand, over a six-month period on the road, had managed to get nothing more than a cold – and that was due to extremely cold air conditioning at the house I stayed in back in Accra.

The bike was now in the back of the truck and I was in my seat by the window, as always. Shortly before getting to Kananga, I'd made a deal with the driver to continue together as far as Mbuji-Mayi, the next big city, where his itinerary ended.

"Do trains work here?", I asked as we passed by the railway tracks, which seemed to be in bad shape. They burst into a deep, hearty laughter, as they always did.

"Sometimes they do, sometimes they don't", they said. The railway network, which sometimes carried merchandise and passengers across the vast country almost in its entirety from one edge to the other, now looked more like a ghost. The tracks were sitting there without the slightest sign of maintenance and the wagons were ramshackle and dirty. From time to time, one of them would set off, but no one knew when it would reach its destination.

"What a shame, I could load on the scooter and travel that way", I said and a second wave of laughter inundated the cabin.

We arrived at Mbuji-Mayi later than I had predicted. In order for the flat tyre to be pulled out and repaired, it took more than six torturing hours, even though the strongest men of the nearby village had come over to help. As the rest of us waited patiently, a group of women with buckets of water and food arrived where we'd been stranded. Right behind them, a little girl, no more than three years old, was running joyfully. As soon as she saw me, she froze! She stood there dumbfounded, stared at me for a few seconds and then burst into tears and rushed behind her mom, who nearly dropped the bucket of water she was carrying on her head. The little girl was crying woefully and, despite her mother's efforts to calm her down, she went on inconsolably.

"She's never seen a white person before", all of them shouted and laughed at the poor girl's scare. With smiles and funny faces, I tried to convince her not to be scared of me. Shortly after, when all my efforts had gone to waste, I decided to hide away so that she couldn't see me. Of course, I couldn't be mad at her. Besides, twenty five years ago at a restaurant back in Thessaloniki, a chubby blond kid put his parents in an awkward position when he stood and stared mesmerised at the first black person he'd ever seen!

MUTOKA MWOYO!

Dawn had just broken. Outside my window, I could hear the whispers of the three new friends I'd made in Mbuji-Mayi. The older one, five years old, had placid eyes and a calm disposition. The middle one, about a year younger, was a little rascal. The little girl, no more than three years old, was coy and kittenish. When I pulled the curtain and winked at them through the glass, their cheerful voices were heard all the way to the ground floor of the crumbing hotel building.

"*Mutoka mwoyo!*" – Hello, white man!

I went down the concrete stairs and went out to the market with the two boys. We left my portable charger at a small store, which was dedicated to that service, and went in search of coffee. All my stuff was in a storage space, back at the truck station and the only thing I yearned for at that moment, my beloved black brew, had to be bought ready-made. The market, a maze of shacks joined together by tin roofs, formed an entire city block without a visible beginning or end, and had it all. Anything your heart could wish for, you could find in bulk or individually packaged. No one stocks supplies, since there are neither conservation means nor enough money for the purchase of big quantities. In Africa life goes by day by day. Nothing is certain and nothing is permanent. Not even food.

"Let's head back, aces", I told the two little kids that were running around me, proud of hitting the town with their temporary, white guardian. We went back to the bar next to the hotel, which looked long deserted, its walls painted in the colours of Primus beer. However, the menu card by the entrance – a photocopied sheet filled out with a marker – read: Skol, 2,000F. Nothing else. Two rival breweries had unexpectedly joined forces in this wreck in Mbuji-Mayi, in which one was advertised while the other served. I pulled a chair out and set up the laptop on the wobbling table. "*Café?*" I asked the owner, though I already knew the answer. I looked at the time. *It's too early for beer*, I thought and decided to wait a little longer.

"I'll get you some coffee!" the neighbour's voice was heard.

"How much for it?" I asked and got my hopes up.

He asked for 1,000 Congolese francs – about one dollar – and though I knew that I could get a generous meal for the same amount, I didn't turn it down. I'd rather give that money to the person who would bring me a cup of coffee, than to any police officer who would ask for it, taking advantage of his position. I drank the milky and syrupy coffee, without losing sight of the kiddies, who were playing rolling around a metal hoop with a wooden stick. The day went by peacefully and when the time came for the beer, the owner served me an ice cold one, asking me if I was going to order another one. The place had no power so he only kept one bottle and, if the customer so demanded, he rushed out in search of a second one. Just like at our favourite joint back in Ilebo. I also bought each of my little aces, who were still playing tirelessly in the yard, a sandwich filled with some unidentifiable deli meat. The man who sold them went around with a bucket of bread buns, in which he shoved small or bigger pieces of the deli meat, depending on the amount of money he received. I had one myself and then headed for my room. Life in places without electricity follows the sun's movement. It starts when the sun rises and it ends when the sun sets.

It was past midnight and I was soundly asleep under my hole-ridden mosquito net, when a sudden thud right above my head made me jump up. I flipped on the flashlight I kept under my pillow and saw a mysterious figure slinking on the fine net before vanishing into the dark. I wasn't sure whether I'd rather it was a giant spider or rat. Good thing I'm leaving tomorrow morning! I said to myself, before drifting back to sleep.

We got to Mbuji-Mayi on a Thursday. No sooner had we parked at the truck station than the driver went out negotiating for the next fare on my account, the one that would get me to Lubumbashi. He found a truck that would depart on Saturday and arranged my fare so the only thing left for me to do was to wait. Early Saturday morning, I went down to the warehouses from where we'd depart to find out the time, but the only information I got was that we weren't going anywhere that day. Or the next. Each of the four days I spent in Mbuji-Mayi, I repeated the same routine: I'd go to the warehouses, ask if anyone knew when we would be leaving and then, empty-handed, I'd go back to the bar and have the only beer available.

LITTLE DIAMONDS

I was told that the name of the city literally meant "*Goat-Water*" in *Tshiluba* and it sure does describe what Mbuji-Mayi abounds with. Indeed – but it also has diamonds.

I strolled around the neighbourhoods near the truck station. The signboards of the stores that offered diamond buy and sell as well as evaluation services, were dominated by pictures of the precious stones. When, back in early 20th Century, it was established that the area was extremely rich in diamonds, the main mining company of the Belgian Congo was quick to seal off the region, thus creating a city that served exclusively the interests of the diamond industry stakeholders.

Trash, tin and clunkers were everywhere I looked as I roamed the streets, killing time until the truck would depart. The skyscrapers of the city centre wouldn't even cast their shadow over the place where I was staying. What I saw looked like a makeshift construction, waiting to get torn down any moment now provided that someone spread the rumour that a diamond was found there. I was pretty far from the centre, and the few paved roads had disappeared so dirt covered everything. Two million people lived where I stood and one should be really naive to think of the residents of the area from which one tenth – in weight – of world-wide diamond production comes, as *fortunate*.

They were slaves to the wealth of their homeland and victims of the corporations and governments which have always sunk their claws deep into anything that smells like money. Ragged but always willing to smile every time they saw my camera, poor devils, smugglers and thousands of despaired, dive into the mud from the moment that they're old enough to toddle to the pits with the shiny stones. I looked at my aces – the only company I'd had over the past few days – scampering behind me as I walked away, and the only thing I wished for was for them to have better luck.

You're the diamonds! I wanted to shout to them as I left.

VIDEOGAME

The old Mercedes roared past the first police block, which obstructed the road at the city's exit. At the second one, it didn't even hit the brakes when we saw the police officer suddenly pop up right in front of us to make us stop. I don't know if I got more scared, convinced that we were going to hit him, or he, who had to leap aside to save himself. I thought I was in a videogame, in which the winner is the player who manages to dodge all police blocks along the way. On one occasion we managed to steer clear of two of them, who were trying to force us to slow down, getting in our way with their motorbikes. I was almost cheering when we finally got out of Mbuji-Mayi, but, the uniformed man at the last block remained unflinching at his position, forcing the driver to freeze a few centimetres before touching the nose of the – courageous and slightly pale with terror – law enforcement officer.

This truck was not smaller than the one that had taken me to Mbuji-Mayi. On the cargo area, about thirty people and a load of merchandise crammed my scooter into a corner. I was in the cabin crammed by a chubby *Big Mama* who got me squeezed onto the co-driver's door. It didn't even occur to me to ask about our arrival at Lubumbashi. Considering that it had taken us five days to travel 350km, knowing how many days it would take us for the remaining 1,050km kind of frightened me.

The thorough police inspection was concluded with a handshake and a bunch of bills and, finally, two hours later, we were back on our way. Countless police blocks followed, usually at the entrance to a village, and to my surprise, I noticed that the truck driver followed the same strategy as I did when I travelled on my bike: whenever possible, he dodged them. However, in those cases when that was not possible, the whole procedure was time-consuming and nerve-racking. The passengers would jump off the truck, stand in line and one by one present their documents along with some money. I had the privilege of refusing to get off and, while I felt guilty about it, I often was glad I could stay inside dozing throughout the process. I showed my passport through the car's window to every police officer, together with any other document he asked for, holding them tight so as to prevent them from ending up in his hands. But the locals weren't that lucky. I don't recall a single occasion on which I didn't get mad at seeing how those who'd somehow gotten to a position of power took advantage of it at the expense of others. The exceptions to the rule of hand-greasing in Africa were regrettably few. Nevertheless, while I knew that the salaries of public officers were unthinkably low or, in some cases, non-existent, I still couldn't justify them making the life of their fellow citizens unbearable. Along the way, I'd met well-educated people who strove to survive in adverse conditions, which, more often than not, were due to the immensely corrupt system. I felt sorry and I empathised with them. For very similar reasons, I'd had lots of doors closed on me back in Greece. Perhaps I shouldn't get so irked when I heard that *"that's how things work"*, but I just couldn't.

1,050 KILOMETRES

It was high noon and the truck moved slowly on the dirt track. We'd gotten off the N1 – which was not much better – to take a shortcut and avoid some police blocks. With my earphones on, I listened to the same classic rock tracklist over and over again, while next to me, *Big Mama* was sound asleep, her head leaning on my left shoulder. I kept my right arm stretched out of the open window and listlessly allowed the annoying little bugs that were flitting around everywhere to perch on it. I counted how many of the little black bugs would try to quench their thirst by sipping on the sweat on my skin and, when the count got out of proportion, I swatted them away. Travelling had become a routine, familiar and boring at the same time. I'd seen and learned a lot about people in the Congo, having no choice but to live like they did, and, although I looked forward to getting to Lubumbashi, I felt sorry that those days would be over.

I laid back and leisurely counted the beans, with or without sugar, I had consumed over the past few days, when, all of a sudden, I was startled by a strong bump. The rear wheels of the truck skidded and within seconds, the vehicle was almost turned over and the passengers started to jump off in panic. Big Mama was abruptly shaken out of her sleep, straightened her wig and gave me a frightened look. When we made sure that there was no risk of flipping over, it was the assistants' turn to get down to business. It took us more than six hours to get back on the road again.

Countless were the times when we'd became stuck in the mud, got a flat tyre and a series of mechanical breakdowns, or arrived at torn down bridges. Every time one of these things happened, we knew exactly what to do. The assistants would either cut down tree trunks to repair the bridge, or grab the shovels to get the truck out of the sand. We'd get off the truck and walk to the nearest settlement, where women waited for us to sell us food. All of my fellow passengers carried a toothbrush and a bar of soap with them and, after the meal was over, the nearby stream would be bursting with bubbles and cheerful voices. Mothers would wash their babies, children and adults would brush their teeth and splash around in the water. I'd follow suit. They'd accepted me as a member of the group and, although the language barrier limited our verbal communication, I really enjoyed being around them.

As the days went by, the landscape changed. The dense tropical forest started to clear up and the climate became drier and drier. Unseen for a long time, the first acacias made their appearance. In the villages at night, the cold was nippy. Endless routes across the savanna in the pitch dark of the night. The headlights of the truck made the eyes of the small animals around shine in the dark. Tumbledown bridges, sand, digging, cutting down trees, baths in the streams, rice, peanuts, bananas, brushing teeth, frozen sleep. The next day, all over again. Time didn't matter. It went by at an indefinable pace, neither slowly nor fast. It just went by.

Until one day the trees almost disappeared. Maybe they'd started to get sparser since the day before and I hadn't noticed it, but we were now at a wide, well-treaded dirt road, surrounded mostly by tall, brown grass.

It seemed to me like a mirage on the horizon and it was only when all four wheels got safely on it that I was actually able to believe it: asphalt!

STONES, METALS AND OTHER CURSES

"Why do have to stop here?" I asked the driver, since we had already unloaded most of the merchandise at Kolwezi. "There's only 300km left to get there" I said with a make-believe whine, aware that it was pointless. The following morning, everyone was in a hurry to get going.

It was the first time I'd ever seen the patient passengers all set so early. We were only a few hours away from our final destination and we really couldn't wait. From the industrial area at the edges of the city, where we'd set camp the previous night, we could see the urban area with its roughly one million residents. Steven was in there somewhere, stuck in some mission, with a mechanical failure that stalled him. *Who could ever imagine that I'd be the first one to get to Lubumbashi!* I thought, as we drove on the asphalt road, the existence of which I still found hard to believe. We even had to pay tolls as we went into the metropolitan area, as if it were the citizens' obligation to finance the scarce kilometres of decent roadway in this country.

I watched the bulky trucks, with French and Chinese logos on their tarpaulins, speed up on the well-made highway. We were now in Katanga, an area rich in mineral wealth in the south, close to the border with Zambia. This is the passage through which almost everything that the inexhaustible subsoil of the Congo provides is carried all the way to South Africa. My mind went back to all those situations I'd witnessed in the long-suffering former Belgian colony, which, regardless of the names it was given throughout its history – Congo Free State, Belgian Congo, Zaire, Democratic Republic of the Congo – never had any luck. Somewhere in the east of the country were the mines where coltan is extracted – the doomed metallic ore that is a valuable component of electronic appliances and indispensable for cellphones. Ten per cent of the entire worldwide production comes from here. Slavery, guerrilla wars, massacres, endless corruption and incalculable environmental damage surround the extraction of minerals and precious stones, drenching the soil of an immense country in blood. Wherever I went I saw dilapidated infrastructure and shortage of goods that would be unthinkable anywhere else in the world. And amidst this state of total neglect, people stoically wait for the next day and smile.

MALAKA, YOU'RE GREEK, AREN'T YOU?

It must have been once in Yaoundé and another time in Brazzaville, when I noticed some Greek presence. I was walking down the street when I saw the sign of an establishment that, dressed in white and blue, read in capital letters: "OUZO"[1]. On another one, I read a surname that couldn't be anything but Greek. I wasn't particularly excited to see them, but I'd convinced myself to take pictures, which were later lost within my already vast collection. All around the world, there are scattered Greek migrants who, at some point packed up everything they had and left, forced out by poverty and the problems of their country, in the pursuit of a better life. I wasn't interested in finding them, I'd not once felt the need to meet compatriots of mine in Africa. When Jean, my host in Lubumbashi, talked to me about the Greek community of his hometown, it was a mix of distrust and curiosity that urged me to look for it, rather than nostalgia for the country I was born in.

I was walking down one of the most central avenues of the city, which bears the name of the country's current president, Laurent-Désiré Kabila. The day before, I'd been there with Jean, who provided me with all the necessary information that would help me find my way around and onto the mini-buses that whirl like spinning tops around the city, without getting lost. The big blue sign above the supermarket entrance left no room for doubt. I stepped inside. On my right, on a wooden podium that looked like those from my school days, four white men were sitting behind desks, yelling over the phone or writing frantically on their logs. Around me, locals were dashing all over the place, carrying pallets with merchandise. I was at the warehouse of a supermarket. I stopped in front of one of the "teachers", who stood up when he saw me.

"*Hello! I'm looking for...*" I uttered in English with a distinctively Greek accent.

[1] *Ouzo is a dry anise-flavoured liqueur, widely consumed in Greece.*

"*Malaka[2]*, you're Greek, aren't you?" he replied with a sly grin on his face.

From that moment on and throughout the entire month that I spent in Lubumbashi, I can't recall a day go by without speaking my mother tongue. The news that a weirdo from Thessaloniki had travelled all the way down there on a scooter spread around almost instantly and, corroborating the Greeks' reputation of being hospitable, they loaded me on a pick-up truck and got me settled in the premises of their community. One of the apartments, otherwise destined for visiting employees, became my home.

I found myself living with all the amenities I could have asked for. I'd already spent a week in the community and I still felt as if I were in a parallel universe. It was only when the first dish of moussaka was served in front of me, and the taste of roasted eggplant, minced meat and béchamel sauce almost brought tears of joy to my eyes that I realised that all that was around me was real. Every evening, when they got off from work, the Greek expats came by the restaurant of the community. We met there and spent hours talking about Africa, Greece and the world. The Greeks that are left in the Congo are no more than five hundred, split between Kinshasa and the distant Lubumbashi, down south. Throughout the country's turbulent history, ever since they were regarded as second-class whites by the Belgian colonists, up to independence and Mobutu's regime, which snatched and reshuffled their properties, the Greek presence there had been constant. Around 1970, nearly seven thousand expats lived in the Congo, but, gradually, ever since the '90s they started to abandon the country due to the turmoil and overall uncertainty. The only ones who remained were those who had serious reasons to do so – which were none others than the thriving businesses they had managed to establish over the years.

"For anything you might need, we're here", they told me and, from the very first moment, they proved that they meant it. I

[2] 'Malakas' (VOC malaka) is, essentially, an offensive slang term, meaning "jerk" or "asshole", widely used in Greek. However, depending on the context, it is also very commonly used as an interjection and/or in an affectionate way among peers, in which case it translates as "dude", "pal" or "mate" – which is precisely the case here.

didn't want to take advantage of their generosity and, unless it was an absolute necessity, I tried not to ask for anything. The president of the community had made a deal with the restaurant managers so that I could get free meals, but I rarely used this privilege, as I preferred to experiment in the kitchen of the apartment. In his garage, Nikos – with whom I started to get along really soon – gave me everything I needed and, two days after receiving the spare parts from Greece, Kitsos' engine sounded again, after a whole month in silence. With their help, I managed to get an extension for my visa that was about to expire, and then I felt comfortable enough to stay, have some rest and reorganise myself, after one month on the road, which now seemed like a dream – like one of the most beautiful dreams.

DIDN'T YOU GET SCARED?

The days went by peacefully in Lubumbashi. In the mornings, I'd make frappé coffee and I'd keep stirring the ice-cubes with the straw, just to hear them clink against the glass. I'd forgotten when the last time I'd seen ice-cubes was. Then, I'd got on the scooter and head out to town. Just that once I got distracted and ran into the police block at Lumumba Avenue. As soon as I saw the armed policemen, out of habit I automatically turned the engine off and put the keys into my pocket. The first thing they did at the controls was to seize the motorbikes' keys and blackmail the owners in order to get them back. With cars, they employed a different technique: if the driver had the doors unlocked, they got in and wouldn't go until the owner of the car would give them something – some change, a soda, a cigarette.

The city streets were wide and the central ones, paved. The old colonial buildings stood with visible signs of decay, imbuing the urban scenery with a sense of bygone glory. The traffic in the city centre was chaotic and, every now and then, a rowdy funeral procession or protest made things even worse. But now I was used to it all. I'd managed to adapt to all that and day after day I tried to get a better grasp of life around me.

The nights at the restaurant, the expats asked me a host of questions about the trip and the impression I'd gotten of Africa so far. Some asked with real interest, while others merely out of curiosity, and very few in a rather discrediting tone, which revealed the intention to discriminate between people and cultures. I'd come across racism so often that it no longer impressed me, but what I'd seen even more often was fear.

"Didn't you get scared?" was most people's question. I didn't know what to say to that. In many cases, I'd answer in one word, "no", which could come off as kind of arrogant. I wasn't fearless; no one is. But the violence I'd experienced on my own skin over the last years in Greece – be it emotional, be it physical – had made me, in a way, unsusceptible to fear. The violence of unemployment, the violation of rights, the despair, and the sense of helplessness against a system that so voraciously exploits everything, had triggered a revolt within me. I'd live my life the way I wanted to, even if the price would be to lose it. I could clearly see that the more people entrench themselves behind their supposed uniqueness, the more expendable they become. *Yes, I may die!* I thought once and, ever since then, something was set free within me and I never thought of it again.

One such evening with food and conversation, two women that I'd never seen before came up and joined us at the dinner table. One of them seemed in her forties and the other about ten years younger. They were Effie and Alexandra. They told me they'd heard from the expats in the community about my story and wanted to meet me. Both of them were simply dressed, in sneakers and jeans, they didn't seem to fit in with the formal look of the rest of them. Effie lived in Johannesburg and was Alexandra's supervisor, who was doing a PhD about the Greeks in the Congo. They were staying in the apartment right next door to mine and, when we finished dinner, we agreed to meet the next day for coffee on my balcony.

"Have you heard of Potagos?" Effie asked me. I had no clue who that guy was. Alexandra smiled. She'd probably guessed her teacher's thought.

"He was, in all likelihood, the only Greek explorer of the 19th Century!" Effie went on enthusiastically. She took a sip of her coffee and started to tell the story of the forgotten man. Disappointed by the sordid situation of his country, he relied on his own powers and between 1867 and 1883, he travelled across Asia and Africa, collecting valuable ethnographic material and information. He charted rivers in Central Africa and contributed to the knowledge of places and cultures that very few had seen. He produced work which however, was never acknowledged in Greece. At the same time as he was honoured by the French Geographical Society and King Leopold II of Belgium, his home country ignored him. Following his death, part of his work was lost forever, without anyone showing any interest in making something out of it.

"You have the same beard!" she concluded, laughing.

DEPARTURES AND ARRIVALS

"I knocked on your door yesterday, but you didn't open" Alexandra complained. I gave her a sleepy look through the half-open door, with my eyes still swollen from sleep.

"I'm leaving the day after tomorrow and I've got loads of things to do", she explained.

"Come inside for one last coffee" I suggested.

Effie had gone back to Johannesburg and Alexandra, during the day was running errands and finishing up her pending tasks. I liked them both. It was the first time in years that I'd met people from my country with whom I felt I had a lot in common. Unfortunately, we never got to go out all together, not once. At nights they used to go out with two friends, Antonis and Lona. I stayed up late, taking advantage of the cheap internet connection, and slept till noon. One July Sunday afternoon, I went back home after a ride around the outskirts of the city and found Alexandra's window closed, and a text message on my cellphone: "*I left without even saying goodbye, but it's OK, because I'm sure the two of us, somewhere in the world out there, will meet again*".

After Alexandra's departure, it was time for a few arrivals. First came Steven, who'd finally managed to fix his carburettor; then it was Katrina's turn who had great trouble getting here. A few days after that Christina and Elias showed up, the Greek couple I'd met back in Burkina Faso and who did roughly the same route as me. We spent hours on end talking about our experiences. Steven joked about the overburdened Kitsos, who gave us a hard time. I feigned getting angry at him, but I never forgot how much he'd helped me, dipping into the mud and pushing me. Every time I talked about the previous month, my eyes welled up. Those had been the most intense experiences, the ones that taught me that I was much more resilient than I thought. There, on trucks and tumbledown bridges, I learned that things I believed to be the same everywhere, were not so. What's a road in the Congo? What's a house? A school? A bathroom? It took effort for me to get to fit these new notions into my mind. But I also learned something else: we may each have our own special way of understanding life, but the way in which we perceive happiness is the same.

After all this, I found myself in an apartment with a fridge and a bed, about to turn the water heater on.

"It's a pity you burned the clutch, though", someone told me. "One extra set of discs and you'd have reached your goal". I laughed. I knew that the goal was reached – if there'd ever been one.

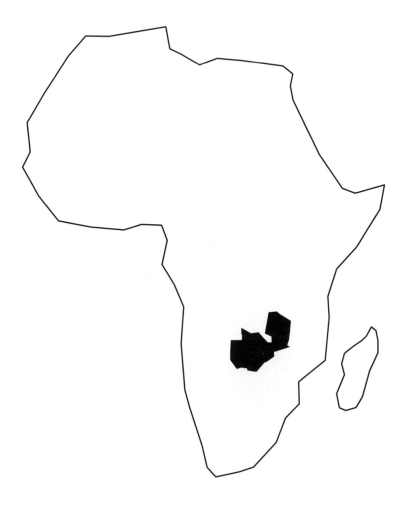

ZAMBIA

VENTURES AND OPPORTUNITIES

We'd agreed to set off early in order to get to the border in time. The distance was no more than 100km, but we had no idea how long the paperwork procedures would take to allow us to enter Zambia. After an entire month as a guest of the Greek community, I'd had all the rest I needed and looked forward to getting back on the road. By the time I'd finished preparing the scooter Christina had already made coffee and was waiting for me. "All set Gogos?" she asked, as I stood the tripod to capture the last moments in Lubumbashi.

The line of trucks at Kasumbalesa, the border town and main passage for crossing over to Zambia, extended over kilometres on the N1. In their huge cargo area the entire mineral wealth of the Congo was loaded and carried all the way to the South African ports and, from there, to the rest of the world. At the buildings of the passport and the customs offices, people went in and out holding documents that had to be checked and sealed. There, we met Nikos' protocoleur – my friend from Lubumbashi. The word "*protocoleur*" sounded kind of weird to me, funnier than "fixer", which was the equivalent term in another language. We'd explained that we didn't need his help – we'd rather go through all this inconvenience on our own – but Nikos insisted that he'd make things easier for us.

Our entry into Zambia took place with great ceremony. I held the colour-printed documents with the embossed watermarks in my hands, which left no room to question their validity. I remembered that time at the border of Mauritania, when the officer ripped us off ten euros in exchange for a shabby old piece of paper with some gibberish scribbled on it, in an attempt to legitimise his transgression.

The plan was to travel along with Christina to the capital of Zambia. From Lusaka, she'd go back to Greece on her motorbike and I'd go on my way. The dark caught us somewhere on the highway so we started to look for a place to spend the night. Our disappointment at the excessive prices of the hotels and the inhospitable treatment we received – since they wouldn't even allow us to camp in their premises – was mitigated when the attendant of a gas station let us spend the night in her backyard.

Everything looked unfamiliar in the new country. After the 2,000 unforgettable kilometres on the indescribable roads of the *big* Congo, and the tons of mud and the hospitality of the locals everywhere I went in the *small* Congo; after the jungle of Cameroon, the police roadblocks and the frightened citizens of Nigeria; after the pristine coasts of Ghana and the nights at the savanna in Mali and Senegal; after all that, I'd arrived in a country with shopping malls and tourism. It'd been a long time since that day at the supermarket in Ouagadougou, when I looked at the price tags on the cheese and wondered where I belonged. Uncertainty: a curse that befalls all Greeks who realise that their race had always been regarded as different by the Europeans, somewhere in between the powerful and the impotent, the privileged and the condemned. I still couldn't wrap my mind around this.

So, when I heard some people speak Greek at a shopping mall in Lusaka, curiosity urged me to stop and introduce myself. Cypriot and Greek businessmen, old and new immigrants have formed a small Greek-speaking community, which, contrary to the one in Lubumbashi, has less clear limits and structure. The sense of a close-knit society, in which the Greek identity is entrenched and safeguarded, at times distorted or magnified without reason – as I experienced it in Lubumbashi – did not exist among the Greeks in Lusaka. Some of them were there temporarily, until they'd gather some money and then leave, others came from South Africa and saw Zambia as a place of opportunity. A third category was made up of those who lived in two or three countries, having life partners and spouses from abroad.

That night, I kept rolling around in my bed, thinking about everything I'd heard all that time.

"The slums are full of useful and cheap human workforce".

"The locals are slow-witted".

"Black women are good at sex".

"Don't think about it too hard, that's just how things are".

"Africa is the land of opportunities".

There wasn't a single person who hadn't taken something from this continent, stepping on its soil. Everyone gets there to increase what they already have. Rich businessmen go there to get richer; scientists go there in search of more knowledge; priests go there to add to their flock; adventurers to live their dream; teachers to transmit their wisdom to minds still untarnished by western culture; merchants to sell more packaged products to people who don't really need them; philanthropists to assure their place on the pantheon of virtuousness and charity. Even I was there for a reason, but I guess I hadn't figured it out yet.

ROCK AND MINES

Every time my father played Led Zeppelin in the car's cassette deck, my brother and I were enthralled by their music and we always ended up with the conclusion that we should form our own rock band. He'd chosen to be the guitarist and I the drummer. We didn't worry about the rest of the members; we'd scout out the best and become famous. On one of our last nights in Lusaka, while digesting the Chinese noodles that Achilles, (one of the Greeks I'd met) had just prepared, we were listening to Led Zeppelin and I asked myself, not why I never became a famous drummer, but instead, why I never learned how to play a musical instrument to begin with.

Achilles hadn't been in Zambia for long. He'd arrived only recently to set up a business, just like so many others. A mining engineer, he triggered my interest right away. When he told me that he used to work at the mines of Chalkidiki, inevitably my mind went back to Skouries, where society has been split into two and the residents have got into an extreme situation. The choking sensation from the tear gas and the police violence against those who disagree with the expansion of the gold mines managed to travel all the way to Lusaka and disturb my outward calmness again.

"The Earth always finds a way to survive", he observed.

"But people don't", I replied bitterly.

He didn't debate that. No matter what humans might do to this planet, on any given day it may well shake them off like a piece of trash and be reborn. The Earth doesn't care about those who inhabit it. Countless forms of life have become extinct throughout time and just as many have been created. However, by spending our fleeting existence destroying it, the only thing we achieve is to destroy ourselves.

"Just so you know, the only ones profiting from the mining in your homeland are the corporation that operates the mines and a bunch of politicians and businessmen". I saw it at the gold mines in Mali, at the diamond mines in the Congo, and the copper industry in Zambia. A threadbare, ruthless state, which never stands on the side of its citizens, is condemned to project its future through examples like these.

"Even Zambia has much more profit than Greece from the deals it makes with multinationals", he concluded and left me numb, rewinding all my last experiences before the trip.

MY GUITAR

Christina, after three weeks, had managed to get a ticket for her and her motorbike, which was now packed up in a cargo container, ready to board a plane. I parted from her at the airport and, before going back to the campsite, I dropped by the *"craftsmen's village"* souvenir bazaar. At the disposal of the tourists there was jewellery and carved decorative figures depicting traditional life and anything else that has been imprinted on Western minds as representative of Africa. I could find the exact same things at a bazaar in Thessaloniki, but I was looking for, and found, a wooden mask to decorate my scooter.

Wearing my colourful shirt, custom-made by a Congolese tailor

230

in Lubumbashi, I sat at a restaurant near the campsite, where I'd been left alone. In front of me, the avenue with huge billboards advertising free AIDS checks. In all big cities I'd see eye-catching posters aiming to raise awareness of the deadly – in Africa – disease. Every gust of wind caused litter to float in the air and reminded me that, despite all the parks and modern shopping malls, around the city centre there were slums. I ordered a portion of *nsima* – the sticky purée from cassava or maize flour – and meat with sauce. In Zambia, the Congolese *bukari* or *fufu* might be called something else, but the taste remains the same. At the restaurant where I sat, it was served on a plate and not from a dirty plastic bowl, pulled out by the cook's hands. I'm not sure if I ate it because the hygiene rules there resembled those of a European restaurant. Maybe I just missed the days when my only food choice was overcooked rice or this.

As I tucked in to my meal I turned and looked at the guitar, which was resting inside its black case. I'd just bought it at a music store for 80 euros. I thought about my brother again and the rock band we never put together. *Sorry, brother, I guess I'll be the guitarist after all!* I apologised to him in my mind.

The time had come to leave Lusaka. With the wooden mask fixed on the windshield and the guitar loaded on the rear part of the seat, I said goodbye to the travellers I'd met a few days ago. Two miniature Basques who had been living for over 20 years in a small 4x4 with a tent attached to the cargo area had taught me how to make real yoghurt. I didn't want to hurt their feelings, so I wrote the recipe down. They seemed so close to each other. They'd managed to find one another and build their own microcosm, where no uninvited guests were allowed. I pictured myself in their place and, for the first time, realised that I'd probably be happy having what they had some day.

"Who cares? My guitar will do for now!", I said to myself as I sat on loyal Kitsos' loins.

IT'S ALL A MATTER OF PERSPECTIVE
When the very last glint of light had vanished from the sky, my ride on the highway to Livingstone became a nightmare. The trucks, totally oblivious to the pitch dark, kept roaring and speeding like

crazy. It looked as if they wanted to efface anything that got in their way. The headlight of the scooter, feeble like a candle, barely managed to reflect light on the bicycles that circulated on the edge of the roadway. Pedestrians carrying haystacks and bulky bundles, walked as if they were indestructible, without any sign of fear of getting crushed by the monstrous truck wheels. As I struggled to find a place to stop, convinced of the stupidity of my idea to travel in the dark, a big animal jumped up in front of me and sprang over to the other side of the road, so close to the scooter that it blocked my visual field completely. The tyres squealed as I hit the brakes sharply and, in a daze, I got off and sat in a field for a while, to pull myself together. *"I survived the trucks to nearly be killed by an antelope!"* I uttered in terror. A few kilometres down the road I stopped at the first campsite I came across.

The following afternoon, in Livingstone, the workaday smile of the boy at the reception and the showcases full of brochures of organised adventures for tourists made my feet want to take a u-turn and make a run for it. Without even looking at me, he handed out the form I was supposed to fill in with my passport information and, just like a well-trained robot, started reciting the amenities provided by the guesthouse.

"Thank you" I said, irritated and decided to heed my initial impulse and dash out of the hospitality factory. When, two hours later I returned, defeated by surrounding tourist developments and the high – for my budget – prices of the rest of the guesthouses, the same robot, who had completely forgotten me, started to advertise rides on helicopters and wild safaris all over again.

The sun was about to set as I was reaching the Victoria Falls and most visitors were looking for a nice restaurant for their dinner. Searching for the entrance, the distracted gazes and vague steps of a group of tourists, who were just entering the Park, lured me along with them, without paying for a ticket. The deafening noise produced by the tons of water cascading down the gigantic, vertical rocks is the reason why the waterfalls are called *"Mosi-oa-Tunya"* – *The Smoke that Thunders*, in the local language. Subsequently, David Livingstone, the explorer and missionary who was probably the first white person ever to see them, named them after his queen. Floating droplets that hazed the atmosphere, rainbows, wet trails and hundreds of visitors completed the scenery of the famous sight.

About 200km to the east, the course of the Zambezi River, trapped by human hand, forms Lake Kariba. I wondered how many of the people around me knew about the effect that the construction of the great dam had, back when Zambia and neighbouring Zimbabwe were still called North and South Rhodesia. How many had heard about the populations that were forcibly driven out of their holy land, without ever getting back on their feet again. The environmental catastrophe that still takes place to this day in the name of development; would anyone care about that? Did they even know who Cecil Rhodes was, the man after whom both countries were named, until they became independent and changed it? Did they care, I wondered, that the "owner" of this land, was a firm believer in the supremacy of his nation and maintained that the English should colonise as many places of the world as possible? I hoped that so much as one of the cheerful visitors posing with selfie sticks would have thought about that.

I quit thinking and got out of the waterfalls park. On my way to my lodgings, I remembered that I once made a selfie stick. A broomstick standing behind my door in Lubumbashi, a plastic support stand for the camera and loads of duct tape were its components. Everybody was laughing their hearts out one afternoon over at my apartment. But now, here in Livingstone, I just wanted to nag. I was moody and withdrawn, and the headache that tormented me wasn't making things any easier. The headaches and migraines that accompanied me ever since I was a kid had been gone completely over the last few months. They only remembered to drop by on really hot and sunny days. What the heck made my head seem like it was about to explode on that day?

The guesthouse kitchen was full of busy tourists. One of them hadn't swept the grease he'd spilled on the floor. With a plate of pasta that I'd just made, I looked around searching for a quiet spot to sit and have dinner. My plastic flip-flop slipped on the greasy stain and, in an instant, I fell flat on my back, while my dinner got smeared all over the place. I cussed out loud in Greek. I had to get the hell out of there as soon as possible. It was the first time during the trip that I'd been in such a bad mood.

With my head pounding, nauseated and starved, I collapsed on the patterned pillows of my bed. A girl from the US, who was either younger than me or more rested, sat next to me. Having witnessed my bad luck, she offered me some of her food. We started talking. She told me about her adventures at the borders, as she'd come from Botswana. Everything that she had to go through in order to cross over to Zambia was completely inconceivable to her, and she wanted to share it with someone who'd had a similar experience at the African land borders. When she finished her narration I understood that the one hour she had to wait until her passport was checked, and got on board a boat which didn't adhere to Western norms of safety, seemed totally unacceptable to her. I didn't know what to tell her. I surely didn't want to come off as an arrogant know-it-all, so I tried to be understanding.

"It's all a matter of perspective" I mumbled, and thanked her for her kindness.

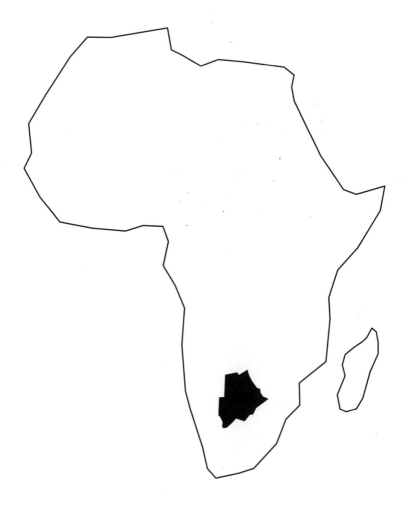

BOTSWANA

WATCH OUT FOR WILD ANIMALS

The waterborne passage to Botswana was so quick and unremarkable that, when I remembered the American girl's description of it as particularly troublesome a few days ago, a smile crossed my lips. I could understand her reaction to what bore little resemblance to the European or North American borders, but I was now convinced that it's up to each one of us to rid our minds of stereotypes and adapt to something different than our own reality. Then again, maybe she needed more time. Or maybe she didn't need to be in Africa.

The 'white saviour complex', the need of many Western citizens to believe that, with a few smiles, some gifts and many hugs, they can save Africans, was as irritating to me as the downright racism of other people. Africans are not children. They are not immature creatures that need the help and guidance of the white man. They're just people, with responsibilities and weaknesses; with wickedness and kindness; with all those features that define every human being. Every time I ran into a 'good Samaritan' who, naively, missing the big picture, got mesmerised by the big round eyes and the genuine smiles of the 'noble savages', I fled. I didn't have a single answer to what I saw around me, but at least I had questions.

From the very first kilometres in Botswana, the signs warning of animals that one might bump into along the way caught my attention. *How many elephants could I actually come across?*

I wondered and, before I got a chance to think it through, an entire extended family of elephants blocked my way. I stood at a safe distance and watched them cross. I was looking at them but something else was on my mind: the weird noise coming out of the engine of the scooter. Since Livingstone, I'd been hearing a ringing metallic sound that didn't seem normal, but I'd kept ignoring it. I hadn't paid much attention to the small spill of gasoline on the ground I'd seen, either. Near Pandamatenga, only 100km past the border and quite a few before the place where I'd planned to be by nightfall, the engine stopped. I got off the roadway to give myself time to consider my options and headed to the thicket nearby. Behind the acacia that I chose to become my WC, I heard a squeak. I lift my head and my eyes met those of a giraffe that was grazing only a few metres away. There was no dilemma; I just had to get the scooter started as soon as possible.

"Aaaah, Kitsos, you little rascal!" I yelled in joy. "You never let me down!". The Vespa started up and managed to carry me all the way to the nearest campsite. After talking to Costas, my infallible mechanic, and thoroughly describing the symptoms, I was confident that nothing could go wrong the following day.

"Did you hear the lions yesterday?", the campsite manager asked as I went over to pay him and leave.

"What lions?", I asked, gawking. Safe inside the fence of the campsite, last night I'd surrendered myself to a sleep so deep, that nothing could interrupt it. Only when the sun was up high enough was I forced by the morning heat to jump out of the tent.

I planned on moving further southwards and then westwards, to the Makgadikgadi salt pans. I was riding along the edges of the Kalahari and I wasn't sure what to expect. The road was a paved perfect straight line through the low, dry vegetation of the savanna. The weather was nice, with no apparent intention of ruining my trip. I wondered where all those trucks that passed me in Zambia and the people on the loaded bicycles that I kept coming across were. I'd read that Botswana is one of the most sparsely populated countries, but I'd never have imagined this desertedness. The vivid green of the tropical forests and the golden-yellow shades of the fields had given way to a rather dull olive green and the earth was now greyish. The landscape itself was the perfect hiding place for the animals, or at least that was what my untrained eyed made me think every time an elephant, a giraffe or an antelope popped up out of nowhere.

The campsite, which the two Basques I'd met back in Lusaka had recommended, was not hard to find. Before sunset, I had put up my tent and was sitting at the bar, which was also an elephant observatory. Lying on comfortable deck chairs, tourists with costly photographic equipment, dressed in explorer-like pants and vests, were waiting for the giant pachyderms to show up. With the tripods set on top of a constructed elevation, placed so as to face the watering hole, they enjoyed their cocktails until the models arrived, most of them from neighbouring South Africa. The scenery was an accurate recreation of the idyllic pictures on the tourist brochures, with the ruby red sunsets and the animal silhouettes against the acacia-lined horizon in the savanna. I took quite a few pictures of elephants that evening by the watering hole. I also had a juicy steak and a glass of wine, and the meal was topped off by a piece of dessert and fruit. I didn't have any rice. I slept in my tent, just as I'd been doing in the countless anonymous villages in the heart of central Africa. Back then I was a guest of people that couldn't imagine that I was passing by their homeland for no particular reason other than just to see what it looked like. I woke up the next morning and saw the spacious tents and the luxury wooden rental cabins around me. *Where was I?*

SALT

I handed my documents to the guard that stood on the bend of the dirt road and moved on among the low brown trees. I was a bit south of the town of Nata, at the point that a local visitor at the elephant campsite had marked on my map. I had to turn there, if I was going to avoid the soft sand ordeal of the main road that leads to the Makgadikgadi salt pans complex.

I rode on towards what, thousands of years ago, used to be a huge lake. The vegetation was getting sparser and sparser. The setting became less hospitable and, although the temperature was not particularly high, the light colour of the soil, as well as the altitude, made the sun heat more intense. When I got to the *Sua Pan*, one of the main salt pans of the complex, I turned the engine off and stood there contemplating the white vastness. I was all alone on the completely flat, arid surface. Only a few birds drifted by making a quick appearance before turning around and heading back to more life-friendly areas.

I'll stay here for the night! was my first thought. I tried to move towards the centre of the Sua Pan, but the thin crust of salt caved in under the weight of the bike, revealing the muddy layer of soil underneath, which made it really hard for the little wheels to move. I unloaded my stuff, set up the tent and, while I was waiting for the potatoes to boil, began to pluck my guitar. The sun was setting and the sky had taken an otherworldly pink hue that was reflected on the salt, lending some colour to the otherwise white surface. When darkness fell, the strong wind that started to blow made my jaw shiver with cold. Before getting into the tent, I took a look around. The pink shades of the sunset had vanished, and millions of stars had appeared above my head, making the pitch-black sky look like an endless shining canvas that I couldn't get my eyes off. I put on my warmest clothes, dumped the guitar and laid down on the salty crust, dazzled by the sight.

The sunrise saw me making hot coffee and thinking of those who once travelled across this land in search of water. Water is so rare and precious in this country. "*Sua*" – salt in the language of the San, the oldest people who have ever lived in the south of the African continent, was the only thing found in abundance. Later on, the industry came along and the extraction of sodium carbonate began. If Zambia had copper, Botswana was full of salt and diamonds, and, inevitably became the favourite target of colonists and multinationals.

Soon after leaving the absolute white nothingness of Makgadikgadi behind, the scarce trees of the waterless savanna showed up again. Since the first baobab I'd seen, somewhere in Senegal, until the day that those enormous trunks dominated the scenery once again, more than eight months had passed. I'd nearly crossed an entire continent. I found it hard to believe that, having travelled through places so different from each other, I'd found myself back in a place dear and familiar. And yet, here everything was different. Through the magnificence of the baobab cropped up signs that indicated the way to tourist lodges. The old clunkers circulating in the last savanna I'd been to, were now replaced by well-built 4x4s with logos of tour operators on their doors. The people I ran into were on holiday, their intention being to rest, see – without risking their ease – a few wild animals and buy colourful souvenirs. I didn't blame them, but I felt there was a distance between us. Maybe they felt the same way, when they lifted their cameras and aimed at me, seeing me as a quirky adventurer, whose story they'd soon forget, once they got back home.

THE FLIGHT

I arrived at Maun, unsure about the reason why. I thought I might visit the Okavango Delta, a place of exceptional beauty and great significance for the wild fauna and flora of Africa. I once read that it is one of the biggest inland river deltas on Earth, and that it received visitors from all over the world. I saw pictures of the canals that form throughout an expanse of many square kilometres, before the water of the Okavango River gets sucked by the permanently parched soil. I'd also seen documentaries about the islands that shelter the numerous and varied animal populations. I was convinced that I really had to go there. By the time I'd reached the city that served as the point of departure of tours to the famous delta, my thoughts were all tangled up in a messy skein and, when I got off at the only cheap campsite that I'd found, the only thing I'd achieved was to get even more confused!

Although there were a few locals that came up to admire the nature of their homeland, once more the majority were white people. The strange mood I was in made the organised tours seem annoyingly expensive and, soon, I started to question my decision to come here. Perhaps if I were at a different stage of my life it wouldn't bother me so much. However, when I realised that the only way to get closer to my destination was to pay a rather high amount and join a group, the thought of leaving crossed my mind. I restrained myself. I remembered that most people that knew me well sometimes appreciated my spontaneity but other times criticised it as self-destructive. I made a quick lunch, which set both my stomach and my mood right, and started to untangle the yarn ball that my thoughts had become, to avoid doing something that I'd bitterly regret.

Around evening time, I got chatting with some other travellers. "Seriously, you came all the way here and you're not going to see the delta?" one of them asked me, astounded. Then it dawned on me that I was following the same drill that everyone else almost inescapably did in places like this one. I was going with the flow, thinking that these were the only options available. On the other hand, in a country where everything looked so organised and predictable, in order to do anything that transgressed the boundaries of the tourist status quo, I had to try really hard. That was the difference that had me so confused. In Nigeria, in the Congo, in Mali, nothing was taken for granted. I had to search around even for the rudimentaries: the routes I'd take, the water I'd drink, the food I'd eat. But now I was at a campsite with the grill full of sausages that I'd bought at the supermarket. And yet my mind roamed back to Cameroon and the Congo, to the day I shared a little liquour sack with the elder of the village and a plate of wretched rice with a family that had allowed me to set my tent next to their shack.

In the morning, a cup of strong coffee and a satiating breakfast, with plenty of bread, olive oil and tomatoes, helped me quit the nagging. People used to say that I had the ability to deal with awkward situations with a sense of humour, and so that day, I chose to do just that. I had no idea of what was going to happen next. After a rigorous search for a relatively economical option that would allow me to see the famous Okavango Delta even for a little while, I finally decided to fly over it. Since Kitsos was categorically banned from going anywhere near the protected area, I figured that a flight was the closest alternative to the pleasure of riding. Five of us gathered up and got into a small six-seater airplane, which, for a full hour would fly us around, enabling us to enjoy the view from above. The pilot's first question was whether we were inclined to being nauseous and whether we had anything to eat before getting there. In an act of ingenuous self-confidence, I ignored his warning and within a few minutes, the plane made a wobbly take-off, shaken about by the wind.

The impressive river delta soon made its appearance. It branched out below us, like the airborne root of some giant plant, across an area the expanse of which I found hard to measure. The pilot, carefully manoeuvring the aircraft and diving every time he wanted to get closer to one of the animal herds that rambled nonchalantly around the peculiar land, was talking about the unique ecosystem. I was looking out the window and kept taking photos of everything. I'd paid around 50 euros and I was determined to make the best of every tiny bit of the flight. Until, suddenly, I felt pressure in my eyes and my blood started to flow away from my head, while cold sweat dampened my bald scalp. My stomach started to turn and images from my childhood came to my mind, back when my brother and I got sick in the family car on our way to the village. I'd never felt nauseous since then, but my symptoms left no room for a different explanation. Within a few minutes, my copious breakfast, coffee included, had been reserved in one of the bags available on the plane specifically for this purpose. My fellow passengers turned out to be in a similarly bad shape, since, right after me, one by one they filled the remaining sick bags. We looked at each other. We were all pasty-faced and worn-out, and only wished for one thing: landing!

DANCE THE LIONS AWAY

I spent one week in Maun, to put all the photos and the videos I had taken in order. When I finished, there was nothing left to do but take my leave. My relationships at the campsite did not evolve at all, since passing-by guests kept coming in and out, oblivious to the people around them. The days I'd spent there, apart from the realisation that it's never too late for someone to get airsick for the first time, also gave me the chance to better understand the reasons why I was in such a bad mood, which I couldn't shake off. I wasn't weary of travelling on my own. What I couldn't stand was the constant repetition of formalities when I met new people, who had neither the time nor the intention to share something beyond a superficial chit-chat. I'd rather be alone than tell the same story over and over again, like a broken record.

I was riding through the savanna of Botswana, undecided on whether I wanted to spend the night all by myself or whether I'd spend some of the time I had left on my visa with other people. I was a few kilometres away from the border with Namibia. As I passed by the village of Nokaneng, where the *Bayei* live peacefully with the *San* – two of the ethnic groups that live in the territory of Botswana – I thought about asking their permission to camp there. The entire settlement was built with materials that the land provides. All grey, with dirt shacks, reed fences and thatch roofs. Despite the overall dreariness of the place, there was something about it that I liked.

I pulled over under the shade of a tall tree, probably the locals' meeting point. Every village in Africa has a spot for that purpose, usually under the biggest tree of the area. There, all the assemblies take place and the important decisions of the community are made. I imagined the villagers having intense discussions in their language. The language that I'd heard for the first time in my life and which I found impossible to speak. Apart from the consonant and vowel sound that we're familiar with, some languages – mostly in the south of the continent – include sounds that, to our ears, sound like a '*click*'. When I attempted to imitate the pronunciation for the first time, flapping my tongue like they did, the result was a complete but hilarious failure. Under the tall tree of Nokaneng, where all important decisions were made, I made my own. I'd move on into the savanna until I'd find a place to set camp all alone.

As the dark set in, among the tall grass and the acacias, the first nocturnal sounds of nature started to sound. For as long as I could see, I wasn't really worried; but when everything around me turned black and surrendered to the dim moonlight, my reflexes sharpened to such an extent that I'd swear I could hear the steps of the ants around my tent. I hung the leftovers from a tree far away and shut each zipper hermetically, thinking that this way I'd keep nosy lions and indiscreet hyenas at bay. I lay down and remained completely still, trying not to make any noise at all, not even by breathing. I remembered the nights in the Senegalese savanna, when Liam used to tell me that, of all animals, only

244

hyenas are capable of detecting food inside a tent. The rest of them see it as an obstacle and just go past it.

I put my headphones on so as not to hear a thing and within a few moments I fell asleep. Around dawn, however, my overflowing bladder left me no choice: there was no way I could put it off any longer, I just had to get out. The noises and shuffling through the dry grass made my heart pound. I was, in all likelihood, surrounded by cattle. Livestock farming is the primary source of income in Botswana and the territory is at risk from overgrazing. At that moment, however, I found it hard to convince myself that whatever was out there wasn't lurking to devour me. My mind went to Maxim, the French cyclist I'd met a few months ago and whose trip had come to an inglorious end in Nigeria: "If you come face to face with a lion, do something that it'd never expect from a human to do: dance!" he once told us. *Poor Maxim!* I thought. *He survived the lions and got done over by a gang in Lagos!* After giving some serious thought though, I reached a decision. I was an awful dancer so I was only left with one option... I zipped the door of the tent open, leaving an opening just wide enough to fit the only part of my body that had to stick out, and, careful not to sprinkle my luggage, I stealthily watered the thirsty soil.

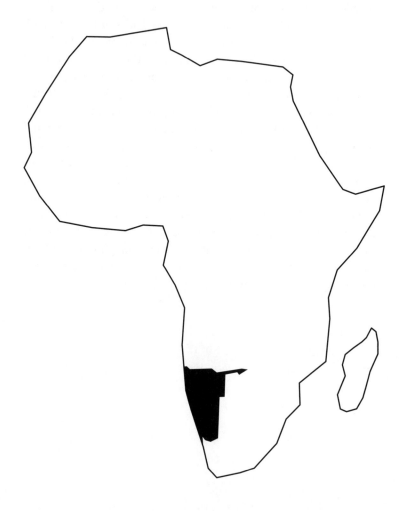

NAMIBIA

BARBED WIRES

The barbed wire over the concrete fence was electric, and hip-hop music came out of the dorms through the open doors. The garden where I'd set my tent however, was surprisingly well looked-after and far enough from the noisy public space, which was full of hung laundry and people talking loudly. The tenants – most of them local men – seemed to have been living in the guesthouse for quite some time and were anything but tourists. They were most likely workers, whose accommodation in the cheap lodgings was paid for by their company.

From the moment I set foot in Namibia, it was impossible to find one quiet spot to put my tent up and spend the night. I'd once read that it is one of the most sparsely populated countries in the world, second to Mongolia, and I'd fantasised about infinite stretches of land where I could stay and enjoy my solitude. But the reality in the north of the country proved to be totally different. I'd either bump into a fenced area – with a couple of barbed wire lines – or into a settlement, which would spread through a large part alongside the road. I'd camped so many times before in villages that I figured it would be just as easy to rely on the hospitality of the villagers there as well. But when I stopped at the first houses, among the cries of the children that ran up to receive me, I made out only one word: "*Money!*" These children seemed much more familiar with begging and foreigners than those I'd come across in the remote regions of Central Africa.

This is how I ended up in the 'jail guesthouse' of Rundu, a fellow tenant of the workers that had got there all the way from their distant villages, in search of a wage. Just a few kilometres away from Angola, on the bank of the Okavango River, Rundu was the first city I ran into. I was curious to see the country that all the travellers I'd met so far insisted that I should visit. With that funny mood that kept following me everywhere since Zambia, I set out the following morning with Tsumeb as my destination.

'More barbed wire!' I thought as I crossed through the gate of the well-hedged guesthouse of the small town. The main reason of Tsumeb's existence was the mineral wealth of the region. Its polymetallic ore brought the white colonists to the area in the early 20th Century. Back then, Namibia was called *German South West Africa*, a name that indicated the identity of those who exploited it. After WWI, it was taken from them by the British South Africans, who made it their own. The entire centre of Tsumeb looked like a typical German town. It was so clean and orderly that I thought I had suddenly been transported to Europe. My neighbours at the guesthouse – all of them white – talked about "hidden" destinations that could only be reached by means of organised tours, car renting and hiring the cheaper tourist agencies. As I heard them talk, I felt I was sinking into an unfathomable apathy. Until suddenly, the most unorthodox solution crossed my numb mind and awoke me: in Namibia, I would become a tourist!

ETOSHA

I left Tsumeb almost immediately, ready to visit the famous Etosha National Park. On the morning of my departure my breath still smelled of garlic and whiskey making me feel sick and nostalgic at the same time. I'd spent the night before as a guest in a Greek home – possibly the only one in the area. My host, who I had met by chance, took me in with excitement. He also asked his wife to make fried fish and *skordalia*[1] , a chance to reminisce – and I quote – 'the flavours of our motherland that kicked us out'. Around 75, once a well-built man with a strong

[1]*Skordalia is a traditional type of dip, the main ingredients of which are mashed potatoes and garlic.*

character, a feature that he still maintained, he told me that he never forgave his fellow countrymen for not fighting hard enough to fix Greece. Every time I tried to suggest that maybe things are more complicated than that, he guzzled down a good gulp of whiskey and, raising his voice, congratulated me for getting out of the country instead of staying and living a miserable life. I didn't feel that way. Even if I had stayed in Greece, I would never have turned into a miserable grouser. I guess it was his need to see himself in me fifty years ago and so I decided to humour him.

As I travelled across the vast fenced stretch of land, I began to think that the barbed wires were not there to protect the cattle from wild animals, but, instead, to prevent me from spending the night outdoors. I finally got a few kilometres away from the entrance to the Park and headed to a campsite nearby. I wanted to have as easy access as possible to the first 4x4 full of tourists that would set out for the protected area the next morning. I slept soundly. Not a care on my mind. Shortly after sunrise, I got onto the specially converted vehicle and started the six-hour safari through Etosha. Any other excursion, longer and more complex, would have been way over my budget, so my tourist experience had to be over within the strictly defined time limit.

The clicking of the cameras of my fellow passengers on the 4x4 sounded like shots from jammed machine guns, every time a herd of antelopes showed up. Giraffes trotted gracefully in front of us turning their heads undisturbed and blinking their enormous eyelashes. Zebras came out of everywhere, filling the dull, waterless scenery with black and white stripes. An elephant, familiar with the presence of humans, stood right in the middle of the road, as if mocking us for being unable to walk around free in his land. It was the dry season of the year and all the animals flocked together around the very few waterholes, which makes them easy targets for observation by the visitors. Jackals, ostriches and big rodents surrounded us and, as much as the permanent presence of other vehicles around us bothered me, when I managed to ignore them, the diversity of nature dazzled me.

The sudden murmur of muffled enthusiasm that broke out after the driver shushed us, made me turn my head abruptly. Two awe-inspiring horns entered my visual field. A couple of rhinos were standing right next to us, watching. The contour of their bodies – the most primitive and powerful thing I'd ever seen – stood out through the dry grass and, taking a few steps further, noticeably disturbed by our presence, they emerged and looked at us with the indifference that derived from their power. I'd only experienced similar feelings at the sight of the elephants, and the thought that both species are slaughtered by man for their horns and tusks filled me with immense sadness.

SKELETONS AND SEALS

"If you burn the clutch now, you're a complete idiot!" I shouted angrily at myself, who didn't have the patience to move a bit further away from the dry creek with the sandy bed. I was glad I'd finally found a spot to set camp all on my own and was so eager to get off the road that, for a moment, I thought that Kitsos would become an enduro bike that would take me across the river effortlessly.

As I moved westward to the Namib Desert, to reach the Atlantic coast, the landscape became more and more arid. The asphalt had disappeared and hundreds of dirt kilometres spread out ahead of me. The utter aridness and the strong winds laid the road completely bare, leaving only rocks in place, and the transit of the ruthless wheels of the 4x4 vehicles that drove on it had caused serious erosion all the way along. Poor Kitsos was bouncing, falling into each one of the vertical furrows and I was holding on to the handlebar as tight as I could, so as not to lose control.

I went past the town of Uis, the population of which had been waning, ever since the pewter reserve of the nearby mine became depleted. I moved on southwards, facing the peak of the Brandberg Mountain, the highest in Namibia. With the ancient rock paintings towering over the landscape, it intensified my desire to camp somewhere around there. About 20km further down, the completely dried up riverbed that I'd run into, beside the road, formed a somehow hidden plane which could conceal my presence. When I jumped onto the flimsy bottom of the river and smelled the smoke coming out of the tormented clutch, I dumped the scooter where it was and started unloading it. I was all alone, except for the bizarre-looking insects of the desert that were walking like acrobats on the bleached dirt. The sun was setting and it tinged the dull, yellowish grass with a shiny golden hue. I watched the colourful patterns in the sky change, until it went pitch black.

On the following day, I'd finally got to see the Atlantic again. I'd soaked my feet in seawater for the last time in March and now it was nearly mid-September. The Skeleton Coast, or, as the locals call it, "*The Land God Made in Anger*", spread out before me. The familiar thrumming of the waves, which I hadn't heard since I drove with Thanos along the edges of the Sahara, compelled me to open up the throttle. When I got there, the mist made the atmosphere at the coast grey and gloomy; some spots of the brown sand were darkened by the water and others brightened by the salt. I was lucky that there was no heavy fog that day; like the one that, over the centuries, had intimidated even the most fearless seafarers. Shipwrecks – victims of the rust and the saltiness – were rotting along with bones of cetaceans, which were washed out on the beach, permeating the place with the smell of death. To this day, although tourists keep flocking here to contemplate the land, they haven't managed to spoil its imposing grandeur.

Moving against the cold wind, I headed to Cape Cross and the seal colony that can be found there. Late in the afternoon I got to the exact spot where, in 1486, Diogo Cão erected a cross, claiming the land he was the first to step foot on, in the name of the Portuguese crown.

The visiting hours of this protected area, home to thousands of seals that gather to mate, rest and be photographed by the tourists, were strict. Within half an hour of walking on to the wooden platforms and observing with interest the behaviour of the cute mammals, I was notified that I had to leave. As I walked away, the smell of the blood from the wounds on the bulls' bodies, a result of their frequent fights with each other, mixed with the stench of the fish and the defeated dead animals, whose carcasses lay on the beach followed me. I chose to photograph the pups that were suckling on their mothers and looking at me with round, curious eyes and then I left, having felt the cruelty of nature in the struggle for dominance. As atrocious as it may seem, I found it reasonable to see animals obey their ancestral instincts. What I couldn't stand was to see the same thing happen among humans.

ONE WHITE, ONE BLACK

My hands and face had completely frozen since the previous night, they just wouldn't warm up no matter what. I'd made an early start to get to Swakopmund. As I moved southward along the coastline, the temperature kept dropping. The cold currents coming from the ocean bring to Namib the much-desired humidity that is so valuable to the few organisms that inhabit it, preventing the scorching heat of the desert from reaching the coast. The night I spent on the beach inside the tent, away from seals and tidal waves, I put on multiple layers of clothes and zipped the sleeping bag all the way over my head, mindless of whether I would be able to breathe or not. The remote wilderness and the big waves accompanied me from the spot where I'd set camp, north of Cape Cross, all the way to the town with the German architecture, the bistros, the shopping malls and the slums that surrounded it.

The only tree in the half-demolished campsite that I found in Swakopmund was an acacia. All campers staying in a tent at the ramshackle yard fought for a spot under its shade. I stupidly did the same, since I found a privileged empty spot when I arrived. The only tenants of the campsite that seemed to be permanent had retreated under the sun. They'd rather keep off those who would only spend a night under the poor acacia. I didn't talk much to my neighbours during the days I spent in Swakopmund. One time, when a Chinese couple kept me awake late at night with their shouts, I limited myself to a reprimanding shush. Another time, when a group of travellers set their tent right next to mine in such a way that it was blocking my entrance, I went up to them and reluctantly explained to them their foolish act. The only presence that spurred my interest was that of two weary bodies – one white, one black.

One of them, the white one, lived in his car, which was parked in a corner of the rickety campsite. Every day we'd bump into each other in the flooded kitchen with the broken windows and the burned power sockets and exchanged a few scattered words. He was around 70, tall and skinny. A piano repairer from South Africa, he'd lived in Namibia for over twenty years. His only source of income was the occasional tuning or fixing of pianos in houses and music schools. He cooked noodles with canned vegetables every day for two weeks straight – that's the time I'd spent there and I hadn't seen him make anything else.

"Why do you eat the same every day?" I asked him, although I could imagine why.

"Cause that's the cheapest meal I can prepare", he replied.

I wanted to help him.

"No it's not!" I said enthusiastically. "The cheapest meal is rice with frozen vegetables". I took out my calculator right away and showed him that, indeed, my option was more economical. He was glad and his snow-white beard, moved slightly sideways by his wide smile, drew open like a curtain, revealing a set of yellow teeth.

The other, the black one, was Stanley Dixon, whose real name was impossible for me to pronounce – and I felt really bad about it. For non-locals, who are incapable of imitating the 'clicks' present in his language, he had to come up with another name. He was a *Damara*, one of the oldest ethnic groups that have lived in the territory of Namibia for centuries. He was originally from Khorixas, a town up north, where I remembered having spent one night, not really worth mentioning. He'd arrived in Swakopmund driven away by the high rates of unemployment in his home region, looking for work. He lived either in the streets or in one of the slums, where the under-privileged of every place are always cast out. The very few days' wages he managed to scrape up here and there he spent on booze.

When he saw me for the first time, I was filming my own mug for a video I wanted to make. He came up and sat next to me on the bench at the beach. We started talking and he talked to me about the hardships of life and poverty. Through his half-drunk

253

words, bitter truths came out. The next time I ran into him, I gave him my jeans, a spare T-shirt and some change, hoping he wouldn't drink it away.

OVAHIMBA

I was wandering around the aisles of the supermarket, browsing through the oversupply of packaged goods. There was nothing particularly cheap. It was the first time I'd missed some chocolate, a package of needless snacks, full of sugar, salt and artificial colourings. In the heart of the Congo, in the jungle of Cameroon and on the dirt trails of Nigeria, I'd almost never craved for all these goodies. I ate rice and mangos that abounded and I was happy. My daily life was so exciting that I never felt like I missed anything. Only when I saw them right in front of me, at unreasonable prices considering the income of the average citizen of Namibia, did I remember what they tasted like and my mouth started drooling. As I walked out empty-handed through the automatic sliding doors, a strange figure standing nearby in total discordance with the shiny packages and the marble floors caught my eye. She was a *Himba*.

At one of the guesthouses I'd stayed, I'd stumbled upon a bunch of brochures advertising the sights of the country to tourists. All of them, along with the rhinos, antelopes and arid moonscapes, featured a few Himba people; a semi-nomadic group that lives in the north of the country and are mostly livestock farmers. Most photos showed young women dressed in animal skins – some of them breastfeeding their babies. Their complexion was auburn from the paste they make using ochre pigment and butterfat, which they spread over their skin to cleanse and protect it from the sun. Their hair is elaborately braided and covered with the same material. They posed in front of earthen huts and seemed untouched by time, as if they were a charming and silent component of the landscape. Seeing those brochures, one would readily wonder whether there are Himba men, hidden somewhere behind the women's exotic beauty. One would wonder whether there are Himba old women, ugly, with wrinkled skin and droopy breasts. Maybe they'd think that somewhere in this world there are still people that remain unspoiled by Western civilisation.

In that supermarket, the answer to every question regarding the 'noble savages' and their exotic portraits was revealed to me. The woman, who was pushing a cart exactly like the one I was pushing along the aisles, shopped for cookies, potato chips and bread, wearing a purple lycra hoodie. Her skin and hair were orange from the ochre and her wrists and ankles were ornamented with jewels that conveyed some sort of information about her social status. I looked more carefully. Among the traditional bracelets, an electronic watch appeared. Outside the supermarket, sitting on the concrete slabs, a few more Himba women with their children were knitting jewellery and spread it out on the ground, for sale to the passing by tourists. They had puffer jackets draped around their shoulders, which they took off to be photographed, mindful of not spoiling the image that others had fabricated of what a 'primitive' Himba, should look like. The babies wore disposable nappies and drank milk from a carton. Next to the eldest of the group, a bottle of alcohol was tucked sloppily in a paper bag. Every now and then, I watched her take a sip. They would spend the night inside the tents they had set nearby; tents that looked just like mine.

I said hello, smiled and asked them to pose. They unwillingly made as if to take their jackets off, but I told them they didn't need to. I wanted the jackets and the watch and the baby's nappy to show. Not once did it occur to me to hire some tourist agency and 'live the Himba experience' in the remote villages – as the brochures said. Not once did it cross my mind to give some change to a fellow human being in order to dance, show me his home, or fake a smile for my camera.

I got back and went straight to the bistro in downtown Swakopmund where I used to hang out. More brochures for organised tours. Among them, a slightly different one: "Township Tours", it read. I took it in my hands and opened it. On its glossy pages there were pictures of the slums that spread around on the outskirts. Tin shacks, filthy roads and stands instead of stores. Among all that, are smiling pariahs welcoming tourists to their daily lives. They sing, dance and offer treats to the visitors in exchange for some change, with the delusion that they'll get something more.

On the one hand, the supposedly pure lifestyle of the 'primitive tribes' – custom-made to fit the Westerner's fantasy – and on the other, organised visits to what may well represent the utmost failure of the Western lifestyle and urbanisation, the slum. And me, drinking my coffee from a nice porcelain cup, I still couldn't wrap my mind around the world.

TRAFFIC LIGHTS, ZEBRA CROSSINGS AND A GENOCIDE

As soon as Steven and Katrina saw me, when we met again after a long time, they burst into laughter.

"What have you done?" my old fellow-traveller asked me, unable to recognise me without the beard.

"It'll grow back, what's the big deal?" I tried to calm him down, touching my face self-consciously.

On my last day in Swakopmund, before heading to Windhoek, the capital, I decided to groom my messy beard a little bit. It had grown way too long and it was becoming a drag. My hair was the easiest part. It was so fine and sparse that it only took a few swipes with the razor for it to vanish from my head. But the beard was rough and dense and had grown in all possible directions. I took the scissors and shortened one side. The other one, though, did not turn out even, so I thought I might correct that. I ended up with a well-trimmed stubble, symmetrical and proper, a discrete five o'clock shadow on my chin. I looked at myself in the mirror. I'd forgotten what I looked like back when I lived in Greece. Then, a crazy thought crossed my mind. I held the razor. Moments later I took another look in the mirror, all clean shaven. *Mistakes like this one take time to fix!* I thought. My rough looks over the past few months – a symbol of my freedom – suited me better.

In Windhoek, I planned to stay only for a few days. Two local white men put me up and I seized the opportunity to learn a bit more about Namibia first-hand. The mines, stock-breeding and tourism had created a middle class, which is rare in most African countries. The dark past, however, was well-hidden from the eyes of visitors and the big corporations didn't care anyway. I felt ashamed for being clueless. The German colonists, in the early 20ᵗʰ Century, wiped out eighty per cent of the *Herero* population and half of the *Nama* people, who had been living in the region for centuries before the European colonists came along. The indigenous populations were exterminated, after being regarded as "non-humans" by the authors of the genocide. The resistance of the people, who saw their land and cattle being snatched from them as they gradually got displaced toward the desert, led to their punishment and almost complete extinction. Germany never apologised for this genocide, until a century later, without, however, committing to compensate the descendants of the victims in any way.

"And South Africa came to help out with the situation", one of my hosts went on to say. "Until it implemented the apartheid regime here, too, that is", he added, lowering his voice.

I left Windhoek and its orderly streets, well-pruned parks, its traffic lights and zebra crossings behind. I felt that, no matter how much I travelled, I never had the time to know the places I saw well enough. Behind every single thing a tangled skein of events and circumstances loomed, invisible and often-times forgotten. With all that in my mind and the difficulty to believe that Namibia became an independent state as recently as in 1990 – after a series of arrogations and armed conflicts – I got off the central road and back on the rutty dirt. This time I headed for Sossusvlei. Steven and Katrina stayed in the capital to see if they could sort out some bureaucratic issues that had come up. I wasn't sad that I'd continued on my own. Perhaps because I preferred it that way, even though I didn't really know why.

HOSPITALITY AND TOURISM

"Please, let me in". "It's dangerous to go on!", were the last words I had time to address to the guard of the lodge, before he turned his back on me and walked nonchalantly back to his shack. It was pitch dark and the corroded dirt road seemed endless.

I'd travelled around 350km, unable to find a single place to set my tent up that was not wrapped up in barbed wire. Since the moment I got off the highway, I'd been riding tinged in white through a cloud of dust, kicked up by the hundreds of 4x4s that passed me. Their destination was the most well-known sight of the area, Sossusvlei. I'd stopped countless times to screw the mirrors and the front fender of the Vespa back on, which kept loosening from the shocks. My arms were sore from the effort I had to make in order to keep the handlebars straight. Even the wooden mask I'd bought in Lusaka to decorate the windshield had broken. At least I had changed the uncomfortable jerrycan I was carrying on the scooter's floor between my legs, and the new one was now well attached with a strap. When it was completely dark, the headlights could only provide visibility a few metres ahead and my weak eyes started to blur.

Worn out, I arrived at the entrance of the luxurious lodge and my relief was ineffable, when I thought that I'd finally found a place to spend the night. But I was left flabbergasted looking at the guard's back who – without once taking his eyes off his cellphone the whole time – explained to me cynically that there was no way he could let me cross the gate and set my tent up, not even for a few hours, until dawn. I was forced to keep riding all the way to the next lodge, which was twenty dark and exhausting kilometres away. At last, I was there. The guard here was only slightly more eager. With his head flashlight on, he showed me the place where I could camp and left me there struggling to find my way around in the darkness.

The weird mood that had been following me for some time now, since I left the Congo for the more "developed" countries, seemed to have abandoned me over the last few days, but that night in the tent, it came back to me. *Who the hell leaves their fellow man alone like that in the middle of the night?* I wondered. I couldn't understand the lodge guard's behaviour, leaving me outside like that, totally unconcerned by the danger I was facing. The tension wouldn't let me sleep so I took my towel and headed for the bathroom. It was only then that I realised that the spot where I have put my tent was at least 800m away from the campsite facilities. I arrived at the restaurant, a big, luxurious thatched hut and asked whether there had been some mistake.

"You have no reservation", came the manager's staggering answer.

"But the campsite is almost empty", I complained.

"Right, but you still have no reservation" he repeated meaninglessly. I went back unrewarded and decided to try and have some sleep.

The next morning, rested and in a better mood, I walked to the reception to find out how I could visit the famous red sand dunes of Sossusvlei, which were around 50km away. The otherworldly formations, dead trees whose carcasses stand like macabre ornaments, and the salt pan that is formed right in the middle of the desert featured in all travel guides and countless movies, commercials and music videos. The rules were clear: I was not allowed to enter in my own vehicle and go wherever I wanted; the only thing I was allowed to do was take the half-hour tour arranged by them. Maybe I would have accepted the rules and not flushed in anger, had the rude office worker looked at me just once, as she went over them idly, all the while fidgeting with her cellphone. I remembered the previous guard, who, in a very similar way, had thrown me out from the other lodge. I remembered the awful dirt road that nearly broke my scooter to pieces and the road taxes I'd paid when I got to Namibia. I remembered that I, too, came from a country that has dipped into the pros and cons of the mass tourism industry. But I also remembered the Congo, the "inhospitable" Congo, where I had been received so warmly.

"Thanks but no thanks, I won't be visiting the sand dunes", I muttered as I walked out.

"You still owe me your entrance fee to Sossusvlei" her irritating voice sounded.

"But I'm not going", I answered, perplexed.

"You don't understand; you see, you're already *inside*" came the infuriating reply. Her kind colleague cut in, in an attempt to calm me down.

"I'm sorry, but, according to the rules, insofar as you have put your name down on the visitors' book, you have to pay."

I looked at him wide-eyed. He lowered his voice and went on explaining, as he showed me out of Sossusvlei. He told me how much tourism had changed his fellow countrymen. He told me that genuine hospitality had been lost, something the locals used to be known for. He and Stanley, the "madman" of Swakopmund, were the only ones who mentioned the low wages, the high cost of living, injustice and social inequality. I paid for my entrance to the sand dunes that I never got to see. Deep down, I empathised with him.

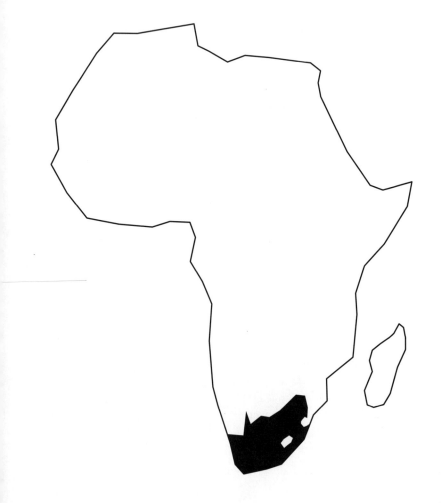

SOUTH AFRICA

WHERE TO FROM HERE?

The hail was bashing relentlessly against the shed under which I'd placed the tent, luckily. The waterless Namibia was saying goodbye to me in the most unexpected way and I couldn't wait for the bad weather to ease so I could set out for South Africa, the only state whose name is nothing but a geographic qualifier. I had no plan. I'd just get into the country and then I'd see what I'd do next.

"I talked to my parents. You'll stay in our house in Pretoria", Naoum assured me. He and his wife had set out some time ago on a trip from their home all the way to Ukraine, her home country. We met at one of the last campsites I stayed at in the south of Namibia, and the only thing that I found surprising about that young couple was their passion about leading a virtuous life, guaranteed only by marriage – according to them. I wished them good luck and our paths parted.

Late in the afternoon, I crossed the border, and the certainty of the officer that there were no documents whatsoever needed for bringing my vehicle into the new country made me worry. Despite my persisting questions, he seemed positive, so I was left with no choice but to trust him.

The paved straight line to Pretoria would have been easy and rather boring to ride on, if it hadn't been for the horrendous driving of the locals and the desperate search for a spot free of barbed wire to erect my tent, which altogether made the time go by really slowly. I rode a little over 1,000km before I got to the doorstep of my host, Naoum's father. Roger was waiting for me with open arms. The squashy mattress on which I lay that night took my weary mind off the one thought that had started to harrow it. I was in South Africa. I was almost at the tip of the huge continent and soon enough I'd have to make a decision: *Where to from here?*

TOO MUCH FREEDOM IS BAD

"Would you mind praying with us?", Roger asked, and the forkful that was already on its way to my mouth was left hovering over the plate. I put it back there together with the juicy steak, whose smell during cooking had brought me to the verge of fainting, and looked at him baffled. Roger and Melanie, his wife, stretched their arms over to me and we held hands in a rather comical – to my eyes – way. The mental circle we drew up enclosed a few chunky steaks, two or three sausages, some fries and a big bottle of cola. Both of them thanked Jesus for the cholesterol he offered them and I smiled and grabbed my fork again.

"Do you believe?" the question was bound to arise.

Within the short interval that elapsed before I uttered something, all kinds of possible answers crossed my mind, but I opted for the most diplomatic one.

"I was baptised an Orthodox Christian, according to the tradition of my country".

That was true. The disarming sincerity of a plain "no" addressed to two people who weren't likely to tolerate it could have me end up looking for a place to spend the night. Besides, I found the opportunity to spend some time close to something so different, intriguing.

For a moment the following morning I thought I was the lead participant in an episode of Candid Camera, the victim of a well-organised prank. Naoum's younger brother came by his parents' house just to meet me.

"Do you know Jesus?" were his first words.

"Well...yes..." I answered without knowing what to say next.

"Do you talk to each other?"

Unconsciously, I turned around to check whether there was

some friend of his hidden somewhere with a camera, filming my astonishment. There was no one around.

"I guess not", was the only thing that occurred to me.

Although he was studying for a university degree in New Technologies, he seemed more concerned about the salvation of his soul.

The following Sunday, I was invited to his church – the one for young people. Perhaps he wanted me to have a chat with his favourite God-man, as well. The room was overflowing with electric guitars, drums and Christian love, and when some of the young devout attendees got caught up into a weeping ecstasy, I felt so uncomfortable that I almost hid myself behind one of the seats. On our way back home, yet another discussion about the presence of Jesus Christ in the daily lives of good people got me so worn out that I immediately started to look for my next destination and to speed up the bureaucratic procedures in Pretoria.

On my way to the Greek Embassy, I stumbled upon a grocery store downtown, with big Greek letters on the door sign. I stopped and went inside. The few Greek customers of the small café tucked in a corner welcomed me and I naively thought they would help me find a place to stay. They were all middle-aged men, convinced they'd discovered the meaning of life.

"We were fine during the Apartheid regime", one of them told me, reminiscing the shameful past of the country that fed them.

"Too much freedom is bad!" the other one pointed out, mindless of what would happen if it were his own freedom that was deemed excessive and in need of restriction. I thanked them for the coffee, promptly turned my back and fled from their hypocrisy.

"Your fellow countrymen are right", was Roger's comment, when I recounted my conversation with the Greeks. The tea that we were having at his yard suddenly turned bitter. My patience was wearing thin. I'd decided not to say anything, but I couldn't hold myself back anymore.

"OK, but still Apartheid was inhumane", I dared say.

"Now that it's over, do you think things are better?" my host asked me in a self-righteous tone. "Look around you; there are blacks everywhere!" I had trouble speaking.

"I pray every day because I want to see my life get better, but blacks can't understand that", he went on. "Some day, with the help of Jesus, I'll have all I need to be happy". Nothing made sense to me anymore.

"What do you need to be happy, Roger?", I asked.

"Money!" At that point I just sat there speechless and looked at him.

"Don't get me wrong, I'm no racist", he added by way of a feigned excuse. "Everyone in this world should know their place". I no longer wanted to continue talking to him. I didn't even want to be there next to him.

"Ever since the blacks mixed with the whites things got tougher", he said, though I wasn't really listening to him anymore.

I looked at his beautiful house and his verdant garden full of flowers and trees in blossom. I looked at his car; his brand-new family car; his freshly ironed clothes. The neighbourhood, which spread beyond the electric barbed wire fence. The black gardener who was pruning the rose bushes. I left the next morning.

RAINBOW NATION

"If you've been with a black woman, you might as well forget about me!" I was at the packed living room of my host, James, in Johannesburg, and I had just finished the presentation of my trip, which I had agreed to deliver to thank him for his hospitality. The projector still cast its light on the wall, displaying the picture of that girl in Ouagadougou, who had got me to buy a bunch of avocados just with her warm smile. I looked at the well-dressed woman who tried to hit on me in the most hideous way. I wanted to stand up and insult her. Make her feel as embarrassed as possible. Tell her that her flirting, instead of being flattering, offended me. But I kept still. Calmly, I started explaining to her that the only reason I hadn't engaged in a relationship of this nature with a black woman was that I just hadn't happened to meet one that would trigger such desire to me.

My words were interrupted by another guest, a young man in his thirties who, after shouting out that only open-minded people could ever fix the mess that the country was in and that people like her were the ones that ruined it, dashed out of the apartment, banging the door behind him.

James, the hospitable South African that put me up – not for being a white Christian, but for being a traveller – stood there clearly uncomfortable. And yet, even though I tried, I couldn't register a trace of surprise on his face. Later that night, he explained that bouts of racism were on the daily agenda of many locals and he was just fed up. The only thing that could keep him going was to cut off those who expressed such views. He apologised for the woman that was among his house guests.

"*Rainbow Nation*" was a term that Desmond Tutu coined for his country when, in 1994, the first democratic elections were held in the post-apartheid South Africa. It referred to the multicultural identity and peaceful co-existence of the country's citizens. Maybe I'd run into the wrong people, but the exceptions to the racist discourse over my first few weeks in this strange country were alarmingly few.

I left James' house as well, and the couple that put me up for a few days – before I retreated into the tranquillity of nature away from Johannesburg – was a pleasant surprise. Two men, married to each other for a long time, talked to me about their lives in such a way that made me forget for a while my foul experiences so far. I wondered how it was possible, in a country that had only recently conceded equal rights to its non-white population, for marriage between people of the same sex to be a constitutional right. I thought about the other African countries I'd been to, where homosexuality is legally prosecuted. I remembered the time when, in Benin and Nigeria, Steven and I had to come up with all sorts of nonsense about being brothers, just to avoid being forced to pay for separate rooms. My mind also ran back to Greece, where many supposedly progressive people insist they have no problem accepting gay people, as long as they make no claim to equal rights.

And just when I started to get all worked up with people's desire to control everything around them, I went out for a stroll and saw how beautiful the place was. I had to focus on something beautiful in order to continue my trip in South Africa. My escape impulses had already started to flare up again.

MELVILLE

The 55km that I had to travel to get back to Melville, the neighbourhood of Johannesburg that I'd left a few days previously, were quite big a deal. I got off the highway and into the streets of one of the greenest cities I'd ever seen. The jacaranda branches with their flowers in full blossom arched over my head forming a purple vault, and the grass that cropped up everywhere on the sidewalks instead of the expected concrete plates, confused my perception of what an urban landscape should look like.

I found it hard to understand how a city so beautiful could possibly have such a dark side. Everyone kept warning me that crime rates in Johannesburg are not just the usual overstatement of the media. Already back in Lubumbashi, Greek businessmen that had dealings with South Africa had told me the worst of stories: stories about robberies, kidnappings and rapes, and I thought I'd enter an endless ghetto, out of which nobody ever gets out alive. Trees and flowers don't belong in a ghetto. I had to carefully observe the inconspicuous strands of daily life to understand that all I'd heard might actually contain more than just a grain of truth. Walls and fences with electric barbed wires hid well behind the blossomed trees. Ragged black people squatted in empty lots, setting up makeshift shacks. Signs on painted fences warned that the private security patrols have the right to shoot real bullets. Car drivers are lawfully allowed to skip a red light, if they feel threatened.

I arrived at my destination. I got into the café on the corner of 4th and 7th Street and started to scan the place in search of the two women. It was hard to believe that over the past few days we'd been living almost next to each other and yet we'd never met. I looked at every table. They were nowhere to be seen. I walked back towards the exit, and, before I even had the time to recognise her, Alexandra popped out of nowhere, spread her arms and hugged me.

"Didn't I tell you that the two of us would meet again somewhere?", she said, and a wide smile brightened her blue eyes. Right behind her was Effie, her teacher from the university, who put her up at the time. She, too, came up to me and kissed me joyfully. We sat at one of the tables and spent the following two hours talking incessantly. We talked about the Congo, about

Lubumbashi, where we first met, about our lives, about our journeys. Our coffee cups soon went empty and we continued with beers at the nearby pub. Then our bottles went empty as well and it was time for dinner, at the nearest restaurant. Then our plates were wiped clean and we just stayed there talking, since there was no place left open for us to go.

"Come stay with us!", Effie suggested before we said goodnight.

"I guess I'll be off to Cape Town soon", I replied, only to regret revealing my plans within seconds. It had been long since I'd last hung out with people who I felt I had a lot in common with and suddenly my need to stick around overpowered my wish to head south.

"I can't find good Greek yoghurt here", Effie complained as she handed the bowl over to us, in order to make the tzatziki[1] I'd promised her. Immediately, she turned back to the frying pan to flip the zucchini fritters. She rarely cooked – so she said – but I didn't believe her. Her zucchini fritters were the tastiest I'd ever tried! Tunes from Mali, the Congo and Ethiopia poured out of the laptop and blended together with the smell of the spices. After three days of torrential rain that kept me stranded in the place where I had been staying, I'd finally made it to her house. It was a true celebration day. Alexandra skimped on the garlic and I teased her, throwing entire garlic cloves into the pot she was stirring. The wine flowed abundantly. Anton, with his scathing sense of humour, made us laugh ceaselessly and Elie with his kind disposition reminded me of my happy days in the Congo. Himself a Congolese, he'd been living in South Africa for years, as a refugee. I wanted to ask him why, but that day, there was no room in Effie's terrace for bad memories. Only laughter. And wine.

STORIES IN THE DARK

It was mid-November and the house was full of suitcases and scattered clothes. Alexandra was sleeping in the small room next

[1] Tzatziki is a sauce served as a dip. It is made of salted strained yogurt mixed with grated cucumber, garlic, olive oil and herbs like dill or fennel.

to the bedroom and I, in the living room. Elie ran off at dawn, every day, to get to work on time; he worked at the warehouse of a supermarket. At night, he'd stay up until his eyes would get really heavy and leave him no choice but to go to sleep. He struggled to finish law school, which he had recently got back to. The image of a careless student sipping on frappé coffee in some small Greek town came to my mind, only to get shattered when I found out about his life. The age of carelessness never came for him. He was *Baluba* and came from Mbuji-Mayi, the Congolese region that had always been coveted by the powerful of this world. Who would ever leave people who sleep on top of diamonds alone? Ever since he was a child, he plunged into the mud together with his brothers and picked the precious stones, to feed his large family. He reminded me of my little aces – the three kiddies that followed me everywhere, during the days I spent there. Of the most persecuted ethnicities in the Congo, the Baluba people were either driven out of their land, or became refugees, so as not to have the same fate as those slaughtered in Kasai. So Elie's course was practically predetermined: he was bound to cross lots of risky borders until getting to South Africa without papers, and end up with any precarious job he could get – mostly as a parking valet. And when, late at night, the cars of the middle-class locals would get scarce, he'd snatch some time and grab his books, hoping to never have to put them down again. It was a book he had in his hands when Effie first met him.

Just like in any country with incompetent governors, in South Africa, too, the *African National Congress*, now bankrupt, has become the means by which a privileged minority feathers its nest. Its subversive, reformist momentum, which gave it the lead in the 1994 multiracial elections, when Mandela was first elected President, had now degenerated in the hands of his successors. President Zuma, to deflect negative attention while he led an outrageously extravagant lifestyle and was completely incapable of doing anything whatsoever to solve the problems of his country, resorted to a discourse of hate. "Immigrants from other African countries come here and steal your jobs from you!", he stated authoritatively and his words made my skin crawl. Every now and then on the news, we heard about black South Africans assaulting black immigrants. *What about the whites?*

"Weren't the homeless people begging at the two traffic lights on the way to the house white?", I asked Effie.

"Things change", she answered.

Money is colourless. So are corruption and power. In South Africa, rich white and black people muddle up the game within a maze of class and racial inequality.

The wine was running short and we were left there staring outside, at the dark terrace. Elie was asleep. Our conversation had woven a thick blanket, like those old woollen ones which, while they muffle you within their warmth, also coop you up under their bristles and don't let you roll over in bed. We were thinking about the future. We liked Africa. Alexandra was considering settling here. Effie had lived here for almost fifteen years and I was still trying to balance between my sense of complete familiarity and my escape impulse, which just wouldn't let go of me. And there we were, daydreaming again.

"What if I stayed here as well?" I wondered.

"If you go to South America, maybe we'll meet again there", said Effie, who had been long looking for a good reason to leave Johannesburg. Alexandra got up and said goodnight. As she walked away, I saw tears in her eyes.

SO WILL YOU JOIN HIM AFTER ALL?

The afternoon summer storm caught us somewhere on the road. "Time to put our rain jackets to test!" I told Alexandra and parked the Vespa hastily. We ran underneath a shed and started getting dressed. My jacket was light green and hers, pink. She wrapped her arm in mine and held on tight to me. Her face was half-hidden under the hood and the only thing I could get a glimpse of was her smile.

"We make a good match in these sassy colours!" she joked. Ever since I'd proposed that she join me on the trip, her mood had changed. She wouldn't stop laughing. Only at night, when it was time for her to get back to her room, her eyes grew darker. I wanted to know why, but it was hard to make her open up.

The rain stopped and the road led us to the notorious city centre.

"Maybe walking around here is not such a good idea", she said as we were looking for the Carlton Center.

"Everyone says it's dangerous!" she added, trying to back up her hesitation.

"If it was that dangerous, would people live here?" I asked her. I was sick and tired of warnings of lethal dangers throughout Africa and I just refused to pay further heed to them. However, that day in Johannesburg, I wasn't alone. I wanted to make Alexandra feel at ease, because I could see her struggle against her own fears. I'd never be a teacher or an obnoxious know-it-all. I would just walk beside her. The decay of the formerly prosperous heart of the city was noticeable in every step. Multi-story buildings that housed multinational corporations' offices, before they abandoned the area, and boulevards with traffic lights and narrow concrete sidewalks, were all in stark contrast with the street vendors and the young people straying around, broken by unemployment and poverty.

The skyscraper we were looking for was not far. We had to lean our heads back until out necks hurt in order to take in its full size. We went up to the top floor and spent quite some time contemplating the world from the *Top of Africa*, as the informative signs read. Below us spread one of the biggest and most special cities I'd ever been to. In a country where only ten per cent of the population is white, black people up until recently struggled to prove that they were human. In a country open to refugees, which grants asylum to the persecuted, which allows same-sex marriage and which has one of the most powerful – according to numbers – economies in the whole continent, people are afraid of getting around. The leafy parks of the metropolis Johannesburg and its blossomed alleys are deserted. The low houses with the pretty yards are surrounded by barbed wire and – with the exception of the very few neighbourhoods where restaurants and bars face the streets – most of the residents prefer spending their free time in guarded shopping malls. Without feeling threatened that day, we wandered around its boulevards, took lots of pictures and late in the afternoon we headed back home.

"So will you join him after all?" Effie asked Alexandra, when she saw the brand new helmet, hanging from her arm. Although it seemed that she had already made up her mind, she still hesitated to make the official announcement.

"Well, I already got the helmet, so..." she replied.

THIS IS WHAT I WAS MISSING!

Effie seemed in a great mood on the day of our departure. She'd been travelling ever since she was young and, although she was now into her fifties, she preserved her readiness and zest intact. She was really glad she'd lent Alexandra clothes and little things that could come in handy during the trip. At the first cranking, Kitsos roared like a lion – or so the noise of the engine sounded in my ears, which were buzzing with enthusiasm. We sat comfortably on the seat and, only when the garage door was shut behind us and we got out on the street, did I realise that it was for real: it was two of us on the Vespa. *Let's wait and see for how long!* I thought, completely clueless of what was yet to come.

Less than an hour since we'd set off, the cellphone GPS, confused by the traffic interchanges within the city, started leading us to the wrong direction. We soon realised that we were just riding in circles around the alleys, unable to locate the highway. I stopped next to a school that, during recess time, was teeming with students, and focused on the screen, trying to find a way out on the map. The place was full of people walking down the paths, while on the streets cars drove along at a leisurely pace. We didn't get off the bike. The warnings about the dangers in Johannesburg were way too many, so it would be naive of me to dismiss them completely. Suddenly, out of the corner of my eye, I saw a group of young men heading towards us, with their hands in their pockets and their heads hidden under their jacket hoods. Their eyes were fixed on us. I immediately handed the cellphone to Alexandra, who, as if expecting it to happen, took it right out of my hands. I put both my feet on the ground and, avoiding any eye contact with them, we rolled down a few metres away, until the engine started – push-starting in second gear – and disappeared. I turned my head back and looked at them. They stood in the middle of the street watching us ride off in the distance.

"Off we go!" sounded the sighing voice of my new fellow traveller as, at last, two hours later, we were getting out of the city. She'd become really scared and frankly, what had nearly happened got me upset, too. Not so much for the imminent robbery that was avoided, but because, for the first time after an entire year on the road, the threat didn't come from some corrupt police or military officer, but from common, everyday people. I remembered Nigeria with all its troubles, but that day in Johannesburg, beside the children and the careless passers-by, the robbery would seem really out of place.

Away from the city, on the rural road we finally chose, our mood started to change and the rice and chickpeas which Effie had made for us and which we ate while staring at the endless meadows and the bright blue sky, made us forget ourselves. Late in the afternoon, we stopped at the first campsite that we stumbled upon and started to unload. I put up the tent joking that, next time, it would be Alexandra's turn to do it and we sat on the ground, to enjoy the view of the lake. The branch tips of the weeping willow that had grown at the shore, reached down over the surface of the crystalline water and looked as if they were floating, drifted along by its faint movement.

"Want some beer?", I said and extended the bottle I had in my hand towards her. She smiled and took it. I watched her take a sip and, right there and then, the ends of the tangled skein of thoughts were pulled out and suddenly the jumbled knot got unravelled. This is what I was missing: a person to share my experiences with!

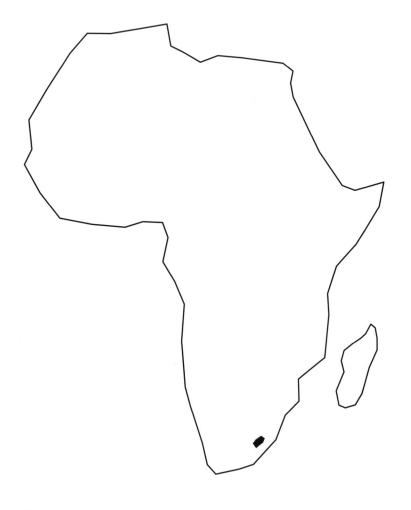

LESOTHO

NO MORE BARBED WIRE!

I was convinced that there couldn't be much of a difference between Lesotho and South Africa. Besides, the tiny Kingdom of two million people – an almost round speck on the map – is an enclaved country that, no matter which part of its borders you cross, you end up back in South Africa.

As usual, I'd read very little about the place we were about to visit. I was mostly interested in practical information: the altitude, the state of the road network, the access to fuel. I wasn't particularly nervous about the latter, though. The horror stories about the shortage of fuel in isolated parts of Africa had long faded away. Even if it came in plastic bottles, I'd always find some. But now I wasn't travelling alone. I shared the seat of the Vespa with Alexandra, and I wasn't at all sure how it would behave with two people on it at high altitude. The change in the performance of the engine became noticeable already when I got to 1,800m above sea level, at the long straight stretches of road in South Africa.

"Well, if it can't climb up I'll have to push it!" Alexandra said when I confessed my worry, and her eagerness filled me with joy.

We crossed over from the northern border, without a set route. Tom, who'd put me up for a few days on the outskirts of Pretoria, had insisted I should travel to Lesotho, while I was trying to get him to understand that, after the Congo, I no longer felt I was in Africa. Zambia, Namibia and South Africa had me fed up with their fences and their tediously predictable structure. However, something felt different here, as soon as I talked to the officers at the border. Maybe it was just me and my need to see something that would make me change my mind. Or maybe it was the fact that Alexandra was with me. It'd been some time since I'd travelled with somebody, but now things were different. Thanos, Liam, Steven and Francis all had their own vehicles and their own route, and when it didn't match mine, they'd just make a turn and leave. I still found it hard to believe that Alexandra had decided to get on the bike and come along with me. She'd warned me though: "If you get too much for me, just drop me off at a train station to get on the next train to Johannesburg!"

Administrative procedures were quick and easy. The passports were stamped there and then and nothing else was needed. The little wheels of the scooter rolled on the narrow yet paved road and the first breaths of Lesotho air I took filled my lungs with optimism. For the first time I felt strongly that I was in a completely different place after crossing a political border. I looked at South Africa behind me. The scenery was, of course, identical. And yet there was a decisive detail which I soon noticed: there was no barbed wire. I was sick of barbed wire. Endless stretches of barriers that, in many cases, I couldn't even find a reason for. Privately owned lands, protected areas, safety. All restrictions are justified if they're in place for "safety reasons", they say. Already since Namibia, the waste of such quantities of metal had begun to get to me. In South Africa, I'd come to terms with them as a reality that seemed impossible to change. Here, they were simply nowhere to be found.

PEACHES AND SMILES

It was late November, summertime in the southern hemisphere, and that day the sun was shining. The road that cut through Butha-Buthe had no traffic at all. As we entered the city, I could no longer hold it in:

"At last, back to Africa!" I shouted to Alexandra, who didn't know what I was talking about yet.

The outdoor market with the stands and the makeshift shacks spread along the road, on the dark-coloured soil and the filthy, broken curb. I'd missed these markets while I was in Johannesburg. Even in Zambia and Namibia, where tourism commands that the folklore tone be neat and tidy, the chaotic bazaars were somewhere out there, but my bad mood had prevented me from scouting them out. But now I just bumped into them. Around us, women arrayed their products, be it fruit and vegetables, or clothes and electrical appliances, and sold them at ideally low – considering my budget – prices. The racket was rather annoying to Alexandra, who, despite having spent a few months in Africa, seemed like she'd much rather pass by the specific place, take pictures of anything that interested her and avoid any transaction whatsoever. I felt the exact opposite.

I pulled over and got off to buy some fruit. Some small peaches caught my eye and made my thirsty mouth drool. However, no sooner had I shared my thoughts with Alexandra than I changed my mind. I wasn't going to buy the fruit, *she* was! A mixture of enthusiasm and nervousness became discernible on her face. Her eyes brightened up. At the same time, she fumbled in her pocket for money, stalling as long as she needed to quickly rehearse a possible dialogue between the saleswoman and herself in her mind. A gentle push was all it took for her to head to the first stand that had peaches on it. With a reluctant smile, she started chatting with the saleswoman, filled a bag and walked away, first taking a couple of steps without turning her back on the crowd that stood up and watched her with some curiosity. *Oh well, we each have our own way of doing things,* I thought. She did get the peaches though.

As we rode through Butha-Buthe, the hubbub, the illusion that there was nothing systematic about the daily grind of the city, the dust that was raised every time a car passed by the sides of the road, all produced a feeling of euphoria in me. We moved at a low speed, which gave the locals enough time to observe us and raise their hands in greeting. I looked at the small buildings, made with cinder blocks and roofed with tin. I looked at the huge brightly-coloured posters warning of the risk of AIDS. I'd once read that the HIV carrier rate among the locals is one of the highest worldwide, while the life expectancy rate is dispiriting. And yet, among the signs of humanitarian organisations and missions, life in Lesotho went on.

A bit further away two mules were patiently waiting for someone to load the cart they were tethered to. I smiled. I felt again the same familiarity with the place and its people that I'd felt in the Congo.

We took the road that led to Maseru – the capital – but we had actually no intention of heading that way. Instead, we moved south-eastwards, to the Katse Dam. From Butha-Buthe to the next town Hlotse, I also realised one more thing: the vegetation around me had nothing to do with the arid savannas and the tropical forests I'd seen so far. We were in a mountainous country with continental climate, which in the winter is covered by snow. Green grass carpeted the mountains and valleys that spread as far as the eye could see, and on them, people and animals seemed to enjoy their everyday life at the familiar, slow-moving pace of Africa.

MORNING YEARNING

The road cut through villages and settlements that seemed to be teeming with life. People everywhere around us walked or led their livestock to the grasslands on horseback. Nowhere in Africa had I ever felt alone. Even when I was convinced I'd found the most remote place, it was a matter of time before I bumped into someone. My mind instantly went all the way back to Cameroon that night when, thinking I was well-hidden, I set up the tent in a berm, on the side of the road. Within moments, I ended up being Gasson's houseguest, trying to subtly elude his match-making scheme that involved his daughter, Marie-Claire.

There were around 70km left to get to the Katse Dam and only when the road started to go uphill did it dawn on me that maybe things would get harder than I'd thought at first. Within the next few minutes, the engine of the Vespa rattled, begging for a lower gear. I shifted from third into second and soon first had to be selected.

"Is everything OK?" Alexandra's voice sounded worried.

"Remember what you promised me?" I asked her.

Without the slightest complaint, she jumped off the seat, grabbed the metal rear rack and started to push. She gave me the momentum I needed to get moving again but was left walking on the side of the road. A few metres further I stopped again. Kitsos had given up, unable to climb up to the top of the slope.

"We won't get too far this way" I said, but she was undeterred.

"You said we could hitch a ride, right?" she reminded me.

The driver of the first car that passed pulled over and we loaded all out luggage in the trunk. The two sturdy Afrikaners that picked us up were on their way back from the annual Cherry Festival in Ficksburg, which took place on the other side of the border, and Alexandra had to share the back seat with dozens of crates full of cherries.

By the time we arrived at the high mountain pass of Mafika Lisiu, my hands were numb with cold and my glasses so opaque that I could no longer tell whether it was due to my breath or the fog. The sun had vanished and little drops of rain started to fall. We were at 3,000m, according to the sign. Alexandra was smiling and nodding to me behind the car window to take a picture of her. I pretended not to understand her. We went on like this all the way to Ha-Lejone. This is where the two Afrikaners, who worked at some diamond-extraction company, lived. The dark had started to fall and the thick fog wouldn't thin out. They dropped Alexandra off at the only hotel of the area and, as soon as they drove away, I got ready to load the stuff back onto the scooter so that we could move on and out of the village limits. I couldn't even remember when I'd last stayed at a hotel. The price of one night's stay at this particular one corresponded to my budget for two days on the road. I turned to Alexandra. The look in her eyes was direct and almost pleading. She wasn't ready yet to camp at some random place in the countryside of Lesotho and I didn't want to disoblige her – not just yet.

The receptionist showed us to the room, which wasn't exactly a room, but an entire house. The location was stunning and after taking a stroll around we realised it was a winter resort for visitors that came mostly from South Africa. We walked up to the village and bought food. We had to choose between grilled chicken feet and some unidentifiable kind of sausage. The sight of the claws on the chicken was rather discouraging so we opted for the sausages, which were handed to us wrapped in a newspaper sheet. I expected Alexandra to eat just the rice we cooked. However, when I saw her cut into the newspaper ink-stained sausage and eat it eagerly, I regretted thinking that she wouldn't last long in Africa. We didn't talk much that night; we didn't plan out the following day, either. We just enjoyed a good night's sleep in the complete stillness of the mountain.

The next day, I woke up with the sensation that I was no longer on the same trip I'd started a year ago. I looked at Alexandra beside me, lazily stretching out on the bed. "Would you like to spend another day here?", I asked her. She smiled and made herself more comfortable under the beddings.

Late that night, we had to go to the hotel bar, since the tap water in our room kept coming out in a variety of brown hues. While waiting for our bottles to be filled with some more healthy-looking water, I was stunned to see my shy companion engage in a conversation with the only customers around. The two women and the man of the group, judging by the way they were dressed and the ease with which they ordered their drinks, seemed well off. They insisted on buying us drinks, too. We accepted and soon found out that the man was a famous singer in Lesotho. After a few shots and drunken keepsake photos, we went back to the room. I was in the bathroom when Alexandra started to play some music on her laptop. We went into the bedroom.

Dawn hadn't broken yet, when I woke up with an unsettling feeling that something was wrong. In the dark, I could make out her silhouette, sitting on the corner of the bed. She was looking outside. The tears rolling down her cheek made it glimmer. I asked no questions, just hugged her. From the living room, Ben Harper's voice was heard singing: "...*With hopes of better days to come, It's a morning yearning...*"

ROADS, DAMS, DEVELOPMENT

In the morning's first light, the night gloom faded and, despite the previous days' rain and the mud which had not dried out yet, we went out to the village. All the residents were outside. Men, wrapped in woollen blankets and wearing white rain boots that made them immune to mud, walked around the market. Older people seemed reserved and unwilling to engage in conversation.

However, it only took a smile for them to open up and talk to us. We didn't spend another day in Ha-Lejone.

With Kitsos all laden up, we only made a last stop to buy gasoline. On the side of the road, a woman was sitting, next to ten plastic bottles or so. We bought as much as we needed, poured it straight into the gas tank and returned the empty bottles, so that she could refill them from a big jerrycan. Alexandra was so blown away by the outdoor sale of fuel that I couldn't stop laughing at the way she looked with her eyes wide open in surprise.

"You... you trust her?", she asked.

"What other choice do I have?", I replied and we set off.

The little scooter, without complaining once, got us to the road to Thaba-Tseka, where, according to my plans, we'd spend the night. The day was sunny and, travelling along the course of the Malibamat'so River, we arrived at the Katse Dam. The human intervention had forcibly tamed the river into a man-made lake. Complete tranquillity reigned in the scenery; the sky was reflecting on the still water and the green slopes reached all the way down to the riverbanks, creating the illusion that the landscape had been like this forever. However, less than ten years had passed since the dam was completed. Populations were displaced against their will, farmlands and grazing lands were flooded. And it was all in the name of financial prosperity, which the export of water to South Africa would allegedly bring to the country. I'd seen destruction under the guise of development countless times before. Mountains, once gutted by excavators, now standing without a trace of life on them; lakes that were drained to wash the ore of some mine. My mind went back to Greece and its golden subsoil, back when I refused to accept the devastation of my homeland. "Everything OK back there?" I asked Alexandra, who had been quiet for a while now.

Shortly before arriving at Thaba-Tseka, Kitsos' wheels, for the first time in months, stepped on dirt. The city was much bigger than I'd thought. I'd been in Africa for a year but I still got confused: sometimes I was under the impression that the alleys and shacks belonged to some village, while an entire urban sprawl was hidden behind them. At other times, the market stalls and the continuous movement of pedestrians on the sides of the streets made me believe that I was at the centre of a city, when a few metres away there was literally nothing.

In Thaba-Tseka we came across, for the first time in Lesotho, a Chinese community. The razing of the tropical forests and the degeneration of the environment to ensure 'progress' was a Chinese affair for sub-Saharan Africa and everywhere we saw road construction works, the machines and the trucks had ideogram logos on them. The unskilled workers of those companies were usually locals, but the rest of them, office workers and contractors, all came straight from China and stayed at least until their job was done. I wondered if they actually wanted to move all the way to Lesotho. Was it their love for travel and their work that pushed them to go there or maybe just their need for a paycheque? For quite some time now, I'd increasingly felt like I could relate more with the immigrants, those forced out from their land, the despondent.

"Look! There's even a supermarket here!" said Alexandra, pointing at an establishment with the basic features of a grocery store. We stopped to get the necessary – non-perishable and long-enduring – provisions. The parking spots outside were occupied by a couple of donkeys and I didn't want to scare them so I parked the eleven noisy horses of the Vespa a bit further down and we stepped into the store. It was owned by Chinese and, among other things, it offered some products imported from their homeland, especially to fulfil the needs of the expat customers. Alexandra amused herself with the price of a pepper, which was almost carved directly on the fruit with a blue ballpoint pen. She insisted on taking a picture of it. I really didn't feel like going out to get the camera, but her laughter left me no choice. The Chinese store assistants, cheerful behind the register counter, looked at us in bewilderment, as we strapped fruit and vegetables on the scooter.

In about 150km, we'd get to the eastern border of the country and then back to South African soil. I was sure about one thing: I didn't want that. I was certainly worried about the dirt road, which seemed endless, but that wasn't enough to make me want to leave Lesotho. Alexandra had turned out particularly efficient at pushing the scooter, so that wasn't such big a deal after all.

"Where do you think we should spend the night?" she asked rather reluctantly, insinuating that she'd rather we spend it at some rental room. I rode unwillingly to the first guesthouse that we'd seen on our way into the town. It was owned by some mission or church – I rarely retained that kind of information. The chubby nun, dressed in white, welcomed us with an uptight, formal smile. She informed us about the price of the room and firmly ruled out the possibility of setting camp, and paying a bit less, in the spacious yard. The place reminded me of the Benedictine monastery I'd stayed at in Yaoundé. I'd camped in the yards of missions, monasteries and even hotels numerous times before, but, apparently this one's policy on the issue was unbending. Back then – in Yaoundé – I was forced to engage in harsh negotiations to bring the price down and that left me with a bitter taste. Dogmas and churches, established all over Africa, promise the salvation of the soul – for a hefty profit – snubbing any ancient African faith.

Alexandra turned and looked at me. The nun's arrogance and intransigence had brought about the effect I hoped for: to make her mad.

"Let's go find a place to camp!" she suggested and, before she even had time to finish her sentence, I opened the throttle and rode off.

IN HEAVEN

Outside Thaba-Tseka we cut across the Orange River and then for a while we rode along its course. I'd told Alexandra to let me know if she saw a place where we could spend the night, but I wasn't sure she'd do it. She preferred to leave this kind of decision to me. The gentle tapping of her finger felt more like a caress underneath the shoulder protector of my jacket. I turned my head slightly to the side and saw her hand stretching out and pointing at a stream in front of us.

"I wish we could stay here" she said.

"Let's do it!" I replied and at once turned in that direction. We started rolling down the steep slope, all the way to the stream bank. She laughed and held me tight and, within the few seconds it took us to get there, I was in seventh heaven.

We unloaded Kitsos and, while I was setting the tent, I was watching Alexandra throw her shoes and socks off and dip her feet into the frozen water. We were all alone and felt great. While there was still some light, we started cooking. I suggested the classic menu: Plain pasta and a – nearly traditional – Greek salad. There was no trace of feta cheese in Lesotho, but tomatoes, peppers and onions were very easy to find.

"You leave the dinner with me and go play with the camera", she said, knowing that I was excited with her camera. I didn't raise any further objections than those strictly necessary for protocol, as I didn't want to risk her changing her mind.

"I'll do the washing-up!" I yelled, as I walked away with my new toy. When dinner was served, I rushed back and found pasta with tuna sauce and a Greek salad with slices of bread waiting for me.

"Looks to me that I won't let you go", I joked, but deep inside of me I knew that I was dead serious. It was not the cooking. Who cares if there'll be sauce on the pasta or not. We'd only spent a few days on the road together and it all seemed perfect.

Darkness fell and the stars showed up in the sky. We remained silent for a while, looking at them and became immersed in our thoughts. Alexandra was the first to get up and head for the tent. It seemed to me that she didn't feel like speaking, like she just wanted to be alone for a while. Ever since we first met in Lubumbashi, we talked. She asked me about my life and she told me about hers, too, but back then I hadn't paid much attention. I now realised that she was looking for a way to escape the life she had in Greece. How could I not see it, since I was running away from that myself. She sometimes seemed like she wanted to open up her soul and let all of her troubles come out, while others, she avoided talking about anything but the present. I followed her to the tent.

The following morning, I was awakened by the sun, which was high in the sky. I wanted to see if the place was still as pretty as I remembered it or if it was my good mood that made it look that way. I pulled the zipper down and popped out of the tent. Indeed, we were in heaven. But we weren't alone anymore. About 50m away, there was a man sitting on a rock. I waved hello and he reciprocated by nodding his head. He didn't stop looking at me. Being discreet and respecting other people's intimacy was not exactly the Africans' strong point. Countless times I'd fallen asleep feeling the eyes and the breaths of the villagers right outside my tent. If I extended my arm against its stretched fabric, I'd sure be able to tickle one of the little kids standing outside.

Alexandra got out of the tent as well, and turned towards the man to say hello.

"I'd swear he was further away a few minutes ago", I said to myself and turned my back to make some coffee. When I looked back again, I couldn't help bursting into laughter. Every time we turned our heads, he snatched the opportunity to get closer. I didn't invite him to join us. I thought that Alexandra might feel uncomfortable. But that wasn't her actual problem: she had just got up and desperately needed to pee. And how could she possibly do that, with two eyes fixed on her? For me things were much simpler. Some time later, she made a decision.

"Well, if he doesn't mind I don't, either" she uttered and, hiding behind a thin bush that barely provided her any cover, she finally relieved herself!

After breakfast, under the man's watchful eye – he was now less than 10m away from us – we packed up and got ready to leave. However, the point where we'd camped was at a lower level than the road and it would be impossible for the scooter to make it there loaded. The only solution was to carry the luggage to the top of the slope. Suddenly, the man, who until that moment remained a bit further away minding his own business, came up to me, grabbed two bags and started to climb along. No matter how used I was to the kindness of Africans, I was always pleasantly surprised when I came across it. I didn't want to take people's kindness for granted, because this way I ran the risk of ignoring it, of no longer noticing it. When we were done carrying our stuff, we thanked him and offered him some of the cookies we had with us. He took them willingly and, before we started to load the bike, he whistled, and suddenly another man showed up out of nowhere.

As both of them walked away towards the stream, eating the biscuits, more whistling sounded. Throughout the whole time, it was not just one or two men that were around us. About five or six more were hidden in the slopes nearby! With their blankets on, which matched the colours of the landscape, they were invisible to the untrained eye. We were about to leave, when we saw the shepherds rolling down the cliffs with their herds and heading to the stream, right where we were a few moments ago. They wanted to water the animals but no-one wanted to disturb our morning peace.

THE PHOTOGRAPHER OF THE VILLAGE

We now rode exclusively on dirt roads and I had the impression that the mountains would never end, that we would stay perched up there forever. My only concern was whether Kitsos would make it up the steep slopes.

"Do you think he'll get us up there?" I asked Alexandra.

"Whatever will be, will be!" she replied, reminding me of a conversation we had back in Johannesburg, during which I questioned the abilities of the tireless little scooter.

"Whatever will be, will be!" I repeated, tired of trying to have everything under control.

The land was lush green, the sky clear blue and cloudless and the camera I had mounted on my helmet didn't stop filming. As we went through a village it coincided with the time when the children got off from school. All of them in their uniforms and with their books in hand, held together with a leather strap. As soon as they saw us, they completely forgot all about their neat, clean clothes and sprang out into the street, in a crazy pursuit of the Vespa. I slowed down a bit, just to give them the pleasure of catching up with us and, when they did, they started to laugh as they ran beside us, mocking the overloaded bike that was no match for their swift little legs.

Had we run into another bunch of kids at the next village, I wouldn't have had to pull any tricks for them to reach us. A few kilometres ahead, the road went up an abrupt incline and Kitsos started panting. Alexandra had to get off and start pushing again. We now worked as a team. She grabbed the rear rack and we went on the count of three to co-ordinate her effort with me getting first gear in, and, after a few metres of pushing, I reached the top of the slope. There, I stopped and waited for her. She caught her breath, got back on the scooter and we moved on.

The villages we passed by were each as pretty as the next, with their matching huts and their small vegetable patches. Now and then, we ran into men and young boys on horseback. In the *Basotho* tradition, horses play an important role. They rear a specific, small-sized breed and most of them learn to ride at a very young age. We'd been told that we'd be lucky if we came across an improvised horse race, but for us it was enough just to see them on the back of their horses, proudly trotting by.

The dirt road wasn't that bad and we were able to look at the hillsides, the valleys and the little villages around us. At the settlements of Lesotho, people usually live in round huts made of mud mixed with cow dung. The sight of the huts with the thatch roofs and the doors and windows painted blue or white made the landscape look like a movie set. Everything seemed to be in perfect order. Even the toilets, which were in some corner of the yards, were built identically. But no place is such a big deal without its people. Women of all ages in Lesotho take care of the house chores. So at the villages, we'd see them do the housework or lie under the shade of a tree in small groups and casually watch passers-by. That's what we were ourselves, and so, every single time, we'd become the object of observation and a source of laughter for women of all ages.

The village we stopped at was no different than the rest. Next to the central road, there was an adobe hut that looked like a grocery store. We stepped inside. There were only a few packaged cookies on the shelf, whose expiry date had long passed. However, both my experience and my sweet tooth had taught me that something has expired, only when its shape, taste or smell is not right.

As soon as they saw us, the villagers started to gather up out on the street. The men, with their blankets and woollen hoods, which left nothing but their eyes exposed, seemed distant. Once they got the hoods off, though, their faces were smiling and kind. Alexandra's presence beside me made the women feel more comfortable and, soon, a conversation started about our helmets and cameras. Those were probably the most interesting things on us. While the men stood a bit further away, alternating glances between their horses and the scooter repeatedly, the women posed in front of the camera and then, when they saw their faces on the screen, they burst into laughter. Then, an idea dawned on me. I hung the camera strap around the neck of one of the women of the group and told her that I wanted her to take a picture of us. She looked at me with eyes full of horror and excitement at the same time. I showed her how to hold it, how to see through the viewfinder and how to make the "click" sound. We stood right in front of her along with her friend, posing at the camera. With a steady hand, she took the picture and, when she looked into the screen, a loud laughter erupted from within her, which was quickly passed on to all of us. I don't really know what that woman did for a living, but on that day, she was a photographer.

UPHILL AND ROCKY

We moved on. The scenery remained charming, but the further along we got, the worse the road became. More and more rocks popped up on the bumpy dirt trail and, as I looked at the uphill slope ahead of us, my concern grew. Alexandra, with the camera in her hands, seemed unaware of the trouble that was about to come our way.

"Look at that huge eagle!" she yelled. "Wow! Did it fly close to us or what!", were her last words before finally realising that not even her pushing could get us to the top. We decided to carry the luggage all the way to the top of the slope. Then she'd have to walk and I'd ride Kitsos, who, with much less weight, would make the climb.

I was staggering with two big bags in my hands, when I heard the sound of a motorbike. It was one of the locals, on a small enduro bike, who was literally flying over the rocks which the scooter had stumbled on. He stopped beside us. He told us that his village was not far from there and that he worked at a humanitarian organisation at Maseru. He had the chance to study and escape the hardship and poverty, but he never forgot where he came from. Once a month he'd visit his village and bring to his family everything they needed. The man had to go back and forth more than twice, carrying our stuff to the top. In the end, he took Alexandra as well, who couldn't stop thanking him for the help he had offered us. Without us knowing, the motorcyclist had helped us through the Menoaneng mountain pass. We were back at 3,000m of altitude, and we hadn't even noticed. "From here on, everything's easy", he reassured us and vanished within a cloud of dust, as he went down the slope.

From the point where we stood, the border with South Africa and the famous Sani pass were less than 70km away. I wanted to spend one more night in Lesotho no matter what, so I wasn't really worried about our slow pace. Shortly after Molumong, where we got without particular trouble, there was a big junction. On the left, the central road led to Mokhotlong, a rather big city. On the right, the same road headed on south-eastwards, to the border. There seem to be no city that way, which is exactly why I turned to that direction. I assured Alexandra that we'd spend the night at some magical place, just like the last time, and we moved on.

Once past the junction, I paid no heed to the roadworks or the warnings thereof along the road. But it wasn't long before I realised that things wouldn't be as easy as I thought. We were still around 2,000m up, but what worried me the most was the mud. I usually fell over in the mud, and it was in the mud that I'd first burned the clutch. And yet the mud and the dirt had made my trip so special. How else would I have lived the unforgettable experience on that truck in the Congo, if it hadn't been for the burned clutch? How else would I have bonded with Steven and Francis, if we hadn't been plunging into the muddy trails together to help each other out? What I didn't know was whether Alexandra would share my enthusiasm about mud. I got a little worried when I showed her a wind-beaten spot, where I'd like us to camp, and she couldn't quite believe that I actually meant it.

WE FELL OFF!

We road along the Sehonghong River. The grass was green, while all sorts of crops appeared near the riverbanks. However, due to the steeply rising ground and because we weren't the only ones that wanted to hang out by the river – the cattle did, too – we couldn't find a place to stop. Darkness had started to fall and the mud layer on the road got thicker and softer. I put my feet constantly on the ground to keep my balance. Alexandra, still inexperienced in long-haul rides, was tense and worried about us falling. The first clouds gathered up in the sky and it soon started to rain, ruining every effort of mine to calm her down. Great! – I thought. *If she reacts like that to a few raindrops, we won't get far.* The sun had now set and in the faint light I suddenly saw a rocky barrier that there was no way the scooter could pass over with both of us on it. Alexandra got off and I carefully started to climb over it. It wasn't that hard, but when I got to the other side of the rocky mound and turned my head around, I saw her coming towards me, angry and scared.

"He scared me witless just to ask me for a dollar!" she said, almost yelling. In the pitch dark, she hadn't seen the man that was sitting on a rock nearby. How could she have? The blankets worn by the Basotho and their hoods make them blend in completely with their surroundings. It was only through the whistling sounds they use to communicate that we perceived their presence. The man's deep, hoarse voice scared the heck out of her. Frankly, though, I don't know whether it was him begging for money or laughing at her reaction that bothered her the most.

We continued to struggle against the mud and the rain. The few vehicles on the road were trucks carrying the workers from the roadworks site back to their villages. The drivers were Chinese, while the workers on the back of the trucks were locals. I wondered whether it was a good thing that the biggest infrastructure works in the country were being undertaken by foreign companies. Some got a job and a wage – even though only for a while – but was it enough? For a moment, I remembered when my salary plummeted when I worked back in Greece, under the pretext of the financial crisis. I got angry and tried to think about anything else. So instead, I started to ask myself where on earth we were going to camp. Everything around us was covered in mud. I tried to see, but the wind and the rain wouldn't let me take my eyes off the road. Until all of a sudden we fell! Our speed was very low and the mud so soft that it absorbed the shock of the fall. I got right up, but Alexandra remained on the ground.

"Are you OK?", I asked her.

Before she had the time to answer, I grabbed her arm to help her up. She got up and stared at me dumbfounded, mudded, her big eyes glimmering, about to cry.

"We fell off!" she complained.

"Well, yes we did!" I replied laughing, after making sure that she wasn't hurt. The fall revealed the spot where we were going to camp, so I lifted the scooter and moved it nearby, to the side of the road. I started setting the tent, while telling Alexandra stories about my hundreds of falls in West and Central Africa. She said nothing, just listened. I guess she was thinking about what else was in store for her.

We got into the tent and I got busy with our dinner. Food, apart from a basic necessity, is also a comfort. There were only a couple of sandwiches of tomato and pepper on the menu, but it worked out just fine. Right when I'd lost all hope, Alexandra finally smiled again.

We hadn't laid down yet and, in the pitch darkness, we heard a voice calling us. It was the guard of the roadworks site, that was about a 100m away. He'd seen us and wanted to know if we needed anything. He invited us to camp closer to the works site in order to feel safer, but we didn't feel any insecurity at all. The human presence was comforting to Alexandra. We fell asleep to the sound of the rain, which kept falling throughout the night, until, in the morning, we were awaken by the groan of the trucks that carried the workers back to their positions. As soon as I popped my head out of the tent, I heard their deep voices say 'good morning'. The day we'd leave Lesotho had arrived.

SANI

As it turned out, we were closer to the border than we thought. The rain and the darkness had made the road seem endless the previous night. Before we even realised it, we reached the descent point. The Sani mountain pass is a steep serpentine slope, right at the border between the two countries. The view up there is said to be dazzling, though ever since I decided to travel to Lesotho, I'd heard that I'd never manage to climb it up on the Vespa. But why wouldn't I be able to climb down it? I'd planned the route in such a way so that I could go through the Sani pass on my way out of the country, and the only thing that I had to tackle was a steep downhill slope with sharp turns.

Alexandra, from the minute she got on the scooter that day, was so nervous that she kept clenching her arms around my waist. When she felt embarrassed and thought she'd gone too far, I heard her breath and knew she was biting her lips so as not to make a sound that would give away her fear. The funniest thing was, though, that every time we ran into a 4x4 loaded with tourists, she mustered all her courage and smiled. She really yearned to get over her fears and anxieties, and this trip was the ideal opportunity to do just that.

After a little miscommunication, typical of all border checkpoints, we crossed over to South African territory. I didn't manage to get the visa extension I needed if I wanted to stay in South Africa while I decided where I'd be heading. I tried not to think about it all the time, but soon I'd be at the southernmost tip of the continent and I still hadn't figured out what I'd do next.

I dispelled all the clouds that insisted on building up over my head and pointed at the paved road ahead with my finger. Alexandra laughed, relieved that she wouldn't have to push any more. But I'd rather we'd spent a little more time up on those infinite mountains. I turned my head around and looked back. The Sani pass was indeed spell-binding but could not compare to the beauty of the rest of Lesotho. Something had happened inside of me. The small, hidden country that struggles to overcome the hardship and put up a resistance to South Africa, which seemed as if it wants to swallow it, had instilled feelings of solidarity within me. The round speck on the map, the land of the Basotho, the people that looked at us proudly as they rode on horseback, was meant to be engraved on my memory for one more reason: it was the place where I travelled with Alexandra for the first time.

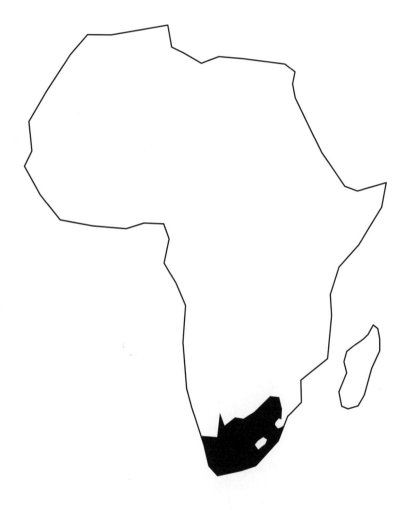

SOUTH AFRICA (AGAIN)

SEPARATE BEDROOMS

Liz, Johan's mother, was waiting for us at the windowsill. No sooner did she open the door than the family's two dogs sprang out to the yard to welcome us, jumping all over us and covering our clothes in drool and hair. Alexandra was really excited. The whole time it took me to unload the luggage, she talked to our hosts, while she didn't stop petting the two pooches who whipped her calves with their tails. She missed the company of her own dog, Marcos. Every chance she got, she proudly showed his pictures. I thought about Rosa and Dolly, the dogs of my family, who were now long gone. I remember how much I cried when, for a moment, we thought we'd lost one of them. We were in the car heading to the village and Dolly, scared by the noise, had sneaked into the corner of the trunk, behind clothes and suitcases. I'd threatened my parents that I'd never forgive them if they lost her.

Johan, himself a motorcyclist, had just returned from his trip across Europe and Africa. On the very first day I met him in Lomé, he promised to put me up when I got to Durban. He lived with his mother, a woman that, despite the health problems that afflicted her, hung in there pretty well. We sat all together for dinner and spent the entire evening talking about travels. When it got late and we were so tired that our eyelids got heavy, our hosts showed us to the bedrooms where we'd sleep. Liz was deeply conservative, so she'd commanded discreetly albeit unyieldingly that we sleep in separate rooms. They were so far away from one another that there was no chance of communication between us once the lights went out. Since we weren't bound by holy matrimony, we had to keep a safe distance from each other.

The following evening, with a glass in my hand and two dogs curled up on my feet, I discovered how unexpectedly interesting Liz' company was. Her strict piousness was at odds with her joyful spirit in the most astonishing way. Johan was out and the three of us opened up a bottle of wine in the kitchen. She also offered Alexandra a cigarette and she, despite not having smoked in years, took it.

"When did your adventure start?" she asked me at some point. It was then that it hit me how uncomfortable the characterisation of "adventurous" made me feel.

"I guess the day I was born", I replied jokingly. From the very first time I used it, at the beginning of the trip, the word "adventure" struck me as odd. What does "adventure" mean? Isn't every life one? Was I more adventurous than my fellow man, the African, who rides his little bike through dirt and mud? Along the way, I ran into people who had to walk for days to get water. I saw others get uprooted from their homes in the pursuit of a better fortune far away. I met women that give birth to their children in the woods. I met men who go out hunting and, if they get lucky enough, bring back a kill to feed an entire village. I don't recall hearing any of them talk about adventure, not once. They all talked about life. I began to wonder. Is the "adventure" a matter of choice? Or luck? If you're born in the *white* world, you're adventurous. But if you're born in the forest of the Congo, you're just lucky to be alive.

BUNNY CHOW

The following morning found me walking with Alexandra along the beach, empty-handed, because I wasn't able to extend my visa for South Africa in the Durban offices. The immense beachfront lapped by the Indian Ocean was dubbed "The Golden Mile" as I saw on some sign. It spread in front of us with the white caps of its waves swelling from a distance and then growing feeble, until they gave the sand a gentle sweep. We were walking along one of the decks and, feeling my skin sticky from the salty sea breeze, I tried to plan out the things I'd do during the time I had left in the country. However, Alexandra made sure to chase the bad thoughts away from my mind. "Let's go grab a coffee!", she suggested.

We turned around and headed back to the beach with the towering buildings and the cafés and we sat at the one that looked the cheapest. With a cup of coffee in my hand, I started answering the messages that had piled up over the last days. In Lesotho I hadn't found an internet connection – not that I'd looked for any.

"Listen out to what Manolis says!" I told Alexandra and read the message to her. "He asks why in the trip reports I send to the app, I use the first person of the plural. Should I unveil the mystery to him?" I asked with a giggle.

I'd met Manolis a few days before leaving Greece. A motorcyclist, a traveller and an inquisitive spirit, he'd developed along with two friends of his, one of those applications which, with the aid of the GPS, you can use to trace the route you follow. Ever since I started using it, we talked increasingly often and, whenever I got distracted, he poked me to encourage me to send a new trip report. I joked about it saying that he was the voice of my consciousness. "Ok, you can tell him. But only because I like him", she replied. I hadn't even told my parents about travelling with Alexandra. Nothing but hints and double-talk. What was I to tell them? I knew what I wanted, but I needed to know what she wanted, first.

By late noon we were back home and Johan received us with a paper bag that gave out a delicious smell of freshly-cooked food.

"You cannot possibly leave Durban without trying the *bunny-chow* first!" he said. We opened the bag and out popped a couple of bread loaves. They were placed upright like deep plates; the crumb had been removed from the inside and had been replaced by a portion of Indian curry. Together with the vegetables and the spicy sauce, chunks of meat made the ingenious delicacy finger-licking good. When, in the late 19th Century, the British colonists brought labourers from India to work at the sugarcane plantations, the latter carried along their culinary customs and, under the influence of local eating habits, they came up with this unique dish. Durban is home to the biggest Hindu expat community, which apparently managed to leave an indelible mark on the city that we'd leave behind on the following day.

GARDEN ROUTE

"You absolutely must do the *Garden Route*!" Liz yelled as we got on Kitsos and said goodbye to our hosts. The dogs ran behind us barking joyfully and we couldn't wait to continue our trip.

"We'll do that, too!", I yelled back and my voice faded out amidst the barks.

Many times, the words we choose to express ourselves reveal the way we think. Just like back when Steven, Francis and I set out to cross the Congo. We read in various travel guides about the routes that we had to "*do*", among which was the "Kinshasa–Lubumbashi" route. I laughed and said that I didn't want to "*do*" it just so I could cross one more chore off my list. I said that I wanted to "*live*" it. And so I did, with a ramshackle scooter in the dirt, and then on the truck. I hadn't forgotten about any single one of the people I met, not a single day of those I spent there, not one plate of rice I ate. On that day, Alexandra and I set out on the Garden Route and the only thing I wondered about was what else we'd *live* together.

From the rainy and foggy Mthatha, we got to East London. The warm night we spent in the verdant campsite by the estuary of one of the numerous rivers that flow to the sea around the city, helped us recover from the unexpected cold of the day before. We were somewhere half-way through the Garden Route and the landscape, though undeniably beautiful, didn't manage to grip me. I thought that once more I was in a place where, in order to admire the natural beauty, I had to search for it far from the road and the cities. Just like in the last few countries I'd travelled across, in South Africa, it seemed to me that the tourist industry had taken it upon itself to tame the environment, reducing it to a mere attraction.

We were looking for an organised campsite to spend the night. Barbed wire held capture almost every patch of unexploited land

and there were villages, hotels and shanty towns all around. Outside Port Elizabeth, yet another city that I didn't really feel like visiting, we realised that we were well into December. Great weather and holiday season for the southern hemisphere. Schools and businesses shut down and hundreds of students and holiday-makers flooded the campsites and guesthouses of the countryside. From one day to the next, the prices at lodges and restaurants shot up and, for once more, I felt that irksome escape urge.

After two or three nights that we spent stranded in the campsite, because of the heavy rain and the soft mud – together with a school excursion group – without asking Alexandra's opinion, I decided to speed up a little bit. I wanted us to get to Struisbaai as soon as possible, the fishing village that was only 10km away from the southernmost tip of Africa.

HOW ARE YOU FEELING?

"It feels like I'm on vacation in Greece!" Alexandra exclaimed, snatching a piece of fried squid off the plate. We were sitting at a makeshift restaurant on the beach and the beer along with the smell of sea food took us back to some Greek island. There was even Greek salad on the menu, which we ordered without complaining about the completely off-topic carrots it included. Struisbaai, a fishing village which has become a popular destination for the excursionists of the area, wasn't packed with people yet. It was right when the locals started to open up their businesses, spruce up their gardens and the sidewalks outside their houses, and freshen up the tourist infrastructures, which awaited the arrival of the first Christmas holiday makers.

With our stomachs full and fairly mellow after one or two pints of beer, we were walking along the beach. Alexandra had rolled her trouser-legs up and was dipping her feet into the water of the Indian Ocean. I was taking pictures of the whitish sand, the turquoise sea and the huge jellyfish that had washed up on the shore. The hot sun and the frozen air made it hard to decide whether to keep our jackets on or not.

"How about visiting Cape Agulhas?" I asked. She nodded.

Sobered up, we got on the Vespa and, a little while later, saw the first sign indicating the way to the southernmost tip of the continent. We left the red and white lighthouse that has been guiding ships since the 19ᵗʰ Century behind, took the dirt trail and got to where Africa ends.

"How are you feeling?", Alexandra asked me as we placed Kitsos next to the stone marker with the metal plate, to take a picture of the two of us. I'd seen countless photos of travellers posing beside this plate. I stood still and looked far ahead, at the swelling sea and the steep black rocks. My left foot stepped next to the inscription that pointed to the Indian Ocean, while my right one was on the Atlantic. How was I feeling?

The truly important moments in life have no need of fireworks and cheering crowds. They sneak in stealthily and touch you, making your skin shiver. One year of my life on the only possession I had left: a Vespa. One year away from a country that felt familiar and foreign at the same time. I'd crossed an entire continent and seen things I could never have imagined. And yet there I was – now! With one foot in the Indian Ocean and the other in the Atlantic; one foot in Africa and the other anywhere else in the world.

HAMBURGER AND CHIPS

The three big cities of South Africa – Johannesburg, Durban and Cape Town – seemed to me like three different worlds. I wasn't so sure about Durban, since we only spent two days there, but the careless walks along the endless stretch of beach of Cape Town, little had to do with the dangerous streets of Johannesburg.

"Here there are also places that you might want to avoid", advised Chris, who put us up in his house uptown. Chris was a *vespista* that I'd met on the internet a long time ago. He'd gone on a trip from South Africa to Ireland, but somewhere halfway through, things didn't go as planned. A series of adverse circumstances cost him his eyesight and it was right at that time that he expected to find out whether the damage was irreparable or whether there was a chance for him to see again.

"I don't know what I'd do if I were in his place", Alexandra whispered almost in shock, when she heard his story.

We stayed in a spacious tent in the yard of the house. So spacious it could fit a double bed and a chest of drawers. Chris' parents had moved in back from Ireland where they lived, and his life partner never left his side. He wouldn't let anyone feel sorry for him. He struggled to get used to his new living conditions, dealing with life exactly like it should be dealt with: with courage and a sense of humour. In his forties, he now had to learn from scratch how to grapple with the small requirements of daily life efficiently. He not only wanted to be able to have lunch without getting all messy by groping for the food in his plate, but also to cook on his own. He'd started to write a book, as well. He didn't want to depend on anyone. He asked us about Europe and confessed that, some day he'd like to travel back there. He loved Cape Town, but the narrow-mindedness of his fellow countrymen and the countless social problems really bothered him. Whenever our conversation took a turn more serious than strictly necessary, he changed the subject.

That afternoon, we were sitting on the terrace moistening our conversation with wine.

"Do you know that joke about the Greek guy who wants to order food in English?" he asked, feeling around for a chair to stretch his legs on.

"It came to me now that I hear you speak English with your funny Greek accent!" he said and started telling the joke. I don't remember how it ended. I only remember that we laughed so hard that Chris dubbed us *Hamburger and Chips* ever since – which was probably what the Greek protagonist of the joke ended up eating.

CAPE TOWN

"Come on, hurry up!", I said impatiently to Alexandra, who was looking for her bag. With the scooter keys in my hand and my helmet on, I waited for her to get ready for a stroll downtown. We got on the highway and headed for the Waterfront, the city's tourist hotspot for leisurely walks along the decks and around the pedestrian zone. At a turn, *Table Mountain* rose up ahead of us. The mountain that owes his name to its characteristic flat-topped shape overlooks the city of Cape Town, along with *Lion's Head* and

303

Devil's Peak, the two bulky rock formations that keep it company.

We got to our designated meeting point and, within a few minutes, the sound of Steven's motorcycle was heard. With his bike and helmet painted in the colours of Africa – yellow, green and red – he showed up with a broad smile on his face. The last time I'd seen him was in Namibia and then our paths had parted again. He now rode on his own – Katrina hadn't been able to get a visa for South Africa – and intended to head up north, to the east side of the continent. We walked around Waterfront and talked about anything that came to mind. He wanted to know the details about how we'd met and ended up travelling together.

"Did you hear about Liam?" he asked at some point.

They'd gotten in touch some time ago, and Liam's news was as interesting as usual. He'd managed to get to the DRC, but the crossing of the Congo River hadn't gone too well. The dugout suddenly rocked as he was loading his bike, and as a result, the poor C90 fell off into the water. Tired of the continuous mishaps, while he could have saved it, he decided to leave it there in the bottom of the river forever.

"Damn it, Liam" I said to myself.

"So what are you going to do?", was Steven's next question. I didn't know what to answer.

"Whatever will be, will be!" Alexandra promptly butted in. Ever since she first uttered it, this phrase had been with her every single day for as long as we'd ridden together.

During the days we spent in Cape Town, there was nothing but leisurely strolls on the schedule. Just the two of us or together with Steven, we got out and wandered around the city streets. Cape Town is a multicultural and interesting place, with a little surprise hidden around every corner, so we didn't get bored for one second. We walked around the Bo-Kaap, the colourful, formerly Muslim neighbourhood, drank beer at the little bars on Long Street and hung around at the Green Market Square, the African souvenirs bazaar. Day after day, I felt more and more familiar with the place.

"Do you think I should try and settle here?" I told Alexandra one day.

"I don't know what you should or shouldn't do, but we should both go get some wine now!" she answered, changing the subject.

She'd been long waiting for me to make a decision, but she didn't want to put any pressure on me. That morning, together with Steven, we rode to the Cape of Good Hope. Passing through the coastal tourist towns, with the food stands selling fish and chips and the fish shops, which piled up their floundering merchandise next to the docks, we arrived at the famous cape.

"The entrance fee is ten euros!" Steven observed, clearly annoyed. We looked at each other, remembering back in Namibia, where in order to see anything, we had to pay. We turned around and left. Besides, it was the fact that we'd gotten there that counted.

"Would you mind not having a photo of the Cape of Good Hope?" I asked Alexandra. She laughed.

That same afternoon we got into Nick's car – he was a local who gave Steven accommodation. We went to Stellenbosch, the neighbouring town with the endless vineyards and the wineries. From the drunken wine tasting we ended up at Nick's house to try a traditional recipe, which he insisted on preparing for us. The entire time it took the *potjie* – meat with vegetables – to simmer in the heavy cast-iron pot that Nick had placed over the fire, our stories kept on going one after the other. It hadn't been long since Steven and I last met, but we'd lived way too many experiences in the meantime. Alexandra and Nick sat in a corner of the yard and watched us, drinking the home-made ginger beer he prepared himself.

"Are you bored?" I asked, when I saw them with their eyes half-closed and almost lying down on their chairs.

"We're travelling along with you", replied Nick, who was always polite and now also a bit dizzy from the alcohol. At last, after a good while, dinner was ready. We sat at the table hoping that food would help us sober up.

"You don't like your dishes too spicy, do you?" I observed at the first mouthful of potjie.

"Nothing's ever spicy enough for you!" Alexandra teased me. She was a bit drunk herself and started telling her own stories.

"Do you know how your friend first caught my attention back in Lubumbashi?" she asked Steven. "He spread an entire spoonful of pili-pili over a piece of bread and ate it!" *Pili-pili* is a hot pepper paste, which caused Alexandra to cry and cough helplessly when she first tried it. I, on the other hand, was accustomed to my mother's spicy food so I actually enjoyed the burning sensation of the chili in my mouth. Every single bite filled with pili-pili took me straight back home and to the family table, when we competed about who could eat more pickles and buyurdi[1] without crying. *It would be nice to sit at that table again!* I thought to myself.

IN KAROO

"There's a golden and a green garland along the chassis and little light bulbs around the handlebar!" described Chris' father to him. He'd come out to the yard to smell the two-stroke oil and hear the engine of the scooter. Christmas was just around the corner, and since we had nothing else to decorate, I came up with the idea of decorating the Vespa. We fixed some garlands on the chassis and wrapped a string of light bulbs around the handlebar and the windshield. At every traffic light we stopped on our way to Chris' house, the drivers of the vehicles beside us laughed and wished us a Merry Christmas. We were about to leave Cape Town and only the sorrow of our host brought me down that day.

"I guess I'll never get back on the Vespa again", he admitted in a low voice, which betrayed how long and hard the struggle ahead of him would be.

"But you'll do lots of other things instead", I said. For some reason, I had great faith in Chris.

"I'll accept the terms of the game and move on" he replied. "I guess I'll be a blind scooter guy!" His dynamism was back. We hugged each other, promised to meet again, and with this promise in our minds, we got back on the road.

There were 1,400km left to Johannesburg. Time was running out for Alexandra. In a few days, she had to go back to Greece and make all those decisions that she had long been avoiding.

---

[1]*Buyurdi (from the Turkish word buyurdu literally meaning "commanded") is a popular Greek hot spicy appetiser consisting of feta cheese, tomatoes, green peppers and olive oil, seasoned with a wide range of spices.*

But things weren't easy for me, either. For the first time I felt the pressure of time on me, as my visa was about to expire, and I had quite a few different options to choose from. Each one of them came with its pros and cons, and I had to choose what to do next all on my own.

The trip had become silent, the only exception being the noise of the engine which, affected by the high altitude, panted at the slightest uphill grade. Absorbed in our own thoughts, we left behind the rich vegetation, the gorges and the rivers of the area around Cape Town and entered a completely different scenery.

The rear shock absorber was bent by the weight and the strain, and I rode carefully without minding the trucks that drove past us. The dry heat and the relentless pounding of the sun wouldn't leave us in peace. Suddenly, the handlebars started shaking. I had replaced the rear tyre, which was worn out, with the front one and in its place I'd used the spare. But I wasn't sure about the shape the inner tube was in.

"What's wrong?" Alexandra's voice sounded concerned.

"Flat tyre!"

I pulled over at the side of the road to fix the puncture which luckily, was deflating slowly, without putting us into serious trouble. We were right in the middle of Karoo – a vast expanse of land in South Africa that looks like a desert – surrounded by an inhospitable waterless environment, with low vegetation and loose fine soil. Trucks drove by so close they almost scraped us and made us shake so hard, that a couple of times Alexandra jumped up on her seat in terror. The smile of the last few days had vanished from her face. I was sure she hoped for something to stall us so that she'd miss her flight to Greece. Unfortunately for her though, the problem was soon solved and we got to the place where we were going to spend the night. It was a campsite within a big farm, a few kilometres away from the Karoo National Park. We pushed the gate open and found ourselves in a place where various domestic animals and poultry wandered around freely, along with semi-wild impalas.

When the farmhouse door opened and a tiny piglet sprang out, Alexandra treated it as joyfully as she would treat a dog.

"Its mom died during birth and so we raise it as a pet", the owner told us proudly. The piglet, however, had a well-developed guarding instinct and decided to vent by biting Alexandra's shoe. I couldn't stop laughing, seeing her flinch with pain while trying to release her shoe from the piglet's firm grip and, at the same time, remaining courteous towards the man who kept smiling affectionately from the doorway.

The piglet managed to cheer us up and once we set the tent Alexandra headed for the showers. The door of the shared shower room was skewed and didn't close properly and the shower trays were only separated from each other by a plastic curtain.

"That stupid goat!" she yelled, as she scampered towards me with a towel wrapped around her head. Right behind her, an adorable and docile impala followed. Cussing and laughing, she got into the tent.

"It just wouldn't leave!" she kept on explaining, while the impala stood a bit further, grazing. While she was relaxing in the shower and enjoying the warm water, the small-built antelope, popped in through the shower curtain and kept on bugging her.

"At least you're laughing again!", I told her.

TEARS

The sun had set and darkness had spread over Bloemfontein, transforming the ride into a true ordeal. The headlights of the cars coming from the opposite direction pointed directly on us and every ray of light was converted into successive blasts of pain in my head. We'd ridden 500km in the unbearable summer heat of the Karoo and my body was getting back at me for having treated it with such cruelty. We were worn out, starving and parched, and still without a place to spend the night. Roaming around the busiest streets in Bloemfontein, we bumped into a big shopping mall.

"There must be something we could eat it here", I told Alexandra and turned towards the parking lot. I left her sitting on the curb beside the scooter and walked into the overly lit-up shopping mall full of store and restaurant signs. I was overcome with grief as I looked for the most economical option on the menu cards that were hanging outside the restaurants. My image, all dusty and tattered, was in stark contrast with the shiny floors and the neon signs. I looked at the cleaning staff in a corner. All of them black. I looked through the windows of the restaurants at the gourmand customers. All white. Me, as always, somewhere in between. White skin and infinite guilt for my privilege to be able to walk into any restaurant I wanted, no matter how dirty I was.

I got back to the parking lot holding two big paper bags full of food: lots of cheap pre-fried fries, burgers that looked as if they were made of plastic and sealed small bags of mayonnaise and ketchup – the icing on our junk food cake. I felt like gobbling down the worst kind of food that day. Ever since I was little, when I was in a really bad mood, my stomach asked for equally bad food. Alexandra, still sitting on the same spot, turned and looked at me. I tossed the paper bags to the ground and ran up to her. Her cheeks were soaked in tears. I made her stand up and hugged her. She burst into inconsolable tears.

"That's it, it's all over!", she kept saying. On the following day we'd arrive in Johannesburg and shortly after, she'd get on the plane back home.

"This is when it all starts!" I corrected her. "I'm not leaving you", I promised her, then grabbed a burger with my hand and brought it right under her nose. In an attempt to amuse me, she bit off a chunk of the burger.

"I'm feeling better now", she said with a snivelling, snot-soaked smile. It only took a good night's sleep at some half-abandoned campsite that we ran across by chance for her to get herself together, but unfortunately, not for my headache to go away.

"Are you sure you can drive?", she asked me with concern the next morning. Ever since I was a kid, I'd suffered from headaches. As I grew older, I became so used to them that at times I couldn't even recall what it was like without them. When I started the trip, they gradually started to subside and, without me realising it, they almost disappeared. That particular day though, I felt as if the universe was making me pay in retrospect for all the headaches that I'd missed over the last few months.

"Let's get going and we'll see" I answered.

Late afternoon, the first houses on the outskirts of Johannesburg became visible. Like in any other city in Africa, the first man-made constructions we saw were the most dehumanising ones. Settlements, shanty towns made of cheap materials without any infrastructure whatsoever are home to equally cheap human resources, who swarm into the big cities for a meagre wage. Their residents are exclusively black.

"Did you know that they set up guided tours to the slums?" Alexandra asked me. I did. I'd first seen it in Namibia, flipping through a tourist brochure at the café I used to hang out in Swakopmund. The *"South Africa Experience"*, can only be complete with a *township tour* – an eye-opening experience, as travel operators put it. One might argue that this way perhaps people would become aware of the unseen sides of reality. I didn't think so.

GRANADILLA AND HALVAS

"The travellers are back!" Effie's voice sounded. She rushed to welcome us, excited. Our sun-tanned faces brightened up with the joy of the encounter. She was followed by Elie and Anton, the beloved friend that was always there. They were all curious to know about our trip.

"I told you that these two were a good match! Anton kept saying, laughing. "I'm curious to see what's up next!", he added, confident that we'd figure out a way to go on together. Anywhere.

I woke up after hours of sleep and having popped in a couple of painkillers with the hope that the headache would subside.

"We got granadillas!", said Alexandra, who'd just come back from shopping with Effie. I got off the couch, rubbed my eyes and put my glasses on to see more clearly.

"You got what?", I asked, dizzy.

"Passion fruit", she translated, checking whether I was actually awake or not. Finally, the explosions in my head had stopped and I felt much better. I headed for the kitchen, grabbed a fruit, cut off the upper tip and dipped my spoon into its gooey flesh. The aroma of the granadilla tickled my nostrils. It was Alexandra's favourite fruit and she was determined to eat as many as she could before leaving. I remembered the juicy mangos that I ceaselessly ate in West Africa. It'd been months since I had one.

"Stergios, honey! Look what I have for you!" said Effie and I turned towards her. She was holding a big, ripe mango and seemed thrilled to fulfil my inner wish.

"We also bought food for the Christmas table!", she added.

Alexandra, with mixing spoons and pots in her hands, was about to prepare the *halva*[2] she'd promised she'd make before leaving. She wanted us to serve it after the Christmas meal, at Anton's place, when she'd already be in Athens. Since that morning, while packing her things into the big suitcase, she'd been making a great effort not to cry, which fortunately had paid off. We'd soon be heading for the airport. She placed the steaming *halva* in a big plate, said goodbye to Elie and Anton and the three of us got into Effie's car. On our way there, we refused to talk about anything that might upset us. There was nothing left to say. She knew that I wanted her by my side and I hoped she wanted the same as well. It was time we parted ways. We hugged each other under the caring eye of Effie, who stood at a discreet distance.

"Whatever will be, will be", she whispered and went through the departure gate.

THE OPPRESSOR'S TONGUE

"Are you up for a ride to Soweto?", said Effie as we got back into the car.

"Let's go", I said listlessly, knowing however, that a little distraction would do me good. We swung by the house, picked Elie up and headed for the historical area of Johannesburg.

It was as though we were in a completely different place. As we drove on the central road, the two characteristic cooling towers of the Orlando Power Station – one of Soweto's landmarks – appeared. The houses around them were low, some of them

---

[2] *Halva is a type of dessert, typical in many countries across the Mediterranean and the Middle East. In Greece, it usually comes in the following two versions: one made with tahini (or other nut butter) and nuts and one made with a mix of grain flour or semolina, olive oil, nuts, and sugar – the latter is the halva referred to in the book.*

humble, reminding me of so many other shanty towns I'd seen, and others neater, with a rather decent infrastructure. The forsaken, at times anonymous townships occupied exclusively by the under-privileged – black labourers – were bound to get the most resounding name. The word "*Soweto*" itself is nothing but an acronym that defines the area both geographically and qualitatively: *South Western Townships*. However, from the 1970s onwards, the voices raised here brought Soweto to the attention of the entire world.

"It is said here that, when Soweto sneezes, South Africa catches a cold", said Effie as we parked the car. We were close to the Hector Pieterson memorial, dedicated to the young schoolboy that was shot dead in 1976 by policemen, when the first massive protests against the change of the language policy in the schools of black South Africans took place. Although the English language had gained significance and was used by increasing numbers of black South Africans, the apartheid regime tried to forcibly impose its own language, Afrikaans, as the main instruction language. Soweto students were the first to react and lead the protests, which, although ending in bloodshed, triggered a series of historical developments beyond all imagination. It might have taken yet another fifteen years for the apartheid regime to be forced to release Mandela from prison, but it all started that day, during the Soweto uprising.

I returned home more concerned than I'd left that same morning. "See what people achieved when they rose up and protested?" I told Effie. I knew that every case in the world is unique and that I'd be naive to think that something similar could happen in Greece. But then again, why not?

I also had other thoughts on my mind...

CHRISTMAS IN JOHANNESBURG

There were so many different dishes spread all over the table that it looked as though we'd invited an entire army over. Each one of the guests that came into Anton's house brought along a few plates, filled with all sorts of delicacies. I was carrying Alexandra's halva. I placed it on the counter right next to the other desserts, hoping to have enough time to serve myself a generous portion, before the rest of the table discovered its existence.

"Are we doing the same thing at your place on New Year's Eve?", I asked Effie.

"But we'll also have melomakarona!" she said cheerfully.

The sun was burning and the breeze that blew in from time to time was soothing. We were all sitting out in the yard, a company of people that looked so different from each other. We ate, laughed and enjoyed the day. When the meal was over, with a glass of wine and a plate of halva in my hands, I got up and went a bit further away, underneath the wooden shed. I took a sip of wine and put the glass down. I had a bite of halva. The sweetness of the honey and the raisins mellowed me down. I sat in an armchair and had another bite. I stroked my beard, which had grown back. *What the hell got into me in Namibia and made me shave it off?*

I started thinking about the previous Christmas. I was in Senegal, at that campsite in Saint-Louis and everything was about to change. Thanos had just announced that he would go back to Greece and I, together with Liam, would move on towards the unknown, the *unfamiliar*. When did the *unfamiliar* become *familiar*? I couldn't tell anymore. Was it in the open-air markets of Burkina Faso? Was it in the muddy blissfulness of the Congo? Was it in the moments of anguish with a gun pointing at me in Nigeria? Or maybe somewhere in the DRC, when I was both in heaven and in hell at the same time? Was it in a moment of tranquillity or in times of trouble, when I put my strength to test – both mental and physical? Perhaps the cold beers I drank in the tumbledown shacks, or in the coffee that the truck driver offered to me that dawn in the forest? Was it among my little aces who were always buzzing around the Vespa everywhere I stopped? Was it in Lesotho next to that creek? And what about Alexandra? When did she come and when did she go? Would I ever see her again?

I turned my eyes to the people that were now scattered all around me. I looked at them one by one: different race, different gender, different life, different language. And yet, there we were, all together in a yard, drinking, laughing and celebrating Christmas, without even knowing whether there actually were any Christians among us. And as I watched them, a thought crossed my mind and I've never worried about what to do since: *In what language do people laugh? In what language do they love? In what language do they hurt?* Wherever I went, I somehow managed to understand any person I met along the way. And they understood me, too.

I made myself comfortable in the armchair and closed my eyes for a while. The following day, I'd call my folks. I also wanted to hear my brother's voice – it had been quite some time since I last had. I'd talk to Alexandra too.

Shuvvy Press

Also from Shuvvy Press

'The Hunt for Puerto del Faglioli'
by PADDY TYSON

The world enters economic meltdown. A global flu pandemic looms. An historical US presidential election is taking place and, somewhere in the Americas, a lone Irishman is coaxing his temperamental Italian motorcycle through another electrical breakdown...

Interspersed with anecdote, social observation and liberal doses of humour, this book follows writer and seasoned overland traveller Paddy Tyson through his battle with bureaucracy, bike breaking road surfaces, illness, accident, gun-toting police and a pasty Celtic complexion remarkably unsuited to the Central American sun.

Published as a collection for the first time, this witty and informative account is essential reading for travellers and would-be adventurers.

ISBN: 978-0-9564305-8-8
£9,99, New edition 2018

'Hit the Road, Jac!'
by JACQUI FURNEAUX

HIT THE ROAD, JAC!

SEVEN YEARS, TWENTY COUNTRIES, NO PLAN

This book should be read by anyone still holding back from taking a risk and pursuing their dreams.

When her conventional life fell apart, Jacqui Furneaux responded in a way that surprised many. Her random global wanderings for seven years astride an apparently obsolete motorcycle, brought beauty, friendship, laughter and romance on the road; when she wasn't fending-off amorous sea-dogs or facing some other adversity with quiet courage.

JACQUI FURNEAUX

ISBN: 978-0-9564305-6-4
£9.99, 2017

'The Road to Mali'
by CRAIG CAREY-CLINCH

This is not just an absorbing narrative about a single trip into North Africa. It outlines a series of events and circumstances between 1991 and 2005 which combined to lead three riders to an isolated road junction in Mali, in the middle of a baking hot baobab forest. One of those did not survive the journey.

It's the story of the exhilarating world of motorcycle politics in the 1990s, of two separate yet intertwined adventures into West Africa, and of a Round The World ride that ended in tragedy, yet which inspired hope, and improved the health of thousands in developing countries.

'The Road to Mali' started long before the African adventures themselves.

ISBN: 978-0-9564305-4-0
£9.99, 2015

'Notes from the Road, Vol IV'
by DEREK MANSFIELD

Like no other travel story you've ever read. These notes from the road were formed mainly within a motorcycle helmet on a journey from London to Ukraine, via the Baltics and Balkans, twice.

Within the first thousand miles the petrol-soaked google maps dissolved and the GPS became intermittent. A thousand miles later the road signs turned from Latin to Cyrillic and the skills for dead-reckoning, remembered from the author's nautical past, proved less than adequate.

No matter, the interior of a motorcyclist's head is lit with flashing synapses long after the ignition is switched off. Thus the author, whose memory is on the brink of age-related failure, stopped regularly to make notes. Reviewing these later he realised they made little sense, but were not without humour, and distilled here they take the reader on an increasingly surreal journey of language, customs and culture.

ISBN: 978-0-9564305-5-7
£9.99, 2015

'Ureka'
by GRAHAM FIELD

Who tries to ride deep into Iraq just to see
if the news reports are accurate, ends up
joining a street demonstration against
someone else's government or sticks their
arm between the jaws of a wild mountain
wolf-dog?

After the success of his first book 'In Search
of Greener Grass', Graham Field hits the
road again with his bargain-basement KLR650, recording
his experiences in his inimitable and revealingly honest diary
style. The Caucasus region is often overlooked by travellers,
but Graham may inadvertently be about to change all that.

A single pivotal event can transform any journey and
accepting rather than fighting that moment can have glorious
consequences for the traveller. In this instant the result
ensures a fantastic exploration of eastern Europe and beyond,
the discovery of a hidden gem in Georgia and meanderings
that leave us all much richer.

Ultimately, 'Ureka' is an almost accidental realisation that we
cannot control our mood on the road, but merely embracing it
can be the most enlightening travel experience of all.

ISBN: 978-0-9564305-3-3
£12.99, 2014

'Old Men Can't Wait'
by SIMON GANDOLFI

Run down by three trucks, leg in plaster, not a good first day...

So begins septuagenarian Simon Gandolfi's ten-month ride on a pizza delivery bike, from the tip of South America to New York. This epic exploration of thirteen countries takes Gandolfi across desert and over mountains, through the Amazon forest and the length of the Appalachians. Guide books may warn of thieves,

bandits, corrupt police and border officials; Gandolfi writes of the remarkable kindness and generosity he encounters. Courtesy, patience and good humour are his passports while hurry is his anathema.

Above all this is a jubilant chronicle of hope and understanding, of new friendships, glorious country, sublime architecture, good food, and ultimately, an old man's determination to surmount his years. Outrageously irresponsible and undeniably liberating, Gandolfi's travels will fire the imaginations of every traveller, young or old.

ISBN: 978-0-9564305-2-6
£9.99, 2011